Compliments of

The Diversified Services Group

WE'RE NOT IN KANSAS ANYMORE

WE'RE NOT IN K

RICH II

WALTER UPDEGRAVE
—*Money* Magazine's Ask the Expert

ANSAS ANYMORE

STRATEGIES FOR RETIRING

TOTALLY CHANGED WORLD

CROWN
BUSINESS
NEW YORK

Published by Crown Business, New York, New York.
Member of the Crown Publishing Group, a division of Random House, Inc.
www.crownpublishing.com

CROWN BUSINESS is a trademark and the Rising Sun colophon is a registered trademark of Random House, Inc.

Printed in the United States of America

Design by Robert C. Olsson

Library of Congress Cataloging-in-Publication Data
Updegrave, Walter L.
   We're not in Kansas anymore :
strategies for retiring rich in a totally changed world / Walter Updegrave.
1. Retirement income—Planning.   2. Finance, Personal.
I. Title.
   HG179.U667 2004
   332.024'014—dc22   2003021247

ISBN 1-4000-4789-7

10 9 8 7 6 5 4 3 2 1

First Edition

*To my wife, Mary, the person with whom
I hope to spend a long and happy retirement,
and to my son, Henry, who,
if all my planning pans out, won't have to
support his parents in their dotage*

ACKNOWLEDGMENTS

I wouldn't have been able to write this book without the help of many other people, just a few of whom I'd like to acknowledge here. First off, I'd like to thank my wife, Mary, and my son, Henry, for being so understanding when I retreated to my office on nights and weekends, cutting into family time. I hope I can make it up. I'd also like to thank my agent, Rich Pine, and my editor at Crown, John Mahaney, for helping me sharpen several vague concepts about retirement planning into a book that, I hope, can help people in one of the most important and difficult financial challenges we face: providing for an enjoyable and secure retirement. Writing a book while holding down a job is always a difficult balancing act, one that I was able to pull off only because my editor at *Money* magazine, Robert Safian, was so accommodating. Finally, I'd like to express my gratitude to Judy Feldman for research assistance; to Buffalo, New York, financial planner Anthony Ogorek for helping me with the "We're Not in Kansas Anymore" retirement-planning worksheet; and to the people at Ibbotson Associates, particularly Alexa Auerbach and Peng Chen, for honoring my seemingly endless requests to provide data and crunch numbers.

CONTENTS

WE'RE NOT IN KANSAS ANYMORE

INTRODUCTION

A TWIST IN THE YELLOW BRICK ROAD

It wasn't too long ago that retirement planning was a pretty straightforward affair. You went to work, you paid your Social Security taxes, and you went about your career, knowing that, without much effort on your part, you were building up retirement benefits you could count on when you left the workaday world. Then, sometime in your early to mid-sixties—or even earlier in many cases—you called it a career, collected a tidy company pension, signed up for your Social Security benefits, and retired to the back porch or the front nine to quietly enjoy the rest of your life.

My, how things have changed. What was once a simple, well-marked, and relatively predictable road to retirement suddenly has some hazardous twists and turns in it. It's almost as if, like Dorothy in *The Wizard of Oz*, we've been transported to a dramatically different landscape where the rules of retirement planning have radically changed.

Where once we could count on paternalistic corporations and the government for a secure retirement, now *we've* got to fashion our own retirement security by contributing money to 401(k)s, IRAs, and the like.

Where once we could let corporate pension managers worry about such matters as how much we should put in stocks or bonds or mutual funds, now *we've* got to decide how to invest our retirement stash.

In short, the days of relying on corporate benevolence and government largesse to support us in our golden years are pretty much gone. Today the responsibility for accumulating a nest egg for retirement has been placed squarely on our shoulders.

More Responsibility . . . but More Opportunity, Too

Clearly, retirement planning in this new reality demands more responsibility on our part, which, understandably, can be somewhat daunting. Many people are uncomfortable choosing investments. They feel overwhelmed by a confusing array of choices and are concerned about the consequences of making the wrong decisions. The stock market, with its unpredictable, gut-wrenching downturns, seems a dangerous place to them. And retirement investing horror stories such as the one at Enron—where thousands of employees who'd loaded their retirement accounts with Enron's stock lost much if not all of their retirement savings when the company's stock collapsed— have only heightened their fears.

But with more responsibility on our part for retirement-planning decisions also comes more *opportunity* to create a comfortable retirement. The tools and resources are definitely there. You've got 401(k)s and other tax-advantaged retirement savings plans that can turbocharge your savings. Indeed, the Bush administration and Congress passed legislation in 2001 that over a period of years significantly boosts the amounts we can contribute to 401(k)s and other retirement plans and makes it easier to take our retirement funds with us as we move from job to job, thus making these savings plans even more valuable. You can choose from a broad smorgasbord of investing choices, including U.S. and international stocks, taxable and tax-free bonds, and a wide variety of mutual funds and annuities. And there are plenty of free or reasonably priced websites around that can help even the most financially challenged among us create a sophisticated road map for our retirement and then monitor our progress.

Similarly, the tax law that Congress passed and President Bush signed in 2003—the Jobs and Growth Tax Relief Reconciliation Act—should also better enable us to prepare for retirement by lowering federal income tax rates as well as the amount of tax we pay on dividends and capital gains. The less of our income we must share with the government, the more we're able to put toward our future financial security. And the lower the tax rate on our investment income and gains, the faster our savings will grow, allowing us to accumulate a larger nest egg for retirement.

But to succeed in this new retirement world, you must also know how to navigate around the new retirement landscape— this new land of Oz, if you will. You must learn how to take advantage of the resources and tools that are out there and how to get maximum use out of the various tax benefits available.

And that's just what this book is designed to do: help you get the most out of the vast array of retirement-planning options open to you. The fact is, whether you like it or not, you are already in charge of your retirement. This book will help you take control of it.

Before we go any further, let's address the guiding principles of this book and your role in planning your retirement.

This Book's Guiding Principles

1. It All Begins with Goals

Planning for retirement without having a goal in mind is like setting off on a journey without a destination. That's fine if you're Jack Kerouac, but most of us actually want to get somewhere, not wander aimlessly on the road to who knows where. For you to be able to make sensible decisions about things like how much money to save each month in retirement accounts and how that money ought to be invested, you have to set goals, such as the age at which you'd like to retire, how much money you will need to accumulate by that age, and how long you want that money to last. Otherwise, there's no way you'll know what kind of chance your savings, combined with Social Security and other sources of income, have of carrying you through your life in retirement, which, given life spans these days, may be twenty, thirty, even forty years or longer.

Granted, it may be difficult to put a number on some goals. Knowing exactly how much income you're going to need when you retire, say, two decades from now, requires a degree of clairvoyance I doubt even the Amazing Kreskin possesses. But you've got to start somewhere, so it is imperative that you create a basic blueprint or retirement plan. Once you've done that, you can refine your plan as conditions change and as your retirement draws nearer.

2. Procrastination Is Your Worst Enemy

The earlier you start planning and saving for retirement, the better off you'll be. This idea is so crucial to creating a successful retirement plan that it's impossible to overstate its importance. Delaying your planning for just a few years can mean the difference between a cushy retirement and a comfortable one, and delaying a few more years can mean the difference between a comfortable retirement and scraping by. The earlier you begin saving and investing, the more opportunity the wonder of compound interest—earning interest on interest or, in the case of stocks and mutual funds, gains on gains—has to build your retirement wealth.

Unfortunately, this essential retirement truth—the importance of saving early and often—escapes many people. Instead, they believe that savvy investing is the single most important factor in building a large retirement nest egg. It's true that investing plays a major role in providing retirement security. And it's also true that regular saving and smart investing are inextricably intertwined when it comes to successful retirement planning. But saving is still the more important of the two. Without the savings, all the investment prowess in the world doesn't mean diddly-squat. There's no way you're going to turn meager savings into a pot of retirement gold by picking stocks or mutual funds that soar to humongous gains. Lots of people thought they could do that during the tech and dot-com heyday back in the late 1990s. And a few years later many found that the tech and Net stocks that had doubled in value within a few months suddenly lost 50, 60, even 80 percent or more of their value just as quickly. Ultimately, we have a lot more control over how much we save than we do over the returns we earn on investments. And the sooner we get started saving, the better chance we have of achieving a comfortable retirement.

3. There Are Many Paths to a Comfortable Retirement

Just as there's an almost limitless number of ways that people plan to enjoy their time in retirement, so are there an almost limitless number of ways to get to these different retirement visions. Throughout this book I'll try to lay out a path that I think gives the most people the best shot at accumulating enough money to live a comfortable and fulfilling life after leaving their career. Which means I'll concentrate on the importance of planning early, saving often, using the tools available to most of us (401(k)s, IRAs, etc.), and putting your money in the types of investments that have proven track records of creating long-term financial security (stocks, mutual funds, bonds, and annuities).

But that doesn't mean you can't deviate at all from the path that I lay out. I recognize that for many people a different path may work better, and you should try to tailor your plan to your own strengths and your own needs. Some people, for example, may prefer starting a business to investing in stocks and bonds. Others may not work for employers who offer a 401(k) or similar retirement savings plan. Some people may be in a line of work in which frequent layoffs or job changes creates financial uncertainty, which makes it difficult to save money on a regular basis. And still others may find it difficult to start saving early in life but may be able to ratchet up their savings after the kids have gone to college and (you hope) left the house.

As much as possible, I'll try to present a variety of alternatives so that you can create a plan that best fits your situation. Of course, I don't recommend you deviate too far from my basic plan of setting a target retirement income goal and then saving and investing as early as possible to achieve it. Similarly, I don't have a bag of magic tricks that will allow you to retire in resplendent luxury if you're barely scraping by now. But I will try to give you enough information and advice to help you achieve the most secure retirement you can with the financial resources and capabilities you have.

4. You're Better Off Thinking in Terms of Probabilities Rather than Certainties

If there's one sure thing in retirement planning, it's the fact that there *are* no sure things. The real world is filled with too many uncertainties to be able to forecast results with anything close to 100 percent accuracy. Fact is, we just don't know whether we'll actually achieve the returns we project on our investments, whether we'll live longer than or fall short of our life expectancy, or whether we'll spend as much or more than we expect in retirement.

So anyone who tells you that by following a certain strategy you'll definitely be able to retire in twenty or thirty years with a specific amount of money that will definitely last you the rest of your life is intentionally or unintentionally misleading you. Ditto for any website, calculator, or software program that delivers a similar message. Fact is, that level of precision is impossible given the inherent variability in the real world.

What you can expect, however, is a sense of how different assumptions and strategies can increase or decrease the *probability* of your reaching targets such as building a six-figure nest egg by the time you retire or receiving a specific level of retirement income from your investment portfolio. In the sections of this book that involve creating a plan, I will explain in detail how to take advantage of resources and tools that use state-of-the-art forecasting techniques to give you the best chances of achieving a secure retirement. What's more, I'll show how changing specific elements of your strategy—saving a bit more money or fine-tuning the mix of your investments, for example—can boost the probability that you'll be able to retire comfortably.

5. It's Never Too Late to Start Planning

Yes, I did say in Guiding Principle 1 that the earlier you begin planning, the better off you'll be. And that's true. But it's also true that, for a variety of reasons, many of us don't get an early start. That's no reason to throw your hands up and do nothing, however. Early may be better, but even a late start is better than not starting at all. I believe that no matter how far behind you may be, no matter how dire your straits, there's always *something* you can do to improve your situation, and I'll have a variety of suggestions that can help the procrastinators among us improve their retirement prospects.

What I Expect from You

Now that you have an idea of what to expect from me in this book, let's get to what's required of you: *You've got to be an active participant in the program.* Here are the five things I expect from you in order to create a retirement plan that really works.

I Expect You to Put Some Thought and Effort into Your Plan

You will increase your chances of success tremendously if you sit down with this book and give some real thought to such questions as how much you need to accumulate to live the way you want in retirement, how much you're really capable of saving on a regular basis, and what kind of investments you're most comfortable with. And then you've got to translate all this into action: sign up for your company's 401(k) plan, open that IRA, start an automatic investing plan at a brokerage or mutual fund company, and choose the investments that will hold your savings.

Once you've done this preparation up front, the heavy work is pretty much done. From then on, it's monitoring your plan to make sure you're still on track, occasionally revising your strategy if it appears you're falling behind, and perhaps doing a bit of fine-tuning to reflect significant changes in your financial circumstances (like deciding how to invest that hundred grand your dear aunt Tillie left you in her will).

I Expect You to Base Your Planning on Your Life, Not Generic Rules of Thumb

The goal here is to create a retirement plan that is tailored to your needs and goals, not something that could apply to some vague everyman. So as much as possible you want to avoid relying on seat-of-the-pants guesstimates and simplistic generalizations.

For example, you've probably heard of the 70 percent rule. This old saw contends that because your work-related expenses disappear in retirement, you can maintain your present standard of living with 70 percent of your preretirement income. There's one problem with the 70 percent rule: It's wrong about 90 percent of the time. Why? Because it's an *average* based on the spending patterns of thousands of people. You are not thousands of people. You are one person. You make your own decisions based on your own resources and needs, not averages.

So the amount of money you'll require in retirement will depend not on what you spend now but what you actually spend after you retire. If you've paid off your mortgage and plan to devote your retirement to documenting the mating habits of the cecropia moths in your backyard, chances are you can easily get by with much less than 70 percent of your income. On the other hand, if you plan to keep a summer home in the country, a winter house on the beach, and a pied-à-terre in town and spend little time in any of them because you're looking forward to globe-trotting around the world in first-class splendor, then you'll probably need more than 100 percent of your preretirement income.

Fortunately, there are enough tools available today for everything from estimating retirement expenses and calculating your insurance needs to creating a diversified portfolio so that you don't have to base your planning on averages based on what other people do. You can—and should—plan on how you live now and how you plan to live once you retire.

I Expect You to Think in Terms of a Portfolio of Investments Rather than Individual Securities

Probably the biggest single mistake investors make when investing for retirement is they think in either/or terms—that is, should the money be in stocks or bonds, technology shares or utilities, large-company stock funds or small-company stock funds? They think they've got to concentrate all or most of their money in one stock or fund or one type of investment. Often, their choice is based on which investment has done the best over the past year, during the most recent quarter, or maybe even in the past month.

That approach is downright dangerous, though, because it's the investment equivalent of rolling the dice. Maybe your choice will come up a winner. Or, as employees of companies such as Enron, WorldCom, and Global Crossing found after loading their 401(k)s with company stock, it could come up a loser.

The better way to go is to build a diversified portfolio that includes a variety of investments that can work together. By spreading your money around, you essentially hedge your bets so that if one part of your portfolio is getting hammered, another part may be chugging along to gains. This process of building a portfolio with different types of investments that complement one another is called asset allocation, and its goal is to help you earn a return high enough to make your retirement accounts grow but at the same time prevent your retirement nest egg from getting shattered. In the sections of this book that deal with creating a retirement investing strategy, I'll explain how you can use any one of a number of easily accessible asset-allocation tools to create a diversified portfolio tailored to your financial circumstances and that's consistent with the amount of risk you're comfortable with when investing.

I Expect You to Take Advantage of Freebies Like Tax-Advantaged Savings

There are few free lunches in the real world. But that's exactly what you get when you take advantage of tax-advantaged savings plans such as 401(k)s and IRAs: a free lunch in the form of tax breaks and other perks that can supersize your retirement portfolio.

That's not to say 401(k)s and other tax-deferred accounts don't have a downside. They do. Probably the biggest is that these plans are creations of Congress, which means that bureaucrats in tax committees have larded them with enough mind-numbing rules and nitpicking regulations to bring even a tax attorney to tears. Still, the pros vastly outweigh the cons. That's especially true since Congress raised the amount you can contribute to 401(k)s, IRAs, and other retirement plans, and even added a provision allowing people fifty and older to make extra, catch-up contributions to their plans.

For some 42 million of us, 401(k) plans, IRAs, and the like will serve as the cornerstone of our retirement plan. So I'll devote two full chapters to explaining how these plans work and how you can you take full advantage of all the benefits they have to offer.

I Expect You to Have the Good Sense to Improvise When Necessary

Let's face it. Today's road to retirement has lots of twists, turns, and obstacles that no plan, no matter how sophisticated, could ever foresee. You'll increase your chances of success immeasurably if you're ready to make adjustments and capitalize on opportunities as they avail themselves.

Early on, for example, when you're starting a career and raising a family, chances are there will be years when you won't be able to contribute the max to your 401(k) or sock away savings in other investments. But it's also likely there will be other years when you come into unexpected cash—a big raise at work or a large tax refund. It's important to take advantage of such occasions to jack up your savings and make up for lost time.

The closer you get to retirement, the less wiggle room you have to make up for lost savings opportunities. But even late in the game there are still plenty of adjustments you can make that will appreciably enhance your quality of life. You can make a concentrated effort to pare expenses so that you can free up more income for saving. You can invest somewhat more aggressively in hopes of earning a bigger return on the money you do manage to accumulate.

Even after you're retired, there are moves you can make. You can give your savings a chance to grow a few more years by joining the ever growing number of retirees whose vision of retirement includes holding some sort of a job. Or you might tap the equity in your home for a tax-free monthly income by taking out a reverse mortgage. You might even consider relocating to a part of the country where lower living costs can stretch your income and extend the life of your retirement portfolio.

I don't want to sound Pollyannaish or imply that there's a magical solution for every problem. But by maintaining a flexible attitude—and being willing to improvise when the situation calls for it—you will be able to wring more out of whatever resources you have and increase your odds for achieving a comfortable and secure retirement.

Of course, I can't guarantee that in the end everything will work out for you as splendidly as it did for Dorothy and her friends in *The Wizard of Oz*. But I can say that your chances of living a financially secure and fulfilling retirement will improve immeasurably if you plan ahead.

Chapter 1

FORGET KANSAS, GET TO KNOW OZ

WE'RE NOT IN KANSAS ANYMORE

It's one of the greatest moments in one of the greatest movies of all time, *The Wizard of Oz*. Dorothy Gale, played by Judy Garland, has just been transported along with her little terrier, Toto, from the Kansas farm where she lives with her auntie Em and uncle Henry to a mysterious place called Oz. The flat, monotone Kansas prairie has been replaced by a bizarre landscape bursting with color and lush with exotic flowers and plants. Bedazzled, Dorothy looks around, trying to gain her bearings in this unfamiliar terrain. And then she utters those famous words to her little dog: "Toto, I have a feeling we're not in Kansas anymore."

When it comes to describing the situation most of us face today when planning for retirement, I can hardly think of a better line: We're not in Kansas anymore. The old, familiar landscape we once took for granted, the cozy, secure world where you could count on the combination of government largesse and an employer-funded pension to provide you with a comfy retirement, has given way to a totally new environment, one as alien to the world we knew before as Oz is to Kansas.

Granted, in this new retirement world we don't have to deal with such nasty creatures as the Wicked Witch of the West or her army of freaky flying monkeys, as Dorothy, the Tin Man, the

Scarecrow, and the Cowardly Lion did. But the twenty-first-century retirement-planning landscape is nonetheless teeming with daunting challenges of a different breed. We must learn how to get the most out of financial instruments that retirees a generation ago never had to concern themselves with, an alphanumeric soup of 401(k)s, 403(b)s, 457 plans, IRAs, Keoghs, SEPs, and so on. (IRAs, Keoghs, and SEPs, oh my!) And then there are the myriad rules concerning IRA rollovers, early withdrawal penalties, borrowing regulations, and RMDs (required minimum distributions). On top of all this, we've got to invest our retirement savings and thus learn to navigate the often treacherous waters of the financial markets, where sudden setbacks can sometimes undo years of diligent saving. In short, just as Dorothy had to familiarize herself with the strange ways of Oz in order to find her way back home, so too must we develop retirement-planning strategies that offer the best chance of success given the new realities we face.

In this chapter I'll bring you up to speed on the new retirement landscape, including a number of distinctly positive developments stemming from recent changes in the tax laws that can increase our chances of achieving a comfortable retirement. Only by coming to grips with the various changes that have transformed the world of retirement planning and understanding how those changes affect you can you sensibly plan for your own retirement.

Changes in the Financial Aspects of Retirement

Social Security Ain't What It Used to Be

Traditionally, retirement-planning experts have told us to think of our income sources during retirement as a three-legged stool, the first leg being Social Security, the second company-funded pensions, and the third personal savings. In fact, however, this stool would have been pretty lopsided because for most people the role of that first leg, Social Security, was much, much bigger than the other two.

But today's and future generations of retirees aren't going to get anything remotely approaching the kind of windfall Social Security recipients received in years past. For one thing, there aren't enough workers paying into the system to provide benefits comparable to those past generations received. You don't have to be a financial whiz to figure out that fewer people putting money into the system and more drawing it out spells trouble. And that, according to the Social Security Administration's own projections, is exactly what lies ahead.

Given the uncertain outlook for this program, some financial planners suggest that people filling out retirement-planning worksheets put a big fat zero on the line where you enter your expected Social Security benefit. I think that's a little extreme. Even if the Social Security trustees' projections are accurate and the trust fund runs dry in 2042 or so, it's not as if the Social Security system will go bankrupt then, as is often suggested in the press. Payroll and income taxes will continue to flow into the system as before. Those taxes just won't be enough to pay full benefits, but they would be able to pay between 65 and 73 percent of currently scheduled benefits over the subsequent thirty-five years.

It's anyone's guess how this will be resolved. At some point in the future the Social Security system could include some version of individual accounts that would allow us to put a portion of our Social Security taxes into stock and bond mutual fund accounts instead of having the money invested solely in U.S. Treasury bonds, as is now the case. That might help some of us earn a higher rate of return on the money we put into the plan and possibly boost what we collect in benefits down the road. Or Congress might try to shore up the existing system by raising payroll taxes or tinkering in other ways. Or maybe we'll see a combination of both approaches. Whatever is done, however, I would expect that future Social Security benefits will be smaller than they've been in the past. If you are relying primarily on Social Security to carry you through retirement, you are (a) counting on a very short retirement, (b) counting on a very grim retirement, (c) fooling yourself, or (d) all of the above. Suffice it to say that planning to make Social Security the cornerstone of your retirement isn't really planning at all.

Corporate Pension Plans Are Going the Way of the Hula Hoop

Remember hula hoops? They were all the rage back in the early 1950s among hip-swiveling young baby boomers. But within a few years, sales of these plastic novelty items fell from the millions to perhaps a few thousand a year, and today the few remaining hula hoops are little more than nostalgic relics of a more innocent era.

Well, the trajectory has been similar, though not nearly as short-lived, for defined-benefit pensions. These are the types of pensions most of us think of (or used to think of) when we hear the term *pension*—that is, one in which the company puts money into an investment fund and, regardless of the performance of the investments, promises to pay you a monthly check for life based on how many years you worked at the company and the size of your salary. Often, after putting in twenty-five or more years at a company, retirees could walk away with pension benefits that guaranteed them upward of half of their salary.

As these types of pension plans were nearing their peak in the late twentieth century, the seeds for their demise were being sewn. For one thing, companies began to realize that with this type of pension they could be on the hook for much bigger liabilities than they'd expected. After all, with more and more people living well into their nineties or even hitting the century mark, companies could end up making monthly payments for thirty or forty years, if not longer, to retirees who stubbornly refused to die. Many companies began to decide they were better off shutting down their defined-benefit plans or at least not starting any new ones. As a result, the number of company-funded pensions fell from 114,000 in 1985 to about 31,000 today, a drop of more than 70 percent.

The old pension arrangement where the company funded the plan and you were guaranteed a monthly check for life is rapidly becoming a vestige of a near-obsolete system. If you are lucky enough to work for a company that still provides such a plan, that's great. But that's not the case for most of us, which means that for the majority of Americans that second leg of the retirement stool has gotten a lot shorter.

More than Ever Before, the Onus Is on Us to Save and Invest for Our Own Retirement

With the first two legs of that three-legged retirement stool contributing less to our retirement security than in the past, we now have to rely more than ever before on that third leg: personal savings.

Fortunately, even as traditional defined-benefit pension plans have been disappearing, most of us have had access to a growing array of other types of retirement savings plans. At the top of the list are defined-contribution plans such as 401(k)s, which allow you to contribute a percentage of your salary before taxes into a variety of investments, typically mutual funds. In many cases, employers will match a portion of what you put into the plan. These are called defined-contribution plans because in accordance with federal pension law the plan stipulates, or defines, how much you can contribute to the plan. No guarantees are made about the benefits the plan will pay, however. Which makes these plans the mirror image in a sense of the defined-benefit plans discussed above, where it was the benefit payment that was defined, while the employers' contribution could change depending on the performance of the plan's investment assets.

401(k)s and other types of plans require us to take on a much bigger role than ever before in planning for retirement in two specific and crucial ways.

First, you've got to take the initiative to put your money into these plans. If you contribute only a small percentage of your salary to your 401(k) plan, then you will have only a little bit of money at work for your retirement. If you don't contribute any of your salary, then the plan is absolutely no help to you at all.

Even in the cases where the employer is willing to kick in some contributions to the plan, those contributions are matching contributions.

Those who are willing to stash away money in these plans, however, got a big break in a piece of legislation known as the Economic Growth and Tax Relief Reconciliation Act of 2001, or more simply the 2001 tax bill. In addition to phasing in cuts in marginal income tax rates, this bill dramatically increased the amount of pretax dollars we can stash away in virtually the entire panoply of retirement savings plans not only this year but stretching out into the future. Those higher contribution allowances, plus other modifications that make it easier to keep tabs on your retirement savings when you switch jobs, have made everything from 401(k)s and 403(b)s to SEPs, Keoghs, and traditional IRAs even more effective retirement savings tools than they were before.

People who are willing to save and invest for their own retirement also got some help from an even more recent change in the tax laws—namely, the Jobs and Growth Tax Relief Reconciliation Act of 2003. This tax bill provided a number of goodies. For one thing, it accelerated across-the-board income tax cuts that had already been enacted in the 2001 tax bill but were not scheduled to kick in until 2006 or later. Result: As of 2003, the top income tax rate immediately dropped from 38.6 percent to 35 percent. But the bill also lowered the tax rate on capital gains—dropping the maximum from 20 percent to 15 percent for gains realized after May 6, 2003—and lowered the tax on most dividends by making the tax rate on dividends the equivalent of that on capital gains. This created a huge cut for many investors, lowering the maximum rate on most dividends from 38.6 percent to 15 percent in 2003. Of course, many lower-income investors will pay lower rates on capital gains and dividends than the newly reduced maximums I've mentioned here.

I'll be the first to admit that both the 2001 and the 2003 tax bills contain a number of squirrelly provisions that undermine their effectiveness and make planning more difficult. The lower tax rates on capital gains and dividends in the 2003 bill tax cuts, for example, revert back to their earlier higher rates in 2009, while the lower income tax rates initiated by the 2001 bill and accelerated by the 2003 bill revert to their older higher levels after 2010—unless Congress votes to keep the lower rates. But even if the relief is only temporary, lower income tax rates still mean less money going into the government's coffers, which leaves more money available to you for retirement saving. Similarly, the less of your investment gains you have to share with the government, the faster your money can compound and the larger a retirement nest egg you can grow with the same amount of savings. And for those of us who like to believe that reason and sound judgment will ultimately win out (and feel that we need every edge we can get when it comes to retirement planning), there's always the chance that Congress will make these tax cuts permanent.

In light of these changes, you'll want to reevaluate your investing strategy to make sure you're getting the maximum possible benefit of the new rules both in terms of the types of investments you buy and which ones you hold in tax-advantaged versus regular taxable accounts. We'll get into that in the investment discussions in Chapter 6. It's important to keep in mind, however, that *no* revisions of the tax laws will change this basic fact: The extent to which you can create a sizable nest egg for retirement these days increasingly depends on how much of your salary you are willing to save today.

Second, you've got to assume responsibility for investing whatever you save. In the old company-funded defined-contribution plans, you didn't have to concern yourself with how the money was invested. The company hired one or more professional investment advisers to deal with questions such as how much of the plan's money should be invested in bonds and how much in stocks, as well as what kinds of each.

But in the world of defined-contribution plans and IRAs, *you are the investment manager.* You've got to decide how much of your money should be in bonds or bond funds, and what kind. You've got to figure out how much to put in stocks or stock funds, and what kind. Which brings us to the final financial change . . .

The Stock Market Isn't as Sure a Thing as It Seemed During the Go-Go '90s

Back during the late great bull market of the 1990s, investing seemed so easy, so simple, so lucrative. All you had to do was put your money in a few high-flying tech stocks—AOL, Cisco, you name it—or pick one of the dozens of top-performing growth-stock mutual funds, and bingo! Your money doubled or even tripled in a matter of a few years. One unfortunate result of that period of what appeared to be easy money is that we got the impression that we could rely on annual returns of 15, 20, even 25 percent or more a year. We came to believe that we could actually earn such high returns without risk. All gain, no pain! And this attitude in turn gave us the erroneous sense that saving isn't the key to achieving a secure retirement, smart investing is. After all, if you can earn high returns on your money, you don't have to save as much to accumulate a sizable nest egg.

Let's say, for example, you're forty years old and want to accumulate $500,000 by age sixty-five. Well, if you could count on annual returns of, say, 15 percent year after year, then putting away just $180 a month would get you to your goal. (For simplicity's sake, I'm ignoring taxes here.) But what if it turns out that 15 percent is unrealistic and that you really shouldn't be counting on more than, say, an 8 percent return on a regular basis? Then to have a shot at accumulating $500,000 by the time you hit sixty-five, you would have to put away more like $550 a month—*or three times as much.*

Neither I nor anyone else knows for sure what returns the financial markets will deliver in the years ahead. But I think it's become pretty clear now that the blimpish returns of the late '90s were an anomaly, little more than a crazy outgrowth of the whole dot-com, New Era, irrational-exuberance phase the country went through. It would be flat-out irresponsible to base one's retirement planning on those kinds of returns. I think most people are resigned to that reality. But what I don't think has necessarily sunk in is the fact that *lower returns mean we've got to save more money to reach the same retirement goals.*

So, financially, we've got two attitude adjustments to make. First, we've got to become a lot more realistic about how much money we've got to put away on a regular basis in 401(k)s, IRAs, and other accounts if we want to attain a reasonably secure retirement. In other words, the stock market isn't going to save us from our poor saving habits. And assuming we make that adjustment, we've then got to get the investing part right, which in and of itself requires a delicate balancing act. After all, if you invest too timidly and plow all your money into "safe" investments such as bank CDs and money market funds, your retirement stash might not grow large enough to fund the living style you aspire to for your golden years. Invest too aggressively and you may find yourself in the position many retirement investors found themselves in after the stock market collapsed in early 2000, with the value of their retirement savings cut by 20, 30, even 50 percent or more and faced with having to rethink their retirement plans or even postpone them indefinitely.

So, the financial changes I've outlined above clearly constitute more than a subtle new twist in the ways we plan for retirement. We're talking about radical change that requires an entirely new mind-set in the way we plan for retirement in the future, as well as new strategies.

Lifestyle Changes in Retirement

At the same time financial changes have been altering the face of retirement planning, so too has the very way we think about retirement undergone a dramatic shift. And to make realistic financial decisions about the future, you've got to take these lifestyle or demographic changes into account as well.

We Are Living Longer than Ever Before

Today a sixty-five-year-old man in decent health can expect to live another twenty years or so, or until age eighty-five, and in many cases much longer. In fact, a sixty-five-year-old man today has about a 13 percent chance of making it to age ninety-five and a 4 percent chance of living to one hundred. And women can expect to live even longer on average than men.

All of which means that unlike in even the relatively recent past, when retirees might have spent ten or fifteen years in retirement before checking out, today it's not uncommon for someone to spend twenty, thirty, or even forty years in retirement. In other words, many people may spend as much time in retirement as they did in their careers. If you'd like to get an estimate of your life expectancy that factors in such variables as your family medical history and lifestyle, check out the Longevity Game in the Calculators section of the Northwestern Mutual website at www.northwesternmutual.com. (If your sense of humor runs to the macabre, you might want to check out the Death Clock—www.deathclock.com—which purports to predict the *exact day* of your demise, based on one of four scenarios you choose: optimistic, normal, pessimistic, or sadistic.)

We're Far More Active During Retirement than Previous Generations

Far from being a time to disengage from life, today's and future generations of retirees will likely see this as a new stage of life: a time for exploration; an opportunity for continued personal growth; a chance to try new sports, hobbies, and activities, to spend time with family, and to set and achieve new goals. In short, today's retirees are not going gently into geezerhood. They may play golf, bingo, and shuffleboard, but you're also likely to find them making pottery, teaching reading to disadvantaged kids, running charities, writing books, registering voters, running for public office, shooting hoops, playing baseball, surfing—both the Net and the Banzai Pipeline at Ehukai Beach Park in Oahu—and returning to college.

The Paychecks No Longer Stop at Retirement

In the mid-'80s through the early '90s, labor economists began to notice two unusual developments. First, the labor force participation rates for people sixty-five and older, which had been steadily declining since World War II, began slowly climbing upward again, rising from 11.8 percent in 1990 to 12.8 percent in 2000, while the Bureau of Labor Statistics projects it will hit almost 15 percent by 2010. What's more, the lines between work and retirement were no longer so distinct. Instead of going one day from work to no work, people began making a gradual transition from the workaday world into retirement, often taking on transitional positions or "bridge jobs" that essentially allowed people to ease their way from their careers into retirement.

But the shift in how people view the relationship between retirement and work has been even more profound. People no longer see the two concepts as mutually exclusive. Although it may seem like an oxymoron, you can work yet still be retired. Indeed, *rehire* may be a better term than *retire* to describe what many people plan to do after calling it a career. When the Gallup Organization polled one thousand nonretired Americans in 2002, more than 80 percent said they planned to work in retirement.

The Retirement Squeeze

Longer life spans and changes in the way we live after leaving our careers make retirement a much more stimulating, challenging, and enjoyable time for us, almost like a shot at a final adventurous journey. But living a longer and more active life than past retirees also means that we're likely to need more money to fund this phase of our lives than previous generations of retirees required.

The style we can afford to live in during retirement comes down to how much we save and how well we invest before we retire. It's really that straightforward. We'll get some help from the government and some help from our employer. But in the final analysis, our actions will determine how comfortable or how grim a retirement we will have.

There are many who haven't faced up to this new reality.

Consider the following findings from recent surveys of American workers:

- Less than two-thirds of workers have tried to calculate how much they must save and accumulate for a comfortable retirement.
- Nearly half of workers have saved less than $50,000 for retirement, and 15 percent have not saved a single cent.
- More than 50 percent of preretirees underestimate their life expectancy.
- Some 40 percent of Americans are counting on the lottery, sweepstakes, getting married, or an inheritance to fund their retirement.

Some people look at statistics such as these and predict that many Americans are headed for a retirement disaster, a version of retirement where the years are more grim than golden. And I'm sure that for many people—especially anyone whose idea of retirement planning is playing the lottery—that will be the case.

But it doesn't have to be that way. Once you understand the new ground rules for retirement, you can create a plan that makes the most of whatever financial resources you have and the retirement-planning tools that are available to you. We will get into the nuts and bolts of that plan in the following chapters. But to get you off to a good start on your retirement-planning journey, I want to suggest that you take a few cues from Dorothy's traveling companions in *The Wizard of Oz:* the Tin Man, the Scarecrow, and the Cowardly Lion.

Start with Your Heart

The Tin Man, as you'll recall, accompanied Dorothy on the trip to Oz because he wanted to ask the Wizard for a heart. He wanted not just to live life but to experience it with emotion and passion.

So what does this have to do with your retirement planning? Well, I think you'll improve your chances of creating a plan and following through with it if you incorporate some passion and emotion into your vision of retirement. In all likelihood you will be spending the last twenty or more years of your life in retirement, so you ought to give plenty of thought ahead of time to how you would like to spend those years. What is likely to challenge you, to excite you, to keep you interested and engaged in life?

Finances aside, it's also critical to think ahead about your retirement lifestyle because you are likely to feel more happy and fulfilled after leaving work if you are making a transition into a life that you have planned and looked forward to. A variety of studies show that retirees who have actively planned for the kind of life they will lead after their careers have a greater sense of control over their lives and tend to enjoy life more than people who simply face retirement without having thought or planned ahead.

So take a few days or weeks to think about how you would like to spend your retirement. And then over the years before you retire, do what you can to make sure those plans are realistic.

Rely on Your Brain

Your heart can help you decide on the kind of life you want to live in retirement, but you're going to have to rely on the old mental processor to put together a plan that will get you what the heart desires. In short, you're going to have to put some thought into such issues as how much you should be saving, how you should be allocating your assets between stocks and bonds, and what stocks, bonds, or mutual funds you should be buying with your retirement savings.

That said, I know that many people are a bit intimidated by things financial. They're worried that they'll make lousy investment decisions or otherwise screw things up and put their retirement savings in jeopardy. But you don't have to be a financial whiz to make reasonable financial decisions for your retirement. Remember in *The Wizard of Oz* how the Scarecrow lamented that his life would be so much better if he only had a brain? Despite that plea, it was the Scarecrow who invariably came up with the best ideas whenever Dorothy and her friends needed to get out of a jam. He actually had the brains all along.

Well, in my experience the same thing is true for most of us when it comes to creating a retirement plan and investing our retirement savings. You don't have to be an Einstein. If you are a reasonably intelligent person capable of making reasonable decisions, you should have no trouble creating and executing a retirement plan. Which is to say that anyone who's successfully managed to do things such as raise a family, hold down a job, and have normal social relationships with other human beings probably has more than enough innate skills for retirement planning. In fact, I'd say the bigger danger comes when people become convinced that they know so much that they've got this investing thing licked. That's when overconfidence rears its head and you find people making lousy planning and investing decisions, as many did by pouring too much of their retirement savings into risky tech and dot-com stocks during the '90s. If you're willing to put a little thought and effort into learning the fundamentals of retirement planning and mastering the basics of investing—and you're willing to set your emotions aside long enough to make your financial decisions in a sober, clear-headed way—you have more than enough brain power to create a successful retirement plan.

Show Some Courage

Here, I don't mean courage in the sense of bravery, which is what the Cowardly Lion was seeking (unnecessarily, as it turns out) in *The Wizard of Oz*. I'm referring to discipline, willpower, and having the courage of your convictions to set a plan and follow it through.

Now, that may sound simple. But in many ways this is the hardest part of retirement planning, something that can't be taught but that each of us must somehow pick up on our own. I'm talking about having the discipline to forgo some treats or indulgences in the present so that you will be able to save for the future. I'm talking about having the willpower to continue your plan to put the maximum percentage of your salary into your company's retirement savings plan when you would rather use the money to buy a new car. I'm talking about keeping your hands off your 401(k) when the balance has grown big enough so that you think maybe it wouldn't hurt to take a few thousand bucks out to pay for a nice, no doubt well-deserved vacation to Europe. And I'm talking about having the willpower when you leave a job to roll over your savings plan balance into an IRA account or into your new employer's plan, rather than simply taking a lump-sum payment and blowing the money, or at least that part of the money that's left after paying taxes and a 10 percent penalty to Uncle Sam.

Okay, so now that we've got the lay of the new retirement landscape and we understand the new rules of the retirement-planning game, let's move on to what you need to know so you can create a plan.

Chapter 2

SAVE AS MUCH AS YOU CAN AS EARLY AS YOU CAN

(BUT DON'T PANIC IF YOU GET A LATE START)

Imagine for a moment that instead of going off to see the wonderful Wizard of Oz to find out how to get back to Kansas, Dorothy had gone to seek his advice about retirement planning. The scene where she and her friends talk to the Wizard the first time in his palace might have gone something like this:

> *Dorothy: O mighty and powerful wizard, please tell me, what is the single most important thing I can do to ensure a comfortable retirement for myself back in Kansas? Is it picking the best stocks and mutual funds? Is it learning the ins and outs of 401(k)s and other retirement savings plans? Is it choosing the right career and the best place to work so I get the best retirement benefits? Is it . . .*
>
> *The Wizard: Silence! A number of people have come seeking the answer to the question you ask. And, like you, they have touched on many of the things one must do to set the stage for a secure retirement. But the great and powerful Oz knows that there is one thing you must do above all others, one thing without which no one can hope to achieve retirement security, one thing that towers above all the others. And that one thing is . . . save! save! save!*
>
> (Flames shoot to the ceiling, and billowing clouds of smoke fill the Wizard's reception hall.)

Okay, the scene may be a little far-fetched, but the basic message is right on. All of the things that Dorothy mentioned, plus many more, are important issues that must be addressed when creating a retirement plan. But mastering the rest of these issues won't get you much in the way of retirement security if you don't also save money from your current income. Social Security, a company pension, or (for most people) an inheritance windfall will not be enough to bridge the gap. According to a study published by the Federal Reserve Bank of Cleveland, statistics show that less than 2 percent of households receive bequests of more than $100,000 and that huge windfalls go to only a very few (and very fortunate) people. What's more, today's retirees are spending down their assets more than previous generations on everything from leisure to medical care. Combine that fact with the propensity for longer life spans, and retirees may well end up going through the assets that would have gone to their kids. Indeed, based on recent Federal Reserve statistics, less than a quarter of households headed by someone over sixty-five expect to leave a substantial bequest. So more than ever before, the lifestyle you will be able to live in retirement in the future comes down to how much you are willing to save today.

Which brings me to my unabashed aim in this chapter—namely, to convince you of the overriding importance of diligent saving, both within retirement vehicles such as 401(k)s and IRAs and outside such accounts. You can be a world-class stock picker and know more about 401(k) plans than a benefits consultant, but you can't put your investing skills to work without money to invest, and the many advantages of tax-favored retirement savings plans are meaningless if you don't contribute to them.

Above all, I want to demonstrate that the sooner you begin saving, the better off you will be. By starting early in your career, you'll vastly increase your chances of accumulating a nice big nest egg for retirement. And you'll also have more flexibility in reacting to the economic and financial bumps you'll inevitably encounter along the way.

Saving Versus Investing

Many people think that the most important factor in building a retirement nest egg is knowing which investments to buy. To be sure, investing does play a big role in boosting the value of our savings. But when you come down to it, we have very little say in what kind of return we can earn from the financial markets. Oh, there are times when we have the *illusion* of being in control, as we did during the tech boom of the late 1990s. But in reality we're just along for the ride, as investors discovered during the market collapse that began in 2000. And while there's plenty of reason to expect that despite such setbacks, the markets will deliver solid long-term returns, there's little we as individuals can do to change the course of the markets in the short term or, for that matter, to boost long-term returns beyond what the markets see fit to deliver.

When it comes to the amount we save, on the other hand, we *are* in driver's seat. For most of us, by cutting back here and there, perhaps opting for a less opulent home, a basic minivan instead of an option-filled Mercedes SUV, and more meals eaten at home, we can exert control over how much we spend and how much we save.

Of course, many of us blame our failure to save on a lack of income. "If only I had a higher salary," we say, "I could begin to save." There are five common excuses, and for most people most of the time they don't hold water.

1. *"I just don't make enough money to save."* Oh, really? Then why do studies show that at every income level, from the very highest to the very lowest, there were always some people who managed to save money and others who managed to spend every cent they earned? There is almost always some way to pare back expenses so that you can put aside even a small amount of money each month. If you're serious about retiring in comfort, you'll find a way to be diligent about saving for the future.

2. *"I can't afford to save now, but I'll definitely get started later."* The problem is that later never arrives. You can always find some reason why now is an inconvenient time to begin saving and why some vague date in the future will be better. So just take the plunge and get started now.

3. *"I want to spend my money now while I'm young and can enjoy life, not when I'm retired and I can't."* There are two fallacies here. First is the idea that you can't enjoy life unless you spend every dime you make. Nonsense. Spending does not equal happiness and fulfillment. Second, the idea that life after you retire isn't quite on a par with that of your youth is being disproven by a whole new generation of retirees who are leading active and fulfilling lives doing the things they never had time to do during their salad days.

4. *"There's no sense in saving because some emergency or setback will force me to spend the money before retirement anyway."* Sure, there's always the chance that unexpected expenses or financial problems might force you to dip into the money you've managed to save. Of course, the financial security of having some money saved can also help you recover more quickly from financial setbacks and allow you to build up your stash again.

5. *"Nobody in my family has ever been a saver. I'm genetically programmed to spend."* When it comes to saving habits, genetics do *not* rule. I, for example, come from a long line of prolific spenders—I'm talking people who spent what they earned and borrowed to spend more. Yet I've still managed to arrive at a reasonable balance between saving and spending. In the end, there's nothing magical or mystical about the ability to save. It comes down to making the choice to save—and then sticking with that choice.

Harnessing the Power of Compounding

One reason that regular saving plays such a powerful role in building wealth for retirement stems directly from the power of compounding. It's very straightforward and simple, boiling down to nothing more than earning interest on interest or earning a gain on a gain you've already earned.

Let's take a simple example. Assume that each year you invest $10,000 in a stock fund that earns a steady 8 percent per year. (In reality, of course, a stock fund's returns will jump around a lot from year to year, but just to make the point, go with me on this. And while we're keeping things simple, let's leave taxes out of the equation.) At the end of the first year, you would have earned $800 and your stock account's value would be $10,800. Assuming you reinvest your gain in the stock fund and earn 8 percent the second year, you would earn another $800 on your original ten grand, plus 8 percent on the $800 you earned the previous year, or another $64. Add that $864 to the $10,800 you started with at the beginning of the second year, and your account value is now $11,664 ($10,800 + $800 + $64). Now, the third year, you would earn 8 percent on your original ten grand ($800), plus 8 percent on the $800 you earned the first year ($64), plus 8 percent on the $800 you earned on your original ten grand the second year ($64), plus 8 percent on the $64 you earned the previous year ($5.12). Add those amounts to the $11,664 you started with at the beginning of the third year, and your account is worth $12,597.12. And the fourth year . . . well, you get the idea.

If you keep this process going over many, many years, the bucks really begin to add up. For example, your original $10,000 would be worth $21,589 at the end of ten years, $46,610 at the end of twenty years, and $100,630 at the end of thirty years. That's more than ten times the value of your original $10,000 investment, all because of the power of compounding.

Start Early with a Little, End Up with a Lot

Of course, turning $10,000 into $100,000 through compounding is great—if you've got ten thousand bucks to start with. But what if you don't happen to have a spare ten grand lying around the house? Or even a spare five grand, or a thousand bucks for that matter?

Not to worry. You don't have to start with a big pile of money to end up with a big pile of money. Indeed, for most of us, the *real* power of compounding comes into play in the way it can make relatively small amounts of money invested on a regular basis add up. And in the case of investing for retirement, the earlier the start you get, the bigger the bucks you'll have waiting for you when you call it a career.

Here's an example of how an early start plus regular savings can create a substantial retirement nest egg.

Let's say that starting at age thirty you begin putting $100 a month into a diversified portfolio of mutual funds that earns 8 percent per year. If you stick with this regimen month after month, year after year, until you retire at age sixty-five, you would have roughly $216,000. Not bad. You put in $42,000—or $100 a month for thirty-five years, or 420 months—and you end up with nearly a quarter of a million.

Of course, if you can manage to put away more than $100 a month, the amount you can accumulate expands tremendously. If you socked away $200 a month starting at age thirty and earned 8 percent annually, you would have about $431,000 by age sixty-five. And if you socked away $500 a month, you would have roughly $1.1 million.

The Cost of a Late Start

The impressive numbers above, however, depend not just on your saving diligently and earning a decent 8 percent return *but on getting an early start.* Indeed, without that early jump, the amount you can accumulate drops off precipitously.

For example, if you didn't start putting away that $100 a month until age thirty-five, then you would have about $142,000 at age sixty-five rather than the $216,000 you would have had if you'd started at thirty. That's right—delaying just five years cost you $74,000. And if you had postponed saving till age forty, then you would have $91,000 at age sixty-five, or $125,000 less. Hold off till fifty, and you would have just $34,000, or $182,000 less.

One of the most unyielding facts of retirement planning is that it is very difficult to make up for lost time. You can boost the amount you save, of course, but it can take quite an increase to get to where you would have been had you started earlier. For example, if you save $300 a month from age thirty and earn 8 percent annually, you would have roughly $647,000 by age sixty-five. Assuming you earn the same 8 percent return but don't begin saving till age forty, you would have to stash away just over $700 a month to accumulate a comparable amount. In short, you would have to more than double your savings—possible but difficult.

Of course, the other way to overcome a late start is to earn a higher return. But to accumulate $647,000 by age sixty-five by saving $300 a month starting at age forty, you would have to boost your return by more than half, to nearly 13.5 percent a year. Possible? Perhaps for a short time. During the market boom of the '90s, investors earned those kinds of returns. Problem is, such high returns also come with high risk, the risk being the chance that stocks that deliver such outsize returns might tank. And that, of course, is exactly what happened in 2000. The overheated stock market collapsed, and the people who thought above-average returns had become the norm found themselves saddled with losses. Despite this gut-wrenching setback, I fully expect that the stock market will continue to deliver solid gains in the future (and I'll explain why in Chapter 6). But to count on anything like 13.5 percent a year for your retirement savings over the long term is, I think, wishful thinking at best. And shooting for such gains in an attempt to make up for a late start, in my view, carries the risk of putting you even further behind.

Dueling Theories of Budgeting

Clearly, the single most important thing you can do to build retirement security for yourself is to embark on a disciplined savings program. Question is, though, how do you do it?

Well, unless you earn so much money that you can buy everything you want and *still* have money left over, then saving for retirement ultimately comes down to some form of budgeting—that is, managing your financial affairs so that the amount of money you have going out is less than the amount you have coming in.

As I see it, there are two basic, though radically different, theories to creating a budget. I wouldn't say that either is inherently superior to the other, although I do have a distinct preference for one of the two, as you'll soon see. The important thing, though, is to choose a budgeting system that seems best suited to your personality and your financial situation, and stick with it.

The Number Cruncher's Budget

Probably the most popular theory of budgeting—or at least the one you see mentioned most often in financial books and magazines—is what I call the Number Cruncher's Budget. Basically, the idea is to break down your spending into a variety of categories, so you can tell exactly where your money is going and how much (if any) is left for saving. You can then set a target—either a dollar amount or, preferably, a percentage of income for savings—and identify specific categories where you might cut back to reach that target.

If you want, you can really throw yourself into this type of budgeting by using software packages that allow you to create electronic worksheets that track your spending not just in typical categories such as housing, health care, education, debt repayment, transportation, and such, but down to the smallest detail—how much you spend on, say, decaf versus caffeinated latte. These programs usually allow you to create elaborate pie charts showing exactly what percentage of your income goes into each of these various categories and how that percentage changes month to month. Armed with this sort of detailed information, you can then begin looking for ways to cut back. If this sort of approach appeals to you, you might try software packages such as Quicken or Microsoft Money. Or you can go to websites that offer free interactive budgeting worksheets. Bankrate.com (www.bankrate.com), for example, offers an online worksheet that lets you plug your spending into ten categories and then shows you how your spending as a percentage of income in each category compares to that of the average U.S. household. The Instant Budget Maker on the CNNMoney site (cgi.money.cnn.com/tools/instantbudget/instantbudget_101.jsp) allows you to break down your spending into even more categories (more than fifty in all) and then compare it to the spending of U.S. households whose members are roughly the same age as you.

You don't have to take this high-tech approach, however. You can do pretty much the same thing with a plain old paper worksheet like the one that appears on the next page. This worksheet, like the online versions you'll find at Bankrate.com and CNN-Money, is based on spending figures compiled for the Bureau of Labor Statistics Consumer Expenditures Survey.

The worksheet on page 37 enables you to see where your income is going and how much is left over for saving—and you can compare your spending habits in various categories with those of other Americans. You shouldn't necessarily be alarmed, however, if your spending as a percentage of income differs from the benchmarks on the table. For one thing, these figures are *averages* and thus mask wide variations from household to household. For more detailed versions of this table, check out the Department of Labor's Consumer Expenditures Survey site (www.bls.gov/cex/home.htm).

Remember, though, the goal here isn't to see how many categories you can slice your spending into or to make your spending conform to some national average. Your spending patterns and needs may be quite a bit different from the average U.S. household's. Perhaps you're willing to spend less than most

ANNUAL INCOME (AVERAGE)

	All Households $44,649		Affluent Households $110,118		Your Household $_____	
	$ AVER-AGE	% OF INCOME	$ AVER-AGE	% OF INCOME	$ AMOUNT	% OF INCOME
Annual Expenses (average)	41,414	92.8	83,700	76.0	_____	____
Housing (total)	10,586	23.7	21,988	20.0	_____	____
Mortgage payments and property taxes	4,897	11.0	11,828	10.7	_____	____
Maintenance, repairs, and insurance	842	1.9	1,503	1.4	_____	____
Household furnishings and equipment	1,652	3.7	3,450	3.1	_____	____
Utilities	2,487	5.6	3,522	3.2	_____	____
Other expenses	708	1.6	1,685	1.5	_____	____
Food (total)	5,857	13.1	9,460	8.6	_____	____
At home	3,577	8.0	5,287	4.8	_____	____
Restaurants, takeout, etc.	2,280	5.1	4,173	3.8	_____	____
Transportation (auto expenses, including fuel and insurance, and public transportation)	7,568	16.9	13,315	12.1	_____	____
Income taxes (federal, state, and local)	3,117	7.0	9,749	8.9	_____	____
Social Security and pensions	3,893	8.7	10,677	9.7	_____	____
Life insurance	415	0.9	880	0.8	_____	____
Apparel and services	2,004	4.5	3,989	3.6	_____	____
Health care (total)	2,120	4.7	2,864	2.6	_____	____
Health insurance	985	2.2	1,254	1.1	_____	____
Health services and supplies	1,135	2.5	1,610	1.5	_____	____
Entertainment	1,958	4.4	3,866	3.5	_____	____
Education	636	1.4	1,462	1.3	_____	____
Gifts and charitable contributions	1,344	3.0	3,050	2.8	_____	____
Miscellaneous expenses	1,916	4.3	2,400	2.2	_____	____

households on transportation because you don't really care whether you have the latest model car and whether it has fine Corinthian leather upholstery and a satellite navigation system. Or maybe a car is important to you because you've got a long commute to work, but you spend far less on entertainment than the average household because you'd rather spend your time reading and gardening than going out to nightclubs or watching Adam Sandler movies. So if you use a Number Cruncher–type approach to budgeting that compares your spending against that of the average household, you should think of the percentages in various categories not so much as targets to hit but as guidelines or red flags that may alert you if your spending in some area is really out of whack. Even if you find that you're spending, say, double the national average on eating out, it may be worth it to you to maintain that expense but cut back somewhere else. Your goal is to wring savings out of your budget overall, not necessarily out of each and every category of spending.

The Two-Line Budget

There is a second theory of budgeting, one that is much simpler and, to my mind at least, much more effective. I call it the Two-Line Budget, and it looks like this:

The amount I want to save	$_____	(% of income)
Everything else	$_____	(% of income)

I'm not being flippant here. I'm dead serious. The aim of budgeting is to help you achieve a target level of savings, right? So the rationale behind this approach is that you can get to that target a lot more easily by immediately docking each paycheck for the target percentage of your income you've decided upon, and then forcing yourself to live on whatever income you have left.

The idea behind this approach is that you can—and should—tailor your lifestyle to your income *after* savings rather than making your savings adjust to your lifestyle.

Let's take an example. Suppose you earn $40,000 a year and you would like to save 10 percent, or $4,000, of that income. That means you'll put away $4,000 a year, allowing you to live on a pretax income of $36,000. Is that doable? Well, think of it this way. Suppose that you didn't make $40,000 a year. Suppose you made $36,000 a year. Would you be able to live on that amount? Of course you would; millions of Americans live on far less. And the reason you would be able to live on that amount is because you would make your spending habits conform to the fact that you have $36,000 a year coming in.

Now let's assume that you get a raise that takes your $36,000 salary to $40,000. If you're like most people, you would probably find all sorts of things you "need" that would use up that extra four grand. If you then get a raise to $50,000, then you would likely find yet more things that you need to use up the extra ten grand. (You don't take home the entire $10,000, of course, because of taxes, but you get the point.) Which brings us to probably the most significant fact about spending and saving—namely, we tend to adjust our spending habits so that we consume virtually whatever income we make.

What I'm suggesting in my Two-Line Budget, however, is that you take a completely different approach: adjust your spending to your income after savings. Granted, this technique amounts to a kind of psychological ploy, attempting to fool yourself into thinking you have an income of, say, $36,000 a year to live on rather than $40,000. But in fact, if you want to build a nest egg that will carry you through retirement, that's exactly what you've got to do. You've got to force yourself to live slightly *below* your means rather than living at or above your means, which is what most of us do. And the easiest way to do that, it seems to me, is to put yourself into a situation where you think of your income as being lower than it is by taking the savings off the top. In effect, this is why payroll deduction savings plans, such as putting money into a 401(k), work so well for so many people. The money is diverted into savings before it gets into their hot little hands.

Of course, if you're already spending virtually every cent of your income, embarking on a forced savings program like this can be a rude shock. After all, once spending patterns are set they can be difficult to break. But it can be done. One way is to start by setting a percentage that you think you can likely handle, say, 5 percent. If it turns out that percentage is too painful for you to adjust to all at once, you can start with a smaller percentage that feels more comfortable and then increase it gradually. If your income is rising at the same time, you may be able to gradually boost the percentage that goes to saving without feeling much of a change in your lifestyle. The important thing, though, is to set a target and achieve it. Once you've done that, you can consider raising your target even more. How high a percentage you eventually shoot for will largely be a matter of how much you're willing to forgo spending today so that you can have a more comfortable retirement tomorrow. You probably don't want to live like an ascetic, and even if you did, your family might not go along with the idea. But setting a goal of saving at least 10 percent of your income certainly seems reasonable, and aiming for 15 percent or more is hardly outlandish. Just remember, the more spending you can forgo now, the more you'll be able to do during retirement.

Ten Tips to Boost Your Savings

There is no "ideal" budget we should all strive to adopt. Nor does putting aside money for retirement mean you've got to live like an ascetic or a pauper. I've seen budgeting and saving newsletters that suggest people can save all kinds of money by doing things like reusing the plastic wrap on leftovers or turning old blue jeans into pot holders and whatnot. I suppose that's fine if you've got the inclination and the time for such extreme measures. But I believe you must approach saving and spending with a reasonable attitude. I mean, you have only one life to live, and presumably you want to enjoy it a bit while you're living it. What fun would a comfortable retirement be if, in order to afford it, you had to miss out on all the fun life has to offer? What memories would you have to look back on with your family? The great times you had sitting in the house knitting your own wardrobe by lamps powered by fifteen-watt bulbs so you could cut your clothing and electricity costs?

Besides, I don't think extreme measures are very realistic in the long run. You'd end up like one of those people who go on a five-hundred-calorie-a-day starvation diet; they stick to it for maybe a couple of weeks and lose ten pounds or so—and then find themselves in the kitchen at three-thirty in the morning shoveling Sara Lee cheesecake into their mouths. Next thing you know, not only have they gained back the ten pounds they lost, they've put on another twenty. Same thing can happen with unrealistic budgets. If you try to live on an unrealistically frugal budget, chances are you'll just give up on saving entirely and be worse off than if you had tried more moderate means of cutting back your spending.

But here are ten ways you might consider paring back spending so that you can bolster your savings and, ultimately, your retirement security.

1. Put Your Savings on Autopilot

The easiest and most efficient way to save is to put the money away before you can get your greedy little hands on it—in other words, sign up for a payroll deduction plan. The best deal on this score—assuming your employer offers one—is a company retirement savings plan such as a 401(k) or a 403(b) plan. These employer-sponsored plans typically allow you to sock away between 6 percent and 15 percent of your salary into investments such as mutual funds—and give you a tax break while you're doing it.

If your employer doesn't offer a tax-deferred plan, see whether money can be automatically deducted from your paycheck and invested in a mutual fund. If that's not possible, then you should look into setting up your own automatic investing plan by having money transferred every two weeks or every month from your checking account to a mutual fund. Most fund

companies offer such a program, many allowing you to participate for as little as $50 a month. Besides the beauty of making
saving simpler, adopting one of these plans also amounts to a
pretty good investing strategy. By investing at regular intervals,
you buy fund shares at a variety of prices, which means you prevent yourself from putting a big chunk of money into the market at a peak, as many investors did back in early 2000, when it
appeared stock prices would continue to soar through the roof.
So an automatic investing plan adds some discipline to your investing strategy.

2. Save Your Raise

Instead of adjusting your standard of living upward the next
time you get a raise, live at the same level you did before you got
the salary boost and save the extra money—preferably through
a payroll deduction plan as described above. Do this and you
will effectively have boosted your savings rate by the amount of
your raise. If that's too ambitious, then at least try to save a portion of your raise, maybe half of it, or perhaps save every other
raise so that you enjoy a rising standard of living but also put
away more for your retirement.

In fact, two well-known economists, Richard Thaler of the
University of Chicago and Shlomo Benartzi of UCLA, have created a savings program based on this premise. It relies on the
principles of behavioral economics to overcome the biggest ob-
stacle to saving—the lack of self-control. The strategy is called
the Save More Tomorrow Plan, and it works like this:

Employees at companies with 401(k) and other payroll deduction savings plans are approached three months before a
scheduled salary increase and asked if they would like to increase the amount they contribute to their savings plan. Those
who agree then set a target savings rate they would eventually
like to achieve. Then, starting with the first paycheck after the
raise, their contribution rate to their savings plan is increased.
Usually, the employees' paycheck remains the same or even
rises since the salary boost offsets the increase in savings. Every

time employees get a raise, their contribution rate to the savings plan continues to rise until they achieve their target savings rate. Employees have the option of dropping out of the program at any time.

The idea is that by agreeing to save in prescheduled amounts in advance, people who normally lack the willpower to save can do so in spite of themselves. And by tying the savings increases to salary hikes, employees are less apt to feel as though they're making financial sacrifices in order to save more. In short, the program more or less tricks employees into doing the right thing—that is, saving more than they otherwise would.

The plan is still in its embryonic stage, but early results are promising. In one company, the average savings rate for people who joined the plan more than tripled, from 3.5 percent of salary to 11.6 percent over a bit more than two years. Thaler and Benartzi hope that eventually Save More Tomorrow will be incorporated into most 401(k) plans.

3. Operate on a Cash Basis

When I buy things with a credit card, it's almost as if I didn't spend anything at all. I don't have the same feeling of separation from my money as I do when shelling out cold hard cash. It makes spending all gain and no pain. What's more, even after I've acquired my booty, I still have cash in my wallet, which means . . . I still have more money to spend! The result, of course, is that I end up spending even more money.

Try to make as many expenditures as possible in cash, either by leaving your credit cards at home or by not reflexively reaching for them every time you buy something. You become much more aware of how much money you're actually going through. That realization alone may help you control your spending more. Second, you'll be less apt to, in effect, spend the same money twice—once in the form of a credit card purchase and a second time when you spend the cash.

The less frequently you use your credit cards, the smaller

the portion of your budget that goes to pay those often outrageous credit card interest rates, which, combined with repayment terms that stretch on for years, have the interest meter ticking for years. Let's say, for example, you've run up $5,000 in credit card charges. If your card charges an 18 percent rate and requires a monthly minimum payment equal to the greater of $10 or 2.5 percent of your outstanding balance (pretty standard terms), then it would take you *more than twenty-five years* to repay that debt, during which time you would have forked over $7,115 in interest on top of the original $5,000 you owed. I think most of us would be surprised to see how much we're paying for the convenience of plastic. Fortunately, there's an easy way to find out. Just go to the calculator section of the Bank Rate Monitor site (www.bankrate.com), select the True Cost of Paying the Minimum link, plug in your balance and repayment terms, and voilà! You'll immediately see how much you'll pay in interest charges. I'll warn you in advance, it's not pretty.

4. Time Your Purchases

As you'll see in the section on investing in Chapter 6, it doesn't pay to time the market—that is, to try to jump in and out of the market based on whether you feel it's ready to go up or down. But it can definitely pay to time your purchases of big-ticket items such as major appliances, cars, computers, and even your wardrobe. Let's say you need to upgrade your computer but, not being a full-blown digital geek, you don't need the latest version with the biggest hard drive, the glitziest graphics, and the most earsplitting sound system. Chances are you can save several hundred to a thousand bucks or more waiting until the major computer manufacturers announce their new systems at the big trade shows—and then buying a system that has just become yesterday's news and therefore has dropped in price. Does this mean you're buying something that's rapidly becoming obsolete? Yes, it does—just as the state-of-the-art systems introduced at the tech trade shows will be obsolete by the time next year's show rolls around. But as long as you're getting enough power to perform the tasks you'll need to carry out on your computer for the next several years, you'll end up with a system that meets your requirements, and you'll have some money you can invest for retirement. This strategy also applies to such things as buying a used car or last year's model instead of one of the new fleet that just arrived in the showroom, and buying your wardrobe when retailers are trying to unload the current season's fashions to make room for the next season's.

One caveat, though. Don't fall into the trap of believing that you're automatically saving money because you're getting a great deal on price. The discounts you get by following this strategy only matter if you are buying items you really need and that you must buy. If you're loading up on goods that you can easily get by without, then you're not saving no matter how good a deal you get.

5. Manage Your Debt

The antithesis of saving is going into debt. But that doesn't necessarily mean you should avoid all borrowing, since debt can be good or bad. Good debt is the debt you incur to acquire an asset that you truly need and can't otherwise afford and that you will put to some productive use. Taking on a mortgage to buy a house would be an example of good debt, as would borrowing to buy a car that makes it easier for you to get to work and live your life. College loans for you or your children are another example of good debt, on the assumption that more education makes for a more interesting life and also represents an investment in that the better educated you are, the higher your earning potential.

Bad debt, on the other hand, is debt you take on to buy things you don't really need. These may include impulse purchases, such as yet another cashmere sweater to add to your collection simply because it's on sale for 40 percent off, or something beyond your means, like a $10,000 three-week first-class tour of Europe when a less expensive vacation is more in line with your finances. Most bad debt is probably incurred through credit cards, although by giving people access via checks to the equity in their homes, home equity lines of credit also make it easy to engage in irresponsible borrowing.

So how can borrowing fit into a savings plan? First, try much as possible to limit yourself to good debt. This will reduce the overall amount of debt you have to carry as well as the amount of your income that will have to go to servicing that debt—that is, paying interest and repaying principal.

Second, whenever you incur debt, good or bad (and let's face it, most of us are probably going to have some bad debt occasionally), try to ensure that you're paying as low a rate as possible. Getting a $150,000 thirty-year fixed-rate mortgage with a rate of, say, 7 percent instead of 7.5 percent would lower your monthly mortgage payments by $50 a month, freeing up cash that you can invest for your retirement.

Similarly, if you're going to borrow against the equity in your home, make sure you're getting a competitive rate. Some home equity lenders charge two or more percentage points above the prime rate (the rate banks charge to their best corporate customers) for their home equity lines of credit. Others charge a rate equal to prime or even a half to a full percentage point below prime. You want to borrow from a bank in that second group (although the rate you get will also be influenced by such factors as your creditworthiness and the amount of equity in your house).

As for credit cards, I recommend avoiding carrying a balance for the reasons I mentioned earlier. But if you must carry a balance, then at least try to find a card that charges a reasonable rate, preferably something in the single digits. To find the best deals on mortgages, home equity lines of credit, credit cards, and other loans, you can go to the Bank Rate Monitor site I mentioned earlier, or you can try the Rate Search tool in the Banking & Borrowing section of the CNNMoney website (money.cnn.com/pf/banking/ratesearch.html).

6. Get to Know Your Kitchen Better

With the hectic schedules that most of us have today, it's no wonder that we often end up dashing into McDonald's or a local restaurant or ordering in pizza or Chinese food instead of fixing dinner ourselves at home. Perfectly understandable. Just keep in mind that these convenience expenditures can add up. According to the Bureau of Labor statistics, a two-income family of four with an after-tax income of $55,000 a year spends nearly a third of its grocery budget, or $3,000 a year, eating out.

Now, it would be unrealistic to think that we can eliminate this expense completely. Sometimes you simply don't have the time to prepare dinner. And while eating out isn't a *necessity,* it's also true that the occasional meal at a nice restaurant can make life more pleasant and put us in a better frame of mind to deal with the world.

That said, you may be able to find ways of cutting back on this expense, perhaps by not making a quick stop at the golden arches an automatic reflex every time you're running a bit late or by going to a less expensive restaurant with "character and ambience" rather than to a monument to haute cuisine that charges prices that match its inflated image of itself. This way you can still indulge in the pleasures that civilized life has to offer but maybe free up a few hundred to several thousand bucks a year that you can invest for the future.

7. Make the Tax Laws Work for You

We tend to overlook the effect taxes have on our budget because of the government's ingenious method of siphoning taxes bit by bit, paycheck by paycheck, instead of presenting us with one big, fat tax bill at the end of the year. But make no mistake: Taxes can soak up a large percentage of your budget. And although we may have somewhat limited maneuvering room for lowering our tax burden, there are a number of perfectly legal steps you can take to lower your contribution to government coffers.

One of the simplest and most effective ways to pare your tax burden is to make full use of tax-advantaged savings vehicles we'll be discussing in the next two chapters, namely, 401(k)s, IRAs, and the like. You get a tax break, *plus* you boost your savings. Another thing you can do is be sure you're taking advantage of every single possible deduction available to you. Some of these deductions are fairly obvious—mortgage interest, property taxes, et cetera. But there are others that may be deductible that are often overlooked, including medical expenses, job search costs, education expenses, the cost of keeping a home office, work-related auto expenses, charitable donations, and many others.

You may also be able to save on taxes related to your investments. If you've sold shares of stock at a profit or you have a mutual fund that's distributed a capital gain to you, you may be able to shelter that gain from taxes by taking a loss in other investments. Barring that, you might also be able to deduct a portion of your loss against noninvestment income such as your salary. Similarly, you may be able to lower your tax bill by investing in what are known as tax-managed funds, that is, funds that employ specific strategies to minimize taxable distributions. I'll discuss some investment-related tax moves when we get to investing strategies in Chapter 6. For more information on deductions you should consider and other ways to lower your overall tax bill, I suggest you check out Yahoo! Tax Center (taxes.yahoo.com) and the Planning & Tax Center at Quicken.com (www.quicken.com/planning/).

8. Keep Car Costs Down

We Americans love our cars. After all, we see them not only as transportation but as a way to express our personalities. And that's fine, except that if you're shelling out upward of $700 a month in loan or lease payments for one of those highly engineered $60,000 Mercedes über-sedans, your self-expression may be interfering with your ability to build an adequate retirement nest egg for yourself. No one is suggesting you drive around town in a beat-up junker. On the other hand, with the wide variety of choices out there in the auto market today, you ought to be able to find a car that's dependable, durable, and attractive at a price that doesn't soak up every cent of your disposable income.

By going to auto buying sites such as Edmunds.com (www. edmunds.com) and IntelliChoice (www.intellichoice.com), you can gets tons of detailed information on hundreds of models of new and used cars that can help you decide whether, given your income and the amount you need to save, you really ought to spend $55,000 for a luxury sedan when you can find perfectly reliable and stylish sedans for $20,000 or less, or for that matter even less expensive used cars. What's more, these sites can help you compare cars not just on the basis of their purchase price but by their total ownership costs—the true cost of the car when you consider expenses such as depreciation, financing cost, taxes, fees, insurance premiums, fuel costs, maintenance, and repairs. Bottom line: By reaching a reasonable compromise between the car of your dreams and a car that looks great and runs well yet doesn't strain your budget, you may be able to save several hundred bucks a month in auto-related expenses that you can funnel into savings.

9. Don't Overinsure

As I'll describe in detail in Chapter 8, insurance is an integral part of any retirement plan. But while you certainly don't want to forgo or even scrimp on the coverage you need to provide a reasonable safety net for you and your family, you also don't want to spend more of your money than you have to.

Fortunately, there are a variety of ways you can save anywhere from a few hundred to a few thousand dollars a year on insurance costs while still maintaining adequate protection. In the case of life insurance, for example, going with a low-cost term life policy rather than a higher-premium whole life policy can easily reduce your insurance outlays by thousands of dollars a year. And in the case of homeowners and auto insurance, raising the policy's deductible—the amount you pay for a claim before the insurer kicks in—from, say, $500 to $1,000 or higher can easily cut costs by 10 to 20 percent. Similarly, linking your home and auto coverage in one company rather than getting policies from two insurers can often save you 10 to 15 percent. Finally, be sure to check with your insurer to see if you qualify for savings for home alarm systems and by having any teenage drivers in your household take a driver's ed course. For specific tips on how you might lower your overall insurance costs, check out sites such as Fidelity Investments' Insurance.com (www. insurance.com), the Auto Insurance Advocate site (www.auto insuranceadvocate.net), Insweb (www.insweb.com), and Quote-smith (www.quotesmith.com).

10. Keep an Expense Log

As I noted earlier, I'm not a big fan of creating incredibly detailed budgets that break your spending down into dozens of categories and subcategories. I'm just not convinced this laborious and time-consuming process actually leads anyone to save money. But I do think it can make sense to keep a detailed expenditure log for a month or so just to give you a good idea of where your money is actually going and to pinpoint some possible areas you might target for savings.

I'm not talking about anything fancy here; just make a note of every time you spend money throughout the day, whether by cash, check, or credit card. And I mean every instance—your morning coffee and doughnut, that late-morning latte, your Blockbuster rentals, filling the gas tank, that newsstand tabloid. (Hey, maybe aliens really have developed a diet that cures cancer and melts away the pounds at the same time.) Then, after a month or so, just read through the log to see if anything grabs your attention. You might find that the little snacks you buy throughout the day are costing you more than $120 a month. Or that your car is a much bigger fuel user than you'd ever imagined, guzzling $200 a month in gas. Or that at the rate you're adding new items to your wardrobe, you're going to have to turn the master bedroom into a walk-in closet. The idea here isn't that you'll necessarily cut out all of these expenses, or for that matter that you'll eliminate even one of them entirely. But by seeing where your money is actually going, you may find places where you can tighten up your spending without making a huge sacrifice and yet free up some cash you can put toward retirement savings.

Playing Catch-up

Failing to get a good jump on savings early in life makes accumulating a sizable nest egg for retirement more difficult. But even though we may know this instinctively, many of us nonetheless don't get started saving until later in life. Sometimes the fault is our own. Retirement seems like a far-off mirage that we can worry about later, so we don't really begin planning for it until the reality is much closer—sometimes too close. Other times it's just the vicissitudes of everyday life that get in the way. We have all good intentions of saving, but the kids' orthodontia bills deplete our savings or the exhaust system on the twelve-year-old Honda Civic begins smoking like a Weber barbecue grill and to pay the repair bill we've got to dip into our retirement stash. Or maybe just as you're getting on your feet financially and about to embark on a disciplined savings program, *boom!* Your employer suddenly "right-sizes" you out of a job and instead of building up your meager pot of savings, you're drawing on it.

But no matter why you find yourself pushing forty, fifty, or even sixty with little or no savings, that's no reason to resign yourself to living out your golden years on a diet of SPAM and Old Milwaukee. Yes, you would have been better off if you had been able to sock away a few dollars earlier in life. But if you didn't, you didn't. Your job now is to make the best you can of your situation. And while you can't completely undo the damage of getting a late start, you can still improve your retirement prospects, often dramatically.

For example, let's say that for whatever reason you find

yourself at age fifty-five with nothing—zilch, *nada*—put away for retirement. Essentially, this puts you between the proverbial rock and a hard place. Assuming you've been working or married to someone who has, you will qualify for Social Security benefits. But those are going to provide a modest existence at best. So, what can you do?

Well, let's say that as a last-ditch effort to build a retirement nest egg, you force yourself at age fifty-five to start saving $200 a month. And to simplify things from a tax standpoint, let's assume you do this saving in one or more tax-advantaged accounts, such as a 401(k), a traditional or Roth IRA, or a tax-managed mutual fund. Maybe you cut back spending to do this, maybe you take a second job, whatever. But somehow or other let's assume you manage to put away $200 a month. And let's say that by investing in a diversified portfolio of stocks and bonds, you earn an annualized 8 percent per year. Where would that put you?

Well, assuming you stuck to this regimen for ten years, you would likely have a nest egg worth just over $36,000 before taxes by age sixty-five. Granted, that's hardly a fortune, but it's certainly better than going into retirement without an extra thirty-six grand. And if you managed to avoid dipping into this stash for another five years, until you were seventy, then your $36,000 would have grown to roughly $53,000. Again, not a fortune but enough to provide at least a bit of a cushion against financial setbacks or to allow you a few creature comforts later in life.

Of course, if you can be a bit more aggressive in your late-start savings program, you can build a larger retirement fund. For example, if you can manage to scrape together $300 a month instead of $200 and earn 8 percent annually, then you would have a nest egg of just over $54,000 at age sixty-five, and if you let that sum ride another five years, you would be sitting on almost $80,000. And if you could boost your savings to, say, $500 a month, you would be looking at a bit more than $90,000 at age sixty-five and roughly $133,000 if you left it untouched till age seventy. This is a pretty decent sum for someone who didn't even begin saving for retirement until way, way late in life.

Of course, all of these amounts would be much larger if we assume a higher rate of return on your savings. For example, if you saved $500 a month and earned a 10 percent annualized rate, then you would have a nest egg worth just over $100,000 at age sixty-five and more than $160,000 if left untouched till age seventy. And if you earned a 12 percent annualized rate, you would have roughly $112,000 by sixty-five and almost $200,000 by seventy.

But I strongly caution you against making projections on the basis of unrealistically high rates of return. Just because some online retirement savings calculator will let you plug in a return of 12 percent, 14 percent, 16 percent, or more doesn't mean it makes sense to do so. We'll get into more detail about rates of return in the investing sections of Chapter 6. But suffice it to say for now that to earn a higher rate of return, you've got to take on more risk. And when you do that, you raise the possibility not just of failing to accumulate as much money as you thought you would but of accumulating much less than you would have had you aimed for a more reasonable rate of return.

So keep your return expectations planted firmly within the realm of reality. Essentially, that means you should probably think in terms of annual returns of 8 to 10 percent or so. If you end up doing better than that and thus accumulate more money than you had expected, fine. That's far better than basing your savings plan on achieving an unrealistically high return and then entering retirement with a tinier nest egg than you expected.

There are a few other moves you might consider that can make a big difference in the retirement lifestyle you'll be able to afford, and I will get into those in Chapter 7. But the single most important thing you can do to ensure a comfortable retirement is to save. And that's true even if you are getting a late start. In the fantasy world of *The Wizard of Oz,* Dorothy was able to rely on help from the Good Witch of the North and her magic ruby slippers. But in the real world of retirement planning in the twenty-first century, there are no supernatural beings or magic formulas to help you accumulate money for retirement. You've got to do it on your own, and one way or another, that means spending less today and investing your savings so you can enjoy them tomorrow.

Chapter 3

MAKE THE MOST OF YOUR 401(K)

Remember in the last chapter I said that there are no *Wizard of Oz*–style supernatural beings, ruby red slippers, or magic formulas to help you accumulate the money you'll need for retirement? Well, that's true. But, fortunately, many of us do have access to a savings vehicle that, although not quite magic, comes pretty damn close: 401(k)s. What's more, as a result of some legislative changes that allow us to stash away more pre-tax dollars into these plans than ever before, 401(k)s have become an even more effective retirement savings tool than they've been in the past, which is saying a lot.

Of course, 401(k) plans can't do our saving for us. *We* still have to come up with the money to put in the account, and *we* have to decide how our contribution will be invested. And by now I'm sure that everyone knows our 401(k) balances are hardly immune from the ups and downs of the stock market. After stock prices began plunging in 2000, for example, many people saw the value of their 401(k) accounts drop precipitously. Still, over the long term, 401(k)s, with their unique tax advantages and other special features, represent our best shot at accumulating the money we'll need for a comfortable retirement.

In fact, at a time when traditional corporate pension plans are becoming anachronisms and the value of the Social Security benefits we'll collect remains a big question mark, the size of our 401(k) will likely determine more than any other single factor what kind of lifestyle we'll be able to afford in retirement.

So the key to a comfortable retirement, clearly, is getting the most we can out of our 401(k). Unfortunately, many of us fail to do that. Whether it's because we don't understand how 401(k)s work or because we don't appreciate the many benefits 401(k)s offer, some 20 percent of us who are eligible for a 401(k) don't even bother to sign up for the plan. And too often, those of us who do enroll don't get nearly as much out of our 401(k) as we should. We don't contribute as much as the plan allows, or if we do contribute the max, we do little to make sure we're taking full advantage of the various investing choices our plan offers. For example, a Mutual of Omaha study a few years ago found that nearly half of 401(k) participants couldn't name a single investment option in their plan, and 75 percent spend less than ten hours a year evaluating and monitoring their 401(k) investments. That's a shame, because the more you know about your 401(k) and the better you manage it, the larger the nest egg you'll be able to accumulate for retirement.

In this chapter, I'll explain the ins and outs of 401(k)s so that you will be able to take full advantage of your plan. I'll start by going over the fundamentals of how these plans work, what investment choices you typically get, how matching contributions work, and how various provisions of the 2001 tax bill have made 401(k)s an even more effective retirement savings tool than they were before. We'll then move on to more advanced issues such as the pros and cons of borrowing from your 401(k), what to do with your 401(k) assets if you switch jobs, and how to lobby your employer for a better plan if yours has shortcomings.

Of course, no discussion of 401(k)s would be complete without addressing the issue of how large (or small) a role company stock should play in your 401(k). That's especially true in the wake of the debacles at companies such as Enron and World-

Com, where thousands of employees who had invested heavily in their employer's stock lost huge portions of their retirement savings. So I'll devote a portion of this chapter to this topic, too.

One final note before we begin our look at 401(k)s. In the wake of the 2003 tax law changes that pushed down the maximum tax rates on dividends and long-term capital gains to 15 percent, many financial experts have been giving the impression that investors might be better off forgoing 401(k)s. The rationale is that since all gains in 401(k)s are taxed at ordinary income tax rates as high as 35 percent, investors would come out ahead investing outside 401(k)s, where long-term capital gains and dividends would qualify for the new lower rates. But this analysis overlooks the fact that most 401(k) contributions are made with pretax dollars, which results in an extremely valuable initial tax break. For that reason alone, you are almost always better off doing a 401(k) than investing in a taxable account, even if the tax rate is somewhat lower. Throw in the matching contributions that many employers give, and 401(k)s are virtually *always* the better option. That's not to say you shouldn't reevaluate certain aspects of your retirement investing strategy in light of the 2003 tax law. (We'll get into that in the investment discussion in Chapter 6.) But don't lose sight of the fact that even after taking the new tax law's lower rates into account, for the overwhelming majority of us the 401(k) remains our most valuable retirement savings option.

Chalk Talk: The ABCs of 401(k)s

You may already be familiar with how 401(k)s work. On the other hand, perhaps you've got a general idea but are a bit vague on specifics such as how the latest revision in the tax laws affects the amount you're allowed to contribute. Just to be on the safe side, I'll give a quick review of 401(k) fundamentals. Oh, and to distinguish what I say from the information you may get from your company's personnel department, I'm going to try to give my explanation in plain English.

A 401(k) is a savings plan—technically, it's a form of a corporate profit-sharing plan—that allows you to invest a percentage of your salary for retirement, typically in mutual funds or other investments. Usually, you're allowed to contribute anywhere from 6 to 15 percent of your salary, and most employers will match a portion of your contribution. The federal government also sets limits on how much you can contribute, although the Economic Growth and Tax Relief Reconciliation Act of 2001 raised those limits, thus allowing many higher-income workers to plow even more into their 401(k)s.

Prior to the 2001 tax law, the most you could contribute to your 401(k) in any one year was $10,500. But the new law boosted the maximum allowable contribution amount to $11,000 in 2002, $12,000 in 2003, $13,000 in 2004, $14,000 in 2005, and $15,000 in 2006. After that, the max will be pegged in $500 increments to inflation. Of course, whether you can actually contribute the maximum depends on the rules laid out in your particular plan. If your plan allows you to contribute no more than, say, 10 percent of your salary to your 401(k), then you could hit 2004's $13,000 ceiling only if you earned a salary of $130,000 or more. If you earn, say, $100,000, your plan's 10 percent-of-salary cap would limit you to a $10,000 contribution.

The 2001 tax law also allows workers fifty and older to make additional "catch-up" contributions to boost their savings prior to retirement. The catch-up amount for 2003 is $2,000 and rises by $1,000 a year until it hits $5,000 in 2006, after which it is pegged to inflation. That means that by 2006 a person fifty or older could conceivably sock away as much as $20,000 a year in a 401(k).

One of the features that makes 401(k)s so appealing is that your contribution is automatically deducted from your paycheck *before* the IRS can lay its hands on it. Which means taxes on your 401(k) contributions—and on any gains your contributions earn—are postponed until you pull the money out of your account. This is why 401(k)s are called tax-deferred savings plans. Just in case you're interested, 401(k)s get their clunky name from the section of the Internal Revenue Code that covers these types of retirement savings plans. After the market collapse in early 2000, when many 401(k) participants saw their 401(k) plans hit for losses of 50 percent or more, some wags began calling these plans "201(k)s," which was kind of funny unless you happened to be one of the people sitting on big losses in your 401(k).

Because 401(k) plans are an employee benefit, you can participate in one only if it's offered by the company you work for. (If your company doesn't offer a 401(k), chances are you're still eligible for one or more of the retirement savings plans discussed in the next chapter, so don't despair.) But even if your company does have a 401(k), your employer may make you wait a while before you're eligible for it. That waiting period can't exceed a year, however, as long as you're over twenty-one. Increasingly, though, companies are allowing employees to sign up sooner rather than later. About 40 percent or so of 401(k) plans now make workers eligible within three months of being hired, and some companies enroll new employees automatically.

You may face one other waiting period. Any money you invest in your 401(k)—plus any earnings on that money—is always yours. But you may have to wait a while before you are vested (employee-benefit jargon for "legally entitled to") in any matching contributions your employer makes in your account, as well as any earnings on the employer's contributions. If your plan uses what's known as "cliff vesting," then your employer's contributions and earnings on those contributions become yours all at once after you've been with the company three years. If your plan has what's known as "graded vesting," then you become vested a bit at a time, although that process can't take more than six years.

This little rundown on rules and regulations tells you what you'll typically find in 401(k)s. You should know, however, that the federal rules governing 401(k)s give employers a good amount of leeway in how they set up their plans and how they enforce rules on everything from how much you can contribute to whether or not you can borrow from your 401(k). So I believe it's a good idea to have a chat with the friendly people in your human resources department to be sure you understand the specifics of how your particular plan works. At the very least, you should ask for a copy of your 401(k)'s Summary Plan Description, a booklet that details the rules governing all aspects of your plan. Employers are required to distribute the Summary Plan Description to plan participants

Now that we've got the basics out of the way, let's get to some of the reasons that for most of us 401(k)s represent our single best shot at accumulating the savings we'll need to fund a secure and comfortable retirement.

The Five Most Important Ways a 401(k) Helps You Save for Retirement

You Get a Tax Break on Your Contributions

Since you contribute pretax dollars to a 401(k), you immediately rack up some serious tax savings. For example, if you're in the 25 percent tax bracket and you put $5,000 into your 401(k) over the course of a year, you've effectively lowered your federal income tax bill by $1,250 for that year. Those tax savings go right to work in your 401(k), so it's almost as if the government is making a contribution to your plan. Of course, taxes are eventually due on your contribution—and on all earnings in your account—when you withdraw the money. But you get to invest those annual tax savings in the meantime, which means you can build up a larger retirement stash than you would be able to do if that money had gone into the U.S. Treasury's coffers instead.

You Defer Taxes on All Gains in Your 401(k) Account

Any gains the investments in your 401(k) generate also escape taxation until you withdraw them. So instead of the IRS and the state siphoning off a piece of your return each year, your entire gain is reinvested. That means you can earn profits on *all* your investing profits, not just on whatever profit you have left over after paying taxes. This process of tax-deferred compounding can boost the value of your savings dramatically. For example, if you invest $500 a month for thirty years in a 401(k) and earn a steady 10 percent annual return, your 401(k) balance would grow to just over $1 million. If you had invested the same $500 a month in a taxable account and paid taxes on *all* your investment's earnings each year, the value of your taxable account would total just under $622,000, assuming you're in the 27 percent combined state and federal tax bracket. Even if you paid all the taxes due on your 401(k) at one time—which is unlikely, since most people withdraw the money gradually during retirement—you would still be ahead of the taxable account by more than $135,000 because of all the money you earned on untaxed profits over that twenty-year span.

You Usually Get Matching Contributions from Your Employer— in Other Words, Free Money

In about 90 percent of 401(k) plans, the company matches at least part of the contribution you make to your 401(k) account. This is essentially free money. The match usually ranges from 25 percent of what you contribute to as much as twice what you contribute. Most often, though, the employer kicks in 50 cents on the dollar for the first 6 percent of your pay that you contribute—in other words, a match equal to 3 percent of your salary.

You Get to Take Your Money with You When You Switch Jobs

One of the least touted but most valuable features of a 401(k) plan is that it's totally portable. Once you're vested in the plan, the money in your account is yours. If you switch jobs, you can roll it over into another employer's 401(k)—assuming it will accept such rollovers—or you can roll the money into an IRA. (We'll discuss rollovers in detail later in this chapter.) With a traditional company pension plan, by contrast, you may have to wait until you actually retire before you can get your hands on the money the company owes you under that plan, and in the meantime you have no say in how the assets of the plan are invested.

You Get to Invest with Professional Money Managers

Virtually all 401(k) plans allow you to direct your 401(k) contributions into a variety of professionally managed investment portfolios. Those investment options might include any of the following.

Mutual funds. Stock, bond, and money-market mutual funds—including well-known portfolios such as Fidelity Magellan and the Vanguard 500 Index Fund—are a staple of 401(k) plans. Usually, 401(k) investors are getting the same deal on funds as investors outside 401(k)s, although in some cases fund companies create a separate—and more expensive—share class for 401(k) investors. (We'll get into 401(k) fees below.)

Commingled pools. It may sound like a nautical term, but a commingled pool is a portfolio run specifically for retirement plans and not available to the general public. Often these pools are managed by a bank trust department or a large investment firm, sometimes even a separate division of a mutual fund firm. These pools often charge lower fees than mutual funds (a good thing), but it can be harder to get details on the pool's holdings (not a good thing).

Stable value funds. Also known as principal preservation funds, stable value funds buy investments known as GICs, or guaranteed investment contracts, which are investments issued by insurance companies that pay rates of interest comparable to those paid by bank CDs. Stable value funds can protect your money from the ups and downs of the stock market. But your money isn't likely to grow anywhere near as much over the long term as it will in a stock fund.

Company stock. Nearly half of 401(k) plans offer company stock as an investment, and many 401(k)s give their matching contribution in the form of company stock. Of all the investing options in 401(k)s, this is the one that you've got to be the most careful with, which is why I'm devoting a special section to company shares later in this chapter.

Brokerage window. This option, which is being offered by a small but growing number of plans, amounts to having your own brokerage account within your 401(k). You get to invest in virtually any of the twelve thousand or so mutual funds available today. Or you can buy individual stocks and bonds, trading them as often as you like. While brokerage windows definitely broaden your investing vistas and give you greater freedom to trade, they must be used with care. They often involve annual fees of $50 to $150, plus trading costs, that can eat into your gains. And while the idea of racking up big trading gains is appealing, it's important to remember that trading can lead to big losses, too.

A broad range of 401(k) investing options doesn't ensure competitive returns, of course. But if you employ those options in a sensible overall investing strategy, such as the one I outline in Chapter 6, you'll certainly tilt the odds in your favor.

The Downsides of 401(k)s

You didn't think Congress was going to bestow all these wonderful 401(k) benefits on you without throwing in a few hitches, did you? Of course not. Like most things in life, 401(k)s also have their drawbacks, although in this case they're relatively minor. In fact, I see only two that are worth talking about, and neither comes close to outweighing the advantages of these accounts.

You Convert Capital Gains to Ordinary Income

Normally, if you sell a mutual fund or a stock for a profit after you've held it longer than a year, your gain is taxed at a long-term capital-gains rate of no higher than 20 percent. That's also true for any long-term capital gains the fund distributes to you while you own the fund. When you pull your money out of a 401(k), however, all investment gains, including long-term capital gains, are taxed at ordinary income rates, which are higher than capital-gains rates (in the case of high-income taxpayers, more than twice as high). So you pay more in taxes on long-term gains in your 401(k) than you would pay on the same investment outside your plan. Still, the combination of the initial tax break you get on your 401(k) contributions and the years of tax deferral on all gains more than makes up for this drawback.

You Face Tough Restrictions on Access to Your Money

For the most part, you can't withdraw money from your 401(k) before age fifty-nine and a half unless you leave your job, become disabled, or experience a financial hardship. The government defines a hardship as "an immediate and heavy financial need," although your plan spells out the specific requirements for hardship withdrawals. Typically you must need the cash for something pretty serious: to pay unreimbursed medical expenses, to meet tuition bills for yourself or your dependents, to buy a primary residence, or to avoid eviction or foreclosure on the mortgage of your principal residence. Even if your plan allows the withdrawal, you will still owe income taxes on the money you pull out, plus a 10 percent penalty. You can avoid the penalty in hardship cases if you're over age fifty-nine and a half or you're disabled. Clearly, a hardship withdrawal is not something to be considered lightly.

The Pitfalls of Borrowing Against Your 401(k)

There is another way to get at your 401(k) early, however, and that's to borrow against it. Nearly 90 percent of plans allow you to take a loan from your 401(k), subject to a variety of limitations. The loan can't be larger than $50,000 or half the balance of your account, whichever is smaller. It must be repaid within five years, although plans usually give you ten to thirty years if the loan is to buy a house. Federal rules require plans to charge a "reasonable" interest rate, a provision most plans interpret as a rate one or two percentage points above the prime lending rate commercial banks charge. Some plans tack on a processing fee of $50 to $100, and some may also charge quarterly or annual fees to keep track of the loan. Employers typically deduct loan payments from your paycheck and funnel those payments right back into your account. So as long as you repay it, a loan is kind of like having an interest-paying IOU to yourself in your 401(k) account.

Considering that these terms are quite attractive—and in many ways better than those you'll get from your local banker—it's hardly surprising that about 25 percent of 401(k) participants have loans outstanding from their plans. Nonetheless, borrowing from your 401(k) has some serious drawbacks.

First, you'll be using after-tax dollars to make those interest payments on your 401(k) loan. Those dollars will then be taxed again when you later withdraw them from your account during retirement. So you end up paying taxes twice on the money you use to repay the loan, which drives up the effective cost of borrowing from your 401(k).

Second, many people find that their budget doesn't allow them to repay the loan *and* continue making new contributions to their plan. As a result, they suspend their contributions, which means they end up accumulating less for retirement.

Finally, if you leave or are fired from your job, most employers will require that you repay any remaining loan balance in full before you depart or shortly thereafter, usually within sixty days. If you fail to do that, the outstanding balance will be considered a distribution subject to income tax, plus a 10 percent penalty if you're under age fifty-nine and a half and not retired.

For all these reasons, I think borrowing from your 401(k) is usually a lousy idea. Remember, a 401(k) is a *retirement* savings vehicle, not a piggy bank to be dipped into every time you need a few extra bucks. The more you raid your 401(k) en route to retirement, the less you'll have available to live on in retirement. So I recommend you exhaust other alternatives before turning to your 401(k). At the very least, you should consider a home equity line of credit first, since the interest rates are usually as low, if not lower, than what you can get on a 401(k), the repayment terms are often more flexible, and the interest on a home equity loan is usually tax-deductible, which isn't the case with 401(k) loans.

What to Do When You Switch Jobs

Most of us probably think of bear markets as the biggest threat to our 401(k) accounts. And there's no doubt that market downturns can wreak havoc on our retirement fund balances. But another big threat to 401(k)s comes when plan participants leave their jobs. And the reason is that's the time when people have easy access to their 401(k) balances, which sometimes leads to decisions that can wipe out years of savings and jeopardize their future financial security.

So what *are* your alternatives when you move from one job to another, and what is the best thing to do with your 401(k) balance when switching employers? Well, you basically have four options—which I see as two good choices, one so-so choice, and another that's almost always flat-out bad. Here's a look at all four.

You Can Take the Money and Run

If you leave a job, there's nothing to prevent you from simply telling your employer to cut you a check for your entire 401(k) balance. *I strongly advise against this option, however.* To begin with, you'll pay income taxes on the withdrawal. And unless you're over age fifty-nine and a half or you're fifty-five or older *and* retiring from your company, you'll also get hit with a 10 percent penalty. (You can also avoid the penalty if you take the cash in equal installments based on your life expectancy, but unless your account is very large, those payments will probably be minuscule.) So in all likelihood the amount you'll actually end up with will be a lot less than the balance on your account statement. If you're in the 25 percent tax bracket, for example, the federal tax-and-penalty combo alone would siphon $17,500 off a $50,000 account, leaving you with just $32,500. And, of course, if you just go ahead and spend whatever's left after taxes, that money won't be there for you after you retire. In short, you'll have undone all the years of savings and tax deferral it took to build your account. So to my mind at least, this option makes no sense unless you're facing a serious financial emergency.

You Can Leave the Money in Your Former Employer's Plan

If your 401(k) balance is more than $5,000, you can choose to leave it in your employer's plan even after you resign. This option is better than the take-the-money-and-run option in that your balance continues to rack up tax-deferred gains. But it also has a drawback. Many companies aren't enthralled with the idea of paying administrative costs on ex-employees' accounts. So while you may be legally entitled to leave your money behind, you may not get service with a smile from a benefits department that considers you a bit of a pain in the neck. This option usually makes sense only if you really love the investing options in your old plan or if you're leaving the money there as a temporary measure until you decide where you eventually want to move it.

You Can Transfer the Money to Your New Employer's 401(k)

If you take another job and your new company's plan accepts rollovers from other 401(k)s—as most plans do—then this may very well be your best move. You'll have all your 401(k) money in one place, which will make managing it much easier. Of course, if you feel the investing options in your new employer's plan are inferior, then this would not be the way to go.

If you move money from a 401(k) with a former employer

to your 401(k) plan at a new job or to an IRA rollover account, you want to take special care to complete this transaction via a direct rollover, also known as a trustee-to-trustee transfer. Essentially, that means the trustee of your old 401(k) account should send your account balance directly to the custodian of your new IRA account or the trustee of your new 401(k) account. Ideally, you won't handle the money at all, although sometimes the trustee at your old 401(k) may opt for a variation of this process in which they send a check to you that's payable to the new trustee or custodian. You would then pass the check along to your new 401(k) or your IRA rollover account.

Whatever you do, you want to avoid a standard rollover. In this version, the trustee at your old 401(k) sends a check directly to you, and you pay no tax on that money as long as you get it into an IRA rollover account or another 401(k) plan within sixty days. This may sound simple enough, but Congress added a nasty and potentially costly little twist to the process in 1993 as an attempt to raise some extra tax revenue. Basically, our legislators added a provision to standard rollovers that requires your old employer to withhold 20 percent of your 401(k) balance for taxes, even if you plan to move the money into an IRA or 401(k). You'll get that 20 percent back when you file your taxes the following year. But in the meantime you'll have to come up with that amount to complete the rollover. If you can't, the IRS will consider that amount a distribution, and you'll have to pay income taxes on the amount withheld, plus a 10 percent penalty unless you're fifty-five or older and retired.

You Can Do an IRA Rollover

If you haven't taken a new job, your new employer doesn't have a 401(k), or your new employer's plan doesn't accept rollovers or has subpar investing options, you can always move your old 401(k) account balance into a rollover IRA. This will preserve the tax-deferred growth of your account and give you access to an even broader range of investments than most 401(k)s offer—virtually all mutual funds, plus individual stocks and bonds. An

IRA rollover can also give you more flexibility in estate planning since you can name any beneficiary you choose. Most 401(k) plans, by contrast, allow you to name only your spouse and, in some cases, your children.

This option has drawbacks, too, however. If you think you might need to borrow against your account balance, you should know that you can't borrow against money in an IRA rollover, as you can with a 401(k). And IRAs also give you less leeway when it comes to deciding when to pull your money out. You must begin making withdrawals from an IRA no later than April 1 of the calendar year following the year you turn seventy and a half. (So if you turned seventy and a half in May 2003, for example, you would have to begin making withdrawals by April 1, 2004.) With a 401(k), you can delay withdrawals—and even continue to contribute—as long as you're still working for the company that sponsors the plan and the plan allows it.

Fortunately, rolling your 401(k) balance into an IRA doesn't prevent you from transferring your money into a new 401(k) sometime down the road. In fact, the 2001 tax law has made it possible to transfer among virtually all different types of tax-advantaged retirement accounts, although the plan itself must acccpt transfers. If you do roll 401(k) money into an IRA, you'll want to make sure you handle the rollover in the way I suggest on page 68.

The Company You Keep: Dealing with Company Stock

For years 401(k) participants viewed company stock as a sort of retirement investing bonanza, a surefire way to fatten the balance of their 401(k) account. After all, many employers liberally doled out company stock as a matching contribution, which meant it was essentially a freebie for employees. And whether due to loyalty to their firm, encouragement from their employer, or because they truly believed the company they worked for had excellent investment prospects, many 401(k) participants willingly loaded up on company stock on their own. Workers at dozens of large firms, including Procter & Gamble,

Texas Instruments, and Abbott Laboratories, at one time held 75 percent or more of their 401(k) assets in company stock.

But the notion of company stock as an all-gain-no-pain 401(k) investment was shattered in the fall of 2001 when Enron, the former high-flying Houston energy company, collapsed into bankruptcy. Suddenly, thousands of workers who had stuffed their 401(k)s with Enron stock found that much if not all of their retirement savings had been wiped out, as plummeting Enron shares erased more than $1 billion from the value of the company's 401(k). And if the Enron debacle wasn't enough of a wake-up call, then certainly similar losses in the 401(k)s of workers at troubled companies such as WorldCom and Global Crossing left no doubt that concentrating a large portion of one's assets in an employer's stock is a risky proposition.

Here are my suggestions for evaluating to what extent company stock should be a part of your 401(k).

Recognize That Owning Company Stock Presents Special Risks No Matter What Company You Work For

Some people still don't get it. They think the problem was with Enron, or WorldCom, or Global Crossing. But their company is strong and has excellent growth prospects, so in their case it makes perfect sense to own lots of company stock. That's nonsense. The basic problem with owning a sizable amount of company stock is that it flouts a bedrock investing principle: diversification. The more company stock you hold in your 401(k)—in fact, the more of *any* single stock you own, your company's or not—the more you subject your portfolio to potentially wide swings in value. And if something happens to the company whose shares you have a big stake in—a collapse in the stock price, a bankruptcy—your savings could be decimated.

Realize That There's No One-Size-Fits-All Solution to the Company Stock Issue

Your decision about company stock must be made in light of your overall financial picture. A 20 percent position in company stock may be suitable if you're well informed about your company's prospects and you also have a large investment portfolio outside your 401(k). That same 20 percent may be wildly inappropriate if you have little or nothing in the way of investments outside your 401(k). That said, however, I think it's generally not a good idea for most people to have more than 10 percent of their 401(k) in their company's stock. Beyond that amount, I believe, the risks usually outweigh the rewards. And if you've got other financial stakes in your employer—a good part of your net worth is tied up in company stock options, say— then owning any company stock in your 401(k) could be a bad idea.

If You Can't Move Out of Your Company Stock, at Least Diversify Around It

In the wake of the Enron debacle, major companies such as Time Warner, Disney, and Gillette have given workers more leeway to diversify out of the company stock in their 401(k)s. But many companies still prevent employees from selling company stock that was given to them as the employer matching contribution until they're in their fifties. If for whatever reason you end up holding more than 10 percent of your retirement stock portfolio in your employer's shares, you should try to adjust your other holdings to compensate for the additional risk of owning company shares. One way is to take a seat-of-the-pants approach. If you work for a large technology company and have, say, 30 percent of your 401(k) invested in company stock, then you might cut back your stake in tech and other large-cap growth stocks in your 401(k) and boost your holdings of small-cap value shares. If your 401(k) doesn't offer enough choices for maneuvering room, then you can make the adjustments in investments outside your 401(k). Alternatively, you could take a more rigorous quantitative approach. If you go to the Risk-Grades site (www.riskgrades.com), you can plug in your retirement holdings, including company stock, and come away with a proprietary risk measure, or RiskGrade, that tells you where your portfolio falls on a scale from conservative to speculative.

If you feel your portfolio is too risky, you can then tinker with your holdings—adding bonds, tilting your mix a bit more toward certain industries or sectors, adding more growth or value, et cetera—and see immediately how your various moves affect your risk score.

Remember That You Are Part of the Mix

Even before you buy your company's shares, you already have a sizable stake in your employer in the form of what economists call your human capital, or the value of the income you generate as a member of the workforce. So, essentially, you are an investment whose return is tied to the health of your company. If your employer's business runs into trouble, the return on your human capital could dwindle—raises might come less frequently—or even disappear completely if you're laid off. If your company's woes also send its stock price south, then the value of the company stock you own would be down just when you are. Which is exactly what happened to thousands of employees at Enron.

So when you're evaluating the risk of holding company stock, don't just consider the value of the stock you own in your 401(k), but consider what might happen if your employer's stock plummeted and you found yourself out of a job at the same time.

Consider the Company Stock Tax Break

When it's time to retire, most people simply roll over their entire 401(k) balance—including company stock—into an IRA. But there's another option that may provide a significant tax break. Take the company shares separately and pay taxes on them, and roll over everything else into the IRA. You will immediately be taxed at the ordinary income rate on your company shares, but that rate will be applied not to the market value of the shares but to their cost basis—that is, their value when they went into your 401(k). When you eventually sell the shares, you pay tax on any appreciation—which is the value above the cost basis—but you are then taxed at capital-gains rates, which max out at 15 percent. If you own company shares whose price has soared over the years, this can be a considerable benefit. But as attractive as those tax savings may be, this option may not be the best bet. Unless you're at least fifty-five years old when you leave your company and take the distribution, you would owe income taxes plus a 10 percent penalty, a combination that would erode much of the benefit of the break. What's more, by taking the stock and holding it, you may be exposing yourself to the higher risks inherent in owning a large position in any single stock. If you have a significant amount of money in company stock, it probably pays to have an adviser run a variety of scenarios and compare the results. Remember, too, that not all companies allow you to take the stock and run. So if you're considering this option, check with your human resources department.

Getting Investing Advice for Your 401(k)

It used to be that 401(k) investing advice consisted of little more than a brief description of the investing options in your 401(k), a boilerplate explanation of the benefits of diversification, and perhaps a heartfelt exhortation from the head of human resources to invest wisely. The reason behind employers' close-mouthed stance on so important an issue stemmed mostly from the fact that employers didn't want to get sued by employees whose 401(k)s got hammered after following company-provided advice.

But as 401(k) balances have grown larger and more companies realize that many of their employees don't know the first thing about creating an overall retirement investing strategy, employers are increasingly looking to increase the amount of financial guidance they offer to plan participants. In a recent survey by the International Society of Certified Employee Benefit Specialists, for example, 48 percent of employers said that one of their top five priorities was to provide retirement-planning tools and information to their employees. The type of advice available still varies tremendously from plan to plan, but here's a rundown of what you're likely to find out there.

General Information About Investing

Although the trend has been for employers to provide more specific information that plan participants can customize to their situation, some 401(k) plans still offer little more than a menu of the investing options, a brief description of what they are ("the growth fund invests in growth stocks"), and perhaps a few pie charts showing how an aggressive investor's mix of stocks, bonds, and cash will differ from that of a conservative investor. While this information is better than none at all, it provides little actual guidance as to what investment options might be right for your particular circumstances or how you should evaluate whether you're better off going with an aggressive or conservative portfolio.

Interactive Online Advice

About a third of employers offer some form of interactive investment advice online, although that number is growing rapidly. This advice typically involves going through an online retirement-planning analysis that starts with your estimate of what size contributions you're likely to make to your 401(k) during your career, then moves on to an assessment of how much income you will need to draw from your 401(k) assets during retirement, and ends with you constructing a portfolio of investments that has a reasonable chance of earning returns high enough to meet your income need. Although this analysis usually doesn't provide recommendations for specific funds or other investment choices, it can get quite sophisticated, allowing you to test a variety of different retirement scenarios so that you can see how different assumptions about contributions, returns, and portfolio makeup might change your retirement prospects. Companies usually turn to specialized investment firms to offer this type of advice, including such well-known companies as Financial Engines, the investment firm started by Nobel prize–winning economist William Sharpe, and Clear-Future, the retirement-planning service from Morningstar, the Chicago-based mutual fund and investment research firm. If your employer doesn't offer this type of advice, you can often sign up for it on your own for a relatively modest fee. In Chapter 5 I'll go into detail about how you can combine the analysis provided by Financial Engines, ClearFuture, and similar online providers with other resources to create your own retirement-planning strategy.

Face-to-Face Meetings with an Adviser

A relatively small percentage of employers—15 to 20 percent—give their employees a chance to sit down and meet with an investment adviser, typically a financial planner. Often, the company picks up all or at least a portion of the tab for this benefit, although sometimes the cost is charged against the assets of the 401(k) plan overall. These kinds of one-on-one sessions offer the potential for participants to receive highly customized advice, although the quality of that advice can vary tremendously depending on the expertise of the financial planner or other adviser offering it. If your 401(k) plan doesn't offer this option, you can always hire a financial planner on your own, although you'll have to pick up the tab. (For tips on how to choose a planner and what you should expect to pay, see "Should You Hire a Pro?" in Chapter 5.)

Online Advice and Specific Recommendations

The latest trend in 401(k) advice is for companies to give participants access to online tools such as those discussed above, but then also provide the option of contacting an adviser for help in putting the online advice into action. So, for example, if the online portfolio analysis tool recommended that you put 45 percent of your assets in large-company stock funds, 15 percent in small-company funds, 10 percent in international stock funds, and the remaining 30 percent in bond funds, you could go to the adviser for specific fund recommendations to create such a portfolio. Merrill Lynch, for example, has begun offering this style of investment advice to the participants of 401(k) plans it manages for employers by partnering with Chicago investment research firm Ibbotson Associates. Under this program, known as AdviceAccess, participants can build a customized portfolio using Ibbotson's tools online and then get additional advice from a Merrill Lynch financial adviser, either in person or online. CitiStreet, a joint venture between Citigroup and State Street Corp., runs a similar program in conjunction with Financial Engines. Ultimately, I think these types of programs will become the norm in 401(k)s since they combine the hard-core number-crunching ability and sophisticated analysis capabilities of the Web with the personal touch of a flesh-and-blood adviser. Even if you opt for advice from an adviser, however, I think it's important that you remain engaged in both managing and monitoring your 401(k). Ultimately, your retirement future is your responsibility, and it is far too important for you to hand off to another person and forget about.

Evaluating Your 401(k)

Ultimately, a 401(k) is part of your compensation package. Which means that you should be evaluating it versus what other employers are offering in their plans, just as you would any other part of your compensation and employee benefits—salary, health insurance coverage, vacation days, family leave policy, et cetera. That's not to say you'll up and leave your company just because its 401(k) plan falls short. On the other hand, your future retirement security *is* directly linked to the amount you can accumulate in plans such as 401(k)s over the course of your working life. So unless your employer makes up for a lousy 401(k) in other ways—like a huge salary or perhaps access to a conventional pension in addition to the 401(k)—spending a large part of your career at a company with a subpar 401(k) plan could seriously diminish your retirement prospects.

To see where your plan falls in the spectrum of 401(k)s operating today, check out the table on the next page. Keep in mind, though, that you've got to evaluate your plan not just on each individual feature but on how it measures up as a whole. Thus, a plan that falls short in less important areas such as loan provisions or hardship withdrawals but offers you a generous contribution limit, a decent match, and a stellar lineup of investing options would still rank high overall. At the very least, however, this table can help you identify weaknesses in your plan that might be improved by lobbying your employer, as I describe below.

Lobbying for a Better Plan

If you don't feel your 401(k) is up to snuff, you always have the option of lobbying your company's benefits or human resources department to improve it. You don't want to do anything obnoxious like nail a list of demands onto the human resources chief's door, however. You'll have a much better chance of success if you go about it in a straightforward, businesslike way.

Your request for improvements will carry a lot more weight if it comes from a group of employees rather than just yourself. So before you approach a company representative, talk to your colleagues to see what changes they would like to have made to the plan. Since a 401(k) is a key employee benefit, I would direct the memo requesting a meeting to the head of employee benefits or human resources. I would also request that the benefits director bring along whoever in the department specifically handles matters relating to the 401(k).

At this meeting, point out as specifically as possible the changes you would like to see, whether it's a higher percentage of salary employees may contribute, a larger employer match, more investment options, lower fees, or all of the above. It's a good idea to have materials on hand to support your request. If you feel the plan's investment fees are too high, you should have data on fees for comparable funds from an independent source such as Morningstar.

Finally, don't be discouraged if you don't get immediate re-

HOW DOES YOUR 401(K) STACK UP?

	INFERIOR PLAN	DECENT PLAN	SUPERIOR PLAN
Contribution	3% of salary or less	4–9%	10% or more
Company match	• No match	• 25–50% of employee contribution (may be limited to first 6% of salary)	• 100% or more of employee contribution (may be limited to first 4–6% of salary) • If match is in company stock, plan allows you to move the match into other investments within a year or less
Waiting period	• One year	• Less than a year	• No waiting period and automatic enrollment
Investment choices	• Fewer than 10 • No index funds or institutional funds • No small-cap, growth, value, or international funds	• 10–15 • Includes index and institutional funds • Small-cap, growth, and value choices, and at least one international fund	• 15 or more • Index and institutional funds • Variety of small-cap, growth, value, and international funds • Brokerage window
Fees	• Expense ratios of 1.5% or higher on most investment options • No low-cost index funds or institutional funds	• Expense ratios less than 1.5% on most options • Offers some low-cost index or institutional funds	• Expense ratios less than 1% on most investment options • Plenty of low-cost index or institutional funds

	INFERIOR PLAN	DECENT PLAN	SUPERIOR PLAN
Advice	• Generic brochures about "balancing risk and reward" handed out at 401(k) sign-up meetings	• Access to one or more of the following: telephone hotline, online investment information, in-person counseling with financial adviser	• Company picks up some or all of the tab for one or more of the following: telephone hotline, online investment information, in-person counseling with financial adviser
Loan provisions	• No loans	• Allows loans but requires $500 to $1,000 minimum • Charges origination fee	• Allows loans with low (less than $500) or no minimum • No origination fee
Hardship withdrawals	• No hardship withdrawals	• Allows hardship withdrawals only for specific purposes, such as buying a home, paying college tuition, or medical expenses	• Allows hardship withdrawals for specific purposes but has discretion to grant loans to alleviate major financial problems

sults. Most firms have an investment committee that helps choose and monitor the plan's investment choices. You can request a meeting with that committee or, for that matter, ask to become part of the committee. Ultimately, you may be able to sway your employer by pointing out that employees who are satisfied with benefits such as their 401(k) are likely to be more loyal and productive. If that approach doesn't work, you always have the option of looking for a more accommodating employer who runs a better plan.

Maximizing Your 401(k)

Considering that for most of us our 401(k) will represent the cornerstone of our retirement savings, it's absolutely crucial that we get the most we possibly can out of our plan. Think of it this way: Your 401(k) account is probably the best chance you have to accumulate some serious bucks for retirement—and it's a onetime shot. There are no do-overs, no reruns, no chances to make up for mistakes by getting it right a second time around. Longevity may be increasing, but the vast majority of us are going to have one working life during which we can save for retirement. So to get it right the first time around, consider the steps below.

Ten Steps to Wringing the Most out of Your 401(k)

1. Sign up for your plan ASAP. Granted, when you're young and starting a new job, retirement may seem like some misty mirage on a distant horizon. And faced with immediate concerns such as paying the mortgage, auto loans, tuition bills, living expenses, and whatnot, saving for retirement may seem like a low priority at best. But if you give in to this natural tendency to procrastinate, you'll seriously limit how much you can accumulate by retirement. Getting started just five years late, for example, can reduce the size of your retirement nest egg by 25 percent—the difference between having, say, $600,000 instead of $800,000 when you retire. So if you're eligible for your company's plan, don't delay—sign up today.

2. Contribute as much as you possibly can. Once you've signed up, you might as well go for all the gusto you can get and pump in as much money as you can possibly afford, preferably as much as your plan allows. Depending on your salary and the maximum percentage of salary set in your plan, you might even be able to take advantage of the higher contribution limits in the 2001 tax law, which boosts the maximum contribution to $15,000 by 2006. Of course, stashing away this kind of cash may mean reining in your current standard of living a bit. But remember: the more you contribute now, the better the standard of living you'll enjoy in retirement. (While maxing out on your 401(k) can never hurt you, there are some instances when you may want to consider dividing your money between a 401(k) and a Roth IRA. I'll discuss that strategy in the next chapter.)

3. If you can't max out, contribute at least enough to get the employer's match. Okay, so maybe you're under so much financial pressure that you can't afford to contribute the 10 percent of your $40,000 salary that your plan allows. But if your employer offers to kick in 50 percent of the first 6 percent you contribute, you want to do everything you can to get that match. If you don't, that's like walking away from free money—$1,200 in this case. Ideally, you should contribute enough to get the full match. But if you can't afford that, at least put in enough to take advantage of some of your employer's largesse.

4. Take advantage of catch-up contributions. If you're fifty or older, you can boost the wealth-building potential of your 401(k) even more by taking advantage of the provision in the 2001 tax law that allows catch-up contributions on top of regular contributions. Those catch-up contributions can total as much as $3,000 in 2004 and as much as $5,000 by 2006. As I'll explain in more detail in Chapter 7, these catch-up additions combined with regular contributions are an excellent way for people getting a late start on retirement to quickly boost the value of their accounts.

5. Allocate your 401(k) assets wisely. Once you've begun socking money away, your attention should then turn to investing that money so that it grows into a retirement fund that can sustain you through your retirement. The key is finding the right balance between stocks and stock funds, which can provide long-term growth and keep the purchasing power of your nest egg ahead of inflation, and bonds and other income investments, which can provide more stability. Invest too aggressively, and you run the risk of seeing your 401(k) balance decimated when the market heads south; invest too conservatively, however, and you may not be able to fund the lifestyle you want for retirement. There's no one-size-fits-all answer to solution to this issue. But in Chapter 6, I'll outline a variety of ways you can build a retirement portfolio that makes sense for you given such factors as the number of years you have until you retire and your tolerance for risk.

6. Don't ignore costs. When choosing investments for our 401(k), we tend to focus on returns. But we have much more control over the investment costs we pay than over the returns we earn. And in fact, choosing low-fee investments such as index funds and institutional portfolios and avoiding ones with bloated expenses can have a dramatic effect on your account balance over time. Consider this: If you invest $50,000 at age forty-five in an investment that earns 10 percent annually and deducts 1.5 percent a year in expenses, you would have just under $256,000 by age sixty-five. That same $50,000 sitting in an investment that earns 10 percent annually but deducts just 0.5 percent a year in expenses would grow to roughly $307,000. In short, saving just 1 percent a year in expenses would give you an extra $50,000 or so for retirement. Lower expenses translates to a bigger retirement stash for you. To learn more about 401(k) fees, check out the Department of Labor's Employee Benefits Security Administration's online booklet "A Look at 401(k) Fees for Employees," which is available at www.dol.gov/pwba/pubs/401k_ employee.html or by phone at 800-998-7542. If your 401(k) offers retail mutual funds, you can check out their expenses at a source such as Morningstar (www.morningstar.com).

7. Avoid dipping into your 401(k) account before retirement. It's nice to have the option of borrowing from your 401(k) or taking a hardship withdrawal to get through a financial rough patch.

But remember, the more you tap your 401(k) *before* you retire, the less money you're likely to have available in your account *when* you retire. So rely as much as possible on other investments to get you through hard times, and tap into your 401(k) only in true emergencies, and only after you've exhausted other resources.

8. Eliminate between-job "leakage." An estimated two-thirds of workers who change jobs simply cash out their 401(k) balances rather than roll the money over into another tax-deferred plan to keep it growing for retirement. Clearly, this is no way to build assets for a secure retirement. Whenever you switch jobs, be sure to roll your 401(k) balance into your new employer's plan or into an IRA rollover account in the way I described earlier. That way, your balance won't be hit with taxes, and it can continue to rack up tax-deferred gains until you retire.

9. Don't overdo it on company stock. The more company stock you own, the greater the risk you're taking with your retirement. So unless you have plenty of other assets you can fall back on, you're probably better off limiting your company stock holdings to no more than 10 percent of your 401(k). If you hold more than that percentage—either because you want to or because company restrictions prevent you from paring your stake—be sure to diversify the rest of your portfolio in a way that compensates for your concentration in company shares.

10. Monitor your account regularly. You don't have to devote every waking moment to tracking your 401(k). On the other hand, you do want to keep tabs on it. For one thing, many companies make improvements to their plans, adding new investment options, increasing the amount you can contribute, increasing the match, et cetera. You want to be able to assess these changes and take advantage of them if they're worthwhile. And, of course, you want to monitor the performance of your investment options occasionally, and at least once a year give your 401(k) portfolio a thorough checkup.

If you follow these ten steps, I can't guarantee with 100 percent certainty that you'll end up with a 401(k) large enough to fund the retirement of your dreams. But I can tell you that if you *don't* follow them, your chances will be a heck of a lot lower.

Chapter 4

MAKE THE MOST OF
OTHER TAX-ADVANTAGED
SAVINGS PLANS

Considering all the attention 401(k)s get in the financial press, you could easily assume that it's a universal retirement savings plan, available to virtually every American who holds a job. Nothing, of course, could be farther from the truth. Fact is, millions of American workers rely on any number of other retirement plans to build their retirement nest eggs, each with its own set of rules and each with its pros and cons. Some of these—403(b)s, 457s, SEP IRAs—we simply don't hear much about. Indeed, the fact that they're covered so little by the media means they often remain a bit of a mystery to the people they're supposed to serve. Other savings vehicles, such as traditional IRAs and Roth IRAs, are definitely more familiar to us. But for a variety of reasons we don't use them to their maximum advantage.

Which is a shame, especially since the passage of the 2001 tax bill—or the Economic Growth and Tax Relief Reconciliation Act of 2001, as it's officially known inside the Beltway—has made all of these plans much more effective retirement savings tools. The amounts you can save on a tax-deferred or even a tax-free basis are higher than ever before, and new regulations now make it much, much easier to shift your assets from one plan to another as you move from job to job throughout your career.

In this chapter we'll go beyond 401(k)s to the broad panoply of other retirement savings plans so that you know what options are available and how to take advantage of them. I'll begin with the vehicles that the largest number of us have access to, that is, traditional and Roth IRAs. From there, I'll move on to 403(b)s, which are available to teachers and employees of nonprofit organizations, and 457s, which cover certain public sector employees. I'll then go on to SEPs, SIMPLE IRAs, and Keoghs, or the retirement plans geared toward the self-employed and small business owners, as well as the people who work for them. Finally, I'll wind up the chapter by trying to shed some much-needed light on annuities, investments that are usually bought for their tax benefits but rarely understood by those who own them. Even if you think you do understand annuities fairly well, you'll want to check out this chapter's section on them because the 2003 tax bill has tilted the playing field against annuities in certain ways.

One more note before we get into the nitty-gritty of the various plans themselves. In today's retirement-planning landscape, where the onus for saving is increasingly placed squarely on our shoulders, it's unlikely that any single savings plan is going to allow you to accumulate enough money for a comfortable retirement. So I strongly urge you to think in terms of contributing to *multiple* retirement savings plans. At the very least you can probably combine a traditional or Roth IRA with whatever plan your company offers. But you should look for other possibilities as well. If you have more than one job and each has a retirement savings plan, take advantage of both. If you have a job but also have some self-employment income on the side, you may be able to contribute to a SEP IRA or a Keogh in addition to whatever you put into your employer's plan. The key is to be resourceful, much as Dorothy and her friends were on the road to Oz, to be ready to seize opportunities in whatever form they arrive in (although in your case that form is more likely to be a tax-advantaged savings plan rather than a friendly witch). The simple fact is that the more you manage to stash away in whatever combination of retirement savings plans you can pull together today, the bigger the nest egg you'll have to support you once you retire.

The Mighty IRA: It's Back—Bigger and Better than Before

When individual retirement accounts were first launched by Congress back in 1974, they were revolutionary. After all, here was a retirement savings plan that allowed you to put away money each year at a bank, a brokerage firm, or a mutual fund company of your choice where it could compound free of taxes as long as the money remained in your IRA account—*and* your contribution got you an immediate tax deduction that lowered your tax bill. On the basis of those two big benefits—plus the fact that 401(k)s wouldn't make their debut for another four years and not become dominant for several more—IRAs became the retirement savings vehicle of choice for Americans who wanted to take responsibility for assuring their retirement security.

Over the years, however, as 401(k)s and other retirement savings plans entered the scene, IRAs began to lose their luster. Even though the maximum allowable contribution was raised from $1,500 to $2,000 in 1981, IRAs simply couldn't compete with the higher limits available in 401(k)s and other vehicles. The addition in 1998 of Roth IRAs, which don't provide a tax deduction but allow for tax-free returns, raised the profile of IRAs somewhat. But there was still the problem of the relatively low contribution ceiling. So aside from money being transferred from 401(k)s and other plans into IRA rollover accounts, IRAs seemed destined to play a relatively minor role in most individuals' retirement savings strategies, a way to increase one's nest egg a bit but not a place to do any serious saving.

But that all changed with the passage of the 2001 tax bill, the Economic Growth and Tax Relief Reconciliation Act of 2001. As it did with 401(k)s and other plans, the bill boosted the amount you can contribute each year to an IRA from the old $2,000 limit to $3,000 in 2003, $4,000 in 2005, and $5,000 in 2008, after which increases are pegged to inflation. What's more, the legislation also allows individuals fifty and older to make additional catch-up contributions that start at $500 a year in 2003 and jump to $1,000 in 2006.

Result: The IRA is back, big-time. Granted, the maximum contribution for IRAs still falls short of that for 401(k)s and the other plans described in this book. But the higher limits have dramatically increased the value of the IRA as a retirement savings tool. If you have access to no other form of tax-advantaged savings, then the IRA's new higher contribution at least gives you a shot at accumulating a decent stash for retirement. And if you already participate in an employer-provided savings plan, then adding an IRA and funding it to the max can truly turbocharge the growth of your retirement nest egg. (To see just how much an IRA can boost your savings even if you get a late start with your retirement planning, see the "Building a Nest Egg at Age Fifty" sidebar in Chapter 7.)

Which IRA Is Right for You?

To make the most of an IRA, however, you've got to know which type is best suited for your circumstances. Basically, IRAs come in three flavors: the traditional deductible IRA, the Roth IRA, and the nondeductible IRA. The real decision, in my opinion, is whether to do a traditional deductible IRA or a Roth (and even there I tend to give the nod to the Roth). You shouldn't even *think* of doing a nondeductible IRA unless you can't qualify for a deductible IRA or a Roth. And even then I don't think it's a given you should do a nondeductible. Why? Because all the investment earnings in an IRA are eventually taxed as ordinary income, which is subject to tax rates that run as high as 35 percent. That's true even if the gain is actually a long-term capital gain, which is normally taxed at rates that max out at 15 percent. The initial tax break in a deductible IRA is enough to make up for this disadvantage, but that's not the case with a nondeductible, which doesn't provide a deduction. So instead of a nondeductible IRA, I recommend investments such as index mutual funds, tax-managed mutual funds, or growth stocks, which deliver all or most of their return in the form of long-term capital gains.

The Deductible IRA

The traditional deductible IRA is similar to the 401(k) in concept. You invest any amount up to the maximum allowable contribution into your IRA account and, assuming you meet the eligibility requirements (see "Are You Eligible for a Deductible or Roth IRA" sidebar), you get a tax deduction for your contribution that lowers your taxable income. So assuming you're in the 25 percent federal tax bracket and you contributed the $3,000 maximum allowed for 2004, you would receive an immediate tax deduction that would lower your federal tax bill by $750.

But there's a second tax break. Any earnings your $3,000 generates—as well as the earnings of future contributions—build tax free as long as they remain inside the account. Escaping the drag of taxes means that your contributions can earn a higher after-tax rate of return than similar investments held outside an IRA, which in turn means you can accumulate a bigger nest egg for retirement than you can investing in regular accounts that don't offer the IRA's tax benefits.

You don't completely escape the bite of taxes by contributing to an IRA, however. When you withdraw money from your IRA account, preferably after you've retired, you'll pay tax on your withdrawal at whatever ordinary income tax rates are prevailing at the time you pull the money out. So let's say, for example, that over the years through a combination of tax-deductible contributions to your IRA and earnings on those contributions your IRA account swells in value to $200,000, and you withdraw $10,000 of that amount the first year of your retirement. If ordinary income tax rates were still 25 percent, you would owe $2,500 in federal taxes on your withdrawal, plus whatever income taxes your state collects.

If you withdraw money from your account before age fifty-nine and a half, however, you'll not only owe ordinary income taxes on the withdrawal, you'll have to pay an additional 10 percent federal tax penalty. In the scenario above, that would mean a tax bill of $3,500 instead of $2,500 on your ten grand withdrawal. In what I suppose amounts to a gesture of magnanimity, the government will waive the penalty in some cases, although not the tax itself. You won't owe the 10 percent penalty if you're taking a withdrawal because you're disabled or because you're using the money to buy, build, or rebuild a first home or to pay medical expenses that exceed 7.5 percent of your adjusted gross income or to pay higher education expenses. You can also avoid the penalty if you take the distribution in a series of substantially equal payments over your life expectancy or the life expectancy of you and a beneficiary.

One more thing: Just as pulling your money out of a deductible IRA too early can result in a penalty, so can pulling your money out too late. Federal regulations require that you begin making minimum withdrawals from an IRA no later than April 1 of the calendar year following the year you turn seventy and a half. If you fail to do this, you can be hit with a whopping penalty equal to 50 percent of the difference between what you should have withdrawn and what you actually withdrew.

ARE YOU ELIGIBLE FOR A DEDUCTIBLE OR ROTH IRA?

Any IRA contribution must come from earned income. (Income from dividends, interest, capital gains, or rent can't be used to fund an IRA, although alimony payments qualify if they're taxable.) Beyond that, here are the rules that determine your eligibility.

Deductible IRA
If you're not eligible to participate in a retirement plan at work and you're under age seventy and a half, you can contribute up to the maximum allowed and deduct the entire contribution. A nonworking spouse under age seventy and a half may also invest up to the max and fully deduct the contribution, provided you have enough earned income to fund both contributions.

If you're eligible to participate in a plan at work (regardless of whether you actually do), you can contribute to the max and fully deduct it if your adjusted gross income (AGI)* is less than $60,000 (if you're married and filing jointly) or less than $40,000 (if you're single). You can take a partial deduction if your income is between $60,000 and $70,000 (married) or $40,000 and $50,000 (single).†

If you're not eligible for a plan at work but your spouse is, you can take a full deduction if you file jointly and your adjusted gross income is less than $150,000 or a partial deduction if your AGI is between $150,000 and $160,000. A nonworking spouse of someone eligible for a plan at work can make a contribution and deduct it, subject to the same income requirements and provided the working spouse has enough income to fund both contributions.

Roth IRA

If you're single, you can make a full contribution at any age regardless of whether you're eligible for a retirement plan at work if your AGI is less than $95,000. You can make a partial contribution if your AGI is between $95,000 and $110,000.

If you're married, you can make a full contribution at any age regardless of whether you or your spouse is eligible for a retirement plan at work if your AGI is less than $150,000. You can make a partial contribution if your AGI is between $150,000 and $160,000. A nonworking spouse can also make a full or partial contribution at any age, subject to the same income requirements and assuming the working spouse has enough income to fund both contributions.

---

*Adjusted gross income (AGI) is the total of income from wages, interest, capital gains, withdrawals from retirement accounts, and alimony paid to you, from which you then subtract deductions for such things as your annual contribution to an IRA account, alimony you paid, and interest on student loans (but not the standard deduction or itemized deductions). For your AGI in previous years, check out line 4 of the 1040EZ tax form, line 21 of the 1040A, or line 35 of the 1040.

†These limits apply to a contribution for the 2003 tax year, which can be made until April 15, 2004. The limits rise annually until 2007 for married couples, when they can take a full deduction if their income is less than $80,000 and a partial deduction if it's between $80,000 and $100,000; the limits rise annually until 2005 for singles, when they can fully deduct their contribution if their income is less than $50,000 and partially deduct it if it's between $50,000 and $60,000.

The Roth IRA

The Roth IRA is almost a reverse image of the traditional IRA in that you get no tax deduction up front. But you don't pay income tax on your contribution or, if you play your cards right, its earnings when you pull the money out. In other words, when you invest money in a Roth IRA, you invest money you've already paid tax on for the promise of tax-free withdrawals in the years ahead. Essentially, this means the money you invest in a Roth earns not a tax-deferred return, as in the case of a traditional IRA, but a tax-free rate of return.

The Roth has another benefit you don't get in a deductible IRA—namely, you don't have to start withdrawing money after age seventy and a half. In fact, you don't have to withdraw it at all, ever, if you don't want to. You can leave the money in your Roth to compound tax free for the rest of your life without any penalty. And you can pass on a Roth to your heirs, who can either pull the money out income-tax free or let it continue to compound away free of taxes. (Depending on the size of your estate, however, it's possible that your Roth could be subject to estate taxes.)

It won't come as a surprise, of course, that the federal government sets some conditions for cashing in on this tax-advantaged bonanza. First, you've got to meet the income eligibility requirements, although that's a much easier hurdle in the case of a Roth than a deductible IRA. And once you've contributed to a Roth, there's also the issue of how long the money must remain in your account before it can be withdrawn without paying taxes on it, although the Roth offers more flexibility than a deductible IRA there as well.

Basically, you're free to withdraw your original annual contributions at any time without paying any tax or penalty. So, for example, if you make the maximum allowable contribution of $3,000 for 2004 today, you can get that money back at any time without paying a cent in taxes or penalties to the government. (Of course, you're not helping your retirement savings program much if you do.)

Once you pull out anything beyond your annual contributions, you're withdrawing earnings. And then things get tricky. Basically, you can withdraw earnings without paying tax and a 10 percent penalty only if your Roth is at least five years old (the clock begins ticking on January 1 of the year you first open a Roth) *and* you meet one of the following criteria: you're fifty-nine and a half or older; you're making the withdrawal because you're disabled or because you're using the withdrawal to buy, build, or rebuild a first home ($10,000 limit); or because the payment is being made after your death, in which case your beneficiary would benefit. Even if you fail to meet the criteria above, it's possible that you can avoid the 10 percent penalty on the withdrawal. If you withdraw money from your Roth to pay higher education expenses for yourself, your spouse, your child, or your grandchild, for example, you would owe tax on the withdrawal but not the 10 percent penalty. Other withdrawals that are taxed but not hit with the 10 percent penalty are ones used to pay medical expenses greater than 7.5 percent of your adjusted gross income, those made to pay health insurance premiums after a layoff, and distributions taken in a series of substantially equal payments over your life expectancy or the life expectancy of you and a beneficiary.

There's one other twist in Roth withdrawal rules that apply if you've converted a deductible IRA to a Roth IRA. (I'll discuss the pros and cons of conversions on pages 96–98). If you convert a deductible to a Roth, you must wait five years from the date of the conversion before you can withdraw the converted funds without incurring a 10 percent penalty. That said, if you're fifty-nine and a half or older or you meet any of the requirements for withdrawing earnings without paying a penalty, you can withdraw the converted funds without paying the 10 percent penalty.

Clearly, all these nitpicking rules are enough to give you a major migraine headache. But there's one easy way to avoid running afoul of them: Don't tap into your Roth IRA (or your deductible IRA if you have one) until you're past age fifty-nine and a half and you need the money for retirement! After all, the whole point of contributing to an IRA and other retirement plans is so you'll have money when you're no longer working. So the more you can refrain from dipping into your IRA stash for current needs, the better your chances of having a comfortable retirement.

The Deductible IRA Versus the Roth

So which type of IRA should you do—a deductible or a Roth? In some cases, the choice may not be yours. If your income is too high for a deductible IRA but within the eligibility requirements for a Roth, then the answer is simple: do the Roth. But what if you're eligible to do both? Which should you do then?

From a purely financial point of view, the answer is go with the Roth if you expect to be in a higher tax bracket in retirement than during your career. That's because you would be paying tax on your contribution when you're in a lower bracket and avoiding tax on the withdrawal when you're in a higher bracket. If you expect to be in a lower tax bracket in retirement than during your career, then you would go with a deductible IRA so you can grab the deduction when you face a higher tax rate and withdraw money when it will be taxed at a lower rate. You can go with either one if you think you'll stay in the same bracket.

But I think this is a case where real-life considerations trump theory—which means I think most people would be better off giving the nod to the Roth. For one thing, I wouldn't take it as a given that you'll end up in a lower tax bracket in retirement. Remember, if you save diligently in an employer savings plan, such as a 401(k), you'll be accumulating a big pot of dollars that will be fully taxable (unless you've made nondeductible contributions to your 401(k)) when you start pulling the money out. At the same time, you won't be contributing to a 401(k) or IRA anymore, so you'll lose those deductions. And you might lose others, such as your mortgage interest deduction if you pay off your mortgage. Add it all up, and I think it's pretty likely you'll stay in the same bracket or possibly slip into a higher one. Besides, there's an element here you have very little control over: Congress. With a deductible IRA, you're at the mercy of Congress's tax policies. If Congress decides to raise income tax rates after you've retired, you'll hand back a bigger slice of the money you've accumulated in a deductible IRA.

With the Roth, on the other hand, you have the assurance that you can withdraw your money tax free. You know how much you'll actually have to spend. Oh, I suppose it's possible Congress could revoke the tax-free status of a Roth if our legislators were really hungry for more tax revenue. But we'd have retirees rioting in the streets if that happened, so I don't think such a scenario is anywhere near as likely as Congress simply hiking tax rates. And there are other reasons to go with the Roth. You aren't required to begin drawing from the account after age seventy and a half, as you are with a deductible IRA. So you can let your money compound tax free as long as you like. And you can even pass it along to your heirs, who also can let it build without the drag of income taxes.

One other thing to consider is that money you pull out of 401(k)s and other plans will be taxed at ordinary income rates. Which means that money is vulnerable to higher tax rates in the future. So it's a good idea to have another stash that is immune to income taxes altogether. If nothing else, it gives you more flexibility in managing your income in retirement. If in a given year it seems that larger-than-usual withdrawals from your 401(k) (or from the rollover IRA you've probably transferred your 401(k) into) will push you into a higher tax bracket, you may be able to avoid moving into the higher bracket by taking withdrawals from your Roth instead. Conversely, in years when your withdrawals aren't so large or in years where you have deductions that can lower your taxable income, you might consider drawing exclusively from your 401(k) or IRA rollover.

When I balance the financial considerations against the real-world realities, I think the Roth most often comes out as the superior choice. It makes planning for retirement income more predictable and gives you more flexibility, and the fact that you don't have to worry about changes in the tax laws chipping away at this part of your nest egg can create a greater sense of financial security later in life when you really need it.

Bottom line: Doing a deductible IRA can be a good choice and certainly better than not doing an IRA at all. But unless all the circumstances in your case stack up overwhelmingly in favor of the deductible, I'd say go with the Roth.

Should You Convert from a Deductible IRA to a Roth?

If you've already been investing in a deductible IRA, you may have the option of transforming your deductible IRA into a Roth IRA. But should you? First, you've got to determine whether you're even eligible to convert your deductible IRA to a Roth. In order to do so, your modified adjusted gross income (adjusted gross income as defined on page 91 with certain items added back in) must fall below $100,000 whether you're single or married. (You can't convert if you're married and file separately.)

Assuming you're eligible, here are a few guidelines that can help you make a decision.

Consider converting to a Roth if:

- **You will be in the same or a higher tax bracket when you retire.** The logic here is that you'll be paying taxes on your deductible IRA stash at a more favorable rate and avoiding a higher tax bill in retirement. You also won't have to worry about future tax hikes depleting this part of your retirement nest egg.
- **You can pay the tax on the conversion from funds outside the IRA.** For one thing, you'll avoid the 10 percent penalty if you're doing the conversion before age fifty-nine and a half. Paying the tax from other funds has another benefit as well: it allows you to transfer more of your deducible IRA balance into the Roth, which means you have more money earning a tax-free rate of return and building a tax-free stash to support you in retirement. If funds are tight, remember that you don't have to roll over your entire deductible IRA balance at once. You can

do it over the years in a series of smaller rollovers. That can make it easier to manage the tax bill and also help prevent the rollover itself from driving you into a higher tax bracket.

• **You want the flexibility and security of having tax-free income during retirement.** As I mentioned in the section on the deductible IRA versus the Roth, there's a lot to be said for knowing exactly how much income you'll actually be able to spend once you've retired. And since you'll likely have money in a 401(k) or other account that will be taxed at ordinary income rates, having a tax-free stash as well can help you manage withdrawals to keep taxes at a minimum.

• **You think you might leave your IRA to your heirs.** One of the big advantages of a Roth is that you don't have to begin making mandatory withdrawals at age seventy and a half, as with a regular IRA. Indeed, you don't have to withdraw the money at all if you don't want to. This makes the Roth an ideal vehicle for leaving a legacy for your heirs—or even just a way to keep some money aside as a backup for late in life just in case other sources start to run dry.

Consider sticking with a deductible IRA if:

• **You're really sure you'll be in a significantly lower tax bracket after you retire.** If that's the case, then you're better off paying tax on your deductible IRA stash later, when you can pay the taxes at a much lower rate.

• **You would have to tap the IRA to pay the tax for the conversion.** A conversion is usually a better deal if you can get the money to pay the tax bill from somewhere other than the IRA itself, especially if tapping the IRA would trigger a 10 percent early withdrawal penalty.

• **You're paranoid about future tax policy.** Some people worry that a future Congress might revoke the tax-free status of Roth accounts, thus rendering the basic premise of a conversion— paying taxes now for the promise of no taxes later—a risky proposition. While I understand this suspicion, I think Congress would actually find it more politically expedient to simply raise tax rates rather than explicitly break a promise to millions of Roth IRA holders, which makes the Roth a sort of defensive measure against higher future taxes. But if you feel that's not the case, then you might feel more comfortable sticking with a deductible IRA.

Before you come to a final decision on the conversion question, it's a good idea to at least run some numbers to see how you would make out under a variety of different assumptions about tax rates before and after retirement as well as other factors. You can do that sort of number crunching at many websites, including the ones at Vanguard (www.vanguard.com), Fidelity (www.fidelity.com), T. Rowe Price (www.troweprice.com), and Schwab (www.schwab.com), to name a few. One final note: As I mentioned earlier, I think there's great value in having a source of funds you can tap in retirement totally free of taxes. So if you run the numbers and don't come up with an absolutely convincing case that you're better off sticking with a deductible IRA, I'd be more inclined to go with the Roth.

The "Oops" or "Second Chance" Rule

What if you've gone ahead and contributed to a Roth IRA instead of a deductible—or vice versa—but you then change your mind? Or what if you decide to convert your deductible IRA to a Roth but later find your income is too high to meet the eligibility requirements for a conversion? Or, for that matter, what if you converted to a Roth early in the year when your deductible IRA balance was $50,000 and then losses in your account took the balance down to $30,000? You've paid taxes on fifty grand. Wouldn't it be nice to be able to undo the conversion and redo it later so you pay less in taxes?

In fact, there is an "oops" or "second chance" rule when it comes to situations like these. If you've contributed to a Roth IRA and later decide you'd be better off with a deductible IRA, or you've contributed to a deductible and would prefer to have done the Roth, you can redo the transaction. Similarly, if you convert from a deductible to a Roth, you can go back to a deductible IRA.

How? By taking advantage of a process called recharacterization. In a display of magnanimity, Congress saw fit to write into the tax code a provision that essentially allows you to change your mind. Basically, a recharacterization allows you to switch your annual contribution from one type of IRA to another or to undo a Roth conversion by transferring the converted funds back to a deductible IRA.

Naturally, there are a few ground rules you must follow. First, there's a time limit for how long you have to pull off this feat, although the deadline is quite generous. Specifically, you have until the due date of your tax return for the tax year for which you make the contribution or do the conversion, including extensions. So if you do the conversion in 2004, for example, you would have until the due date for your 2004 tax return, plus extensions. That would give you until October 15, 2005, assuming you took advantage of the two allowable filing extensions.

You should also know that in the case of switching a contribution from a deductible IRA to a Roth (or vice versa), the decision is irrevocable. You can't change your mind again (although if you've switched a Roth contribution to a deductible IRA, you could still choose to convert that IRA to a Roth at a later date, assuming you meet the usual criteria for a conversion). As for undoing a Roth conversion, you can change your mind later about that decision and convert back to a Roth later on. But you must hold off at least for thirty days or until the beginning of the next year following the date of the recharacterization, whichever is longer.

So certainly in the case of a conversion at least, you'll want to keep track of the balance you transferred to a Roth to see how it's fared. If you happened to do a conversion before a big downturn in the market, you may be able to save some dough by undoing the conversion and then redoing it again with a smaller balance that results in a smaller tax tab.

Beyond IRAs and 401(k)s

While 401(k)s and IRAs get most of the attention in the financial press, there's a whole world out there of retirement plans we seldom hear about but that nonetheless represent for millions of Americans their best shot at retirement security. While plans such as the 403(b) were not nearly as attractive as 401(k)s in the past, the 2001 tax law immensely improved things for people relying on non-401(k) employer plans. It eliminated much of the needless confusion and complexity surrounding some of these plans and significantly raised the amount one can contribute to such plans as well. While it would be a gross overstatement to suggest these changes come close to guaranteeing a comfortable retirement to people who participate in non-401(k) plans, it's certainly accurate to say that participants now have a much better shot at achieving retirement security if they take full advantage of them.

403(b) Plans: Kind of Like 401(k)s, but Then Again . . .

If you work as a teacher, a university professor, or a school administrator, or you're employed by a nonprofit hospital or other nonprofit organization, chances are you're covered by a retirement savings plan known as a 403(b). In many ways, a 403(b) works pretty much like a 401(k). You contribute pretax dollars (in other words, you get an immediate tax break, as with a 401(k)), and the earnings on your contributions compound free of taxes until you withdraw them. Your employer may offer matching contributions as well. As with a 401(k), each year you can contribute up to a specified dollar amount each year—the limits are the same as those for 401(k)s—or a certain percentage of your salary, whichever is less. (That percentage of salary is determined by your particular plan but cannot exceed a government ceiling of 20 percent.) Participants fifty and older can also make catch-up contributions to 403(b) plans. The maximum amount for such contributions is the same as for 401(k)s:

$3,000 in 2004, climbing to $4,000 in 2005 and $5,000 in 2006, after which the max is pegged to inflation. Participants who have at least fifteen years of service at a qualifying organization and also have a history of low contributions may also be able to take advantage of a separate lifetime catch-up provision that allows them to contribute up to a total of $15,000. (The formula for figuring the lifetime catch-up is complicated and the IRS hasn't specifically said whether you can take advantage of both catch-up provisions, although some organizations are telling participants they can take both if they qualify. If you think you might qualify for the lifetime catch-up, I recommend you seek some guidance from your plan's sponsor.)

So, fundamentally, the 403(b) plan plays a role very similar to that of the 401(k) in a retirement-planning strategy: It allows you to rack up more money than you probably otherwise could for retirement by allowing you to save regularly in a convenient tax-advantaged way. That said, however, 403(b)s have two shortcomings that, in my opinion, make them inferior to 401(k)s. One is that 403(b) providers don't act as gatekeepers. In a 401(k) plan, the employer takes some responsibility for screening and choosing the investment choices that will be offered to plan participants. This doesn't completely ensure high-quality reasonably priced investment choices, of course. But at least it tends to weed out truly awful ones and, if nothing else, gives participants a manageable menu of choices to work with.

While some 403(b) providers take this approach, many admit the products of almost any investment, brokerage, or insurance firm into the plan. The result is that participants can face a vast and confusing array of investment choices, often with little help available to them about how to separate the worthy ones from the duds.

The second drawback is that the investment choices are often limited to annuities. Annuities, hybrid creatures that contain elements of both investments and insurance, are far and away the predominant investment choice in the 403(b) world, although mutual funds have been gaining ground.

While annuities can play a role in retirement planning, they don't deserve much of a role in the saving stage of retirement. The reason is that annuities typically come with onerous fees that drag down their returns and make them less effective vehicles than, say, mutual funds for accumulating wealth for retirement. There are exceptions. TIAA-CREF, the organization that runs the 403(b) plans for most of the nation's colleges and universities, offers annuities with razor-thin expense levels. But the fees on most annuities exceed those on mutual funds by a wide margin. Annuities are also sold outside of 403(b) plans and often touted (mostly by annuity providers) as an ideal way to save for retirement outside of employer plans. I'll delve more into the specifics about how annuities work and what they charge later in this chapter.

By using your smarts and exercising some initiative, you may be able to get around these shortcomings. First, check with your employer to see if there's a mutual fund firm on your 403(b) plan's menu of eligible investment providers. You may have the option of investing in mutual funds and not even know it. If your plan doesn't have a fund firm on its list of investment providers, ask your human resources or personnel department rep to add one or two fund companies. Some employers are quite willing to honor such requests, especially if they come from an organized group of employees. If you can't get your employer to improve the quality of the offerings in your 403(b), then you may be able to periodically withdraw funds from your 403(b) account and transfer them to another 403(b) you've set up outside your employer's plan. To do this, you'll have to set up your own 403(b) account in advance with a mutual fund company or other investment firm that maintains a 403(b) plan. (Most of the large fund companies and investment firms do.) You'll also have to make sure your employer's 403(b) allows such transfers. Finally, before transferring any money, you'll want to see whether you'll be hit with a "surrender charge," a penalty for early exit that often starts at 7 to 10 percent. To see if a surrender charge will apply in your case, call the company that issued the annuity you own in your 403(b).

457 Plans: Retirement Plans That Aren't Really Retirement Plans

The 457 plan is a savings vehicle that allows state and local government workers and some employees of tax-exempt or non-profit organizations such as charities and hospitals to sock away a portion of their income on a pretax basis and shelter earnings on those contributions until they're withdrawn. Technically, though, a 457 plan is not really a retirement savings plan but a deferred compensation plan—that is, a plan that allows you to defer part of your paycheck and pay taxes later on that income. This distinction used to have some serious ramifications for all 457 plans, namely, in the event the organization offering the plan went into bankruptcy, the plan's assets could be seized by creditors. Congress changed the laws to offer 457 plans of government workers greater protection, but assets of 457 plans offered by tax-exempt organizations may still be vulnerable.

Typically, a 457 plan will offer investing options similar to those in a 401(k)—a menu of stock and bond mutual funds, plus one or more options designed to preserve capital, such as a money market fund or a stable value fund. As with a 401(k), you agree to have a percentage of your salary automatically contributed to your 457 plan, subject to a maximum dollar amount. Previously, the dollar ceiling for 457 plans had been much lower than the maximum that applied to 401(k) plans, which made 457s much less effective vehicles for accumulating money for retirement. But the 2001 tax law eliminated that shortcoming by making 457s subject to the same maximum contribution levels that apply to 401(k) and, as noted above, 403(b) plans. Employers may match workers' contributions, but it's not as common as in 401(k)s.

You may also be able to make catch-up contributions to your 457. In fact, there are two types of catch-up contributions. First, if you're fifty or older, you can make the same type of catch-up contributions that the 2001 tax law approved for 401(k) and 403(b) plans and that are outlined in the section on 403(b)s above. But there's also another type of catch-up contribution for 457s that's been around for years. If you're within three years of retirement and haven't contributed the maximum to your 457 plan in the past, you can contribute up to your normal limit for the year *plus* any unused amounts from prior years. Your combined contribution cannot exceed a specified ceiling, however, The ceiling is $26,000 for 2004 and rises to $30,000 by 2006. This is an either-or proposition, though. You can do only one or the other in a given year. So if you're eligible for catch-up contributions, you'll probably want to consult with your personnel department to see which type has the higher limit.

There's one other feature of 457s worth mentioning. Like other retirement plans, most 457s have a provision that allows you to withdraw money before age fifty-nine and a half for unforeseen emergencies, usually for situations like an accident or unexpected illness. If you do make such a withdrawal, you'll have to pay income tax. Unlike with a 401(k), however, you won't be hit with a 10 percent penalty. Similarly, if you leave your job and instead of rolling your 457 money into an IRA or new retirement plan you start spending it, you'll pay income tax only, not tax and a 10 percent penalty as you would with a 401(k). I suppose this is a plus in that it gives you more financial flexibility. But if you think of the assets in your 457 plan as money earmarked specifically for retirement, then this is a feature you won't want to take advantage of, if you can possibly avoid it.

Retirement Plans for Small Businesses and the Self-Employed

It wasn't too long ago that working for a small business meant you had a good chance of being shortchanged on the retirement savings front. The amounts that workers at small companies could accumulate in retirement plans often paled in comparison to what people who worked at larger companies with 401(k) plans could amass. And while self-employed individuals have long had access to plans that allowed them to stash away impressive amounts of money on a pretax basis, the plans themselves were often complicated to set up and were nothing short of a paperwork nightmare to maintain.

But the 2001 tax bill has made retirement planning, if not a breeze, at least somewhat easier for small business owners and the self-employed, which means that things have improved for their employees as well. Setting up plans has become easier, and, even more important, the amounts that one can contribute on a pretax basis to these plans has also increased, making them much more viable ways to stockpile a retirement stash. As a result of the new law, self-employed individuals and small business owners with fewer than one hundred employees can even qualify for a tax credit of up to $500 toward the cost of establishing a retirement plan—granted, not a to-die-for perk but one that could at least encourage more small businesses to offer plans to their employees. Which is to say that, overall, things have been looking good for small businesses and their employees when it comes to saving for retirement at the workplace.

In this section, we'll take a look at the savings opportunities available in the three most popular plans specifically geared toward small businesses and their employees: the SEP IRA, the SIMPLE IRA, and the Keogh.

SEP IRA

Many people who work for a small business are covered by a Simplified Employee Pension IRA (SEP IRA) instead of a 401(k), since they are much easier for small business owners and self-employed individuals to set up and maintain. Here's how they work.

After the employer creates an overall SEP IRA plan to cover the firm's workers and the employer himself, employees then set up their own SEP IRAs at an investment firm of their choice. The employer funds the employee account with pretax dollars, up to a maximum of 25 percent of compensation or $40,000, whichever is less. In fact, the employer is the only one who can put money into the account. That money then compounds without the drag of taxes until the employee withdraws it, at which point income taxes on the withdrawal are due. (SEP IRAs are subject to the same withdrawal rules as traditional IRAs, which we'll get into later in this chapter.)

If you're the employee of a small business that doesn't offer a 401(k), then having access to a SEP IRA can be a good deal. Depending on how much you make and the percentage of salary the employer contributes to the plan on your behalf, the annual contributions to your account could be larger than what you could make on your own to a 401(k) or a regular IRA account. And since you decide where to open your SEP IRA, you have much more latitude in terms of investing choices than people in 401(k)s, who typically must choose from a preset menu of options created by their employer.

But SEP IRAs also have a disadvantage. Unlike a 401(k), where you have the choice of contributing every year, in lean years the employer could decide to forgo making contributions altogether.

SIMPLE IRA

The Savings Incentive Match Plan for Employees IRA, or SIMPLE IRA, is another way self-employed individuals and small companies, in this case ones with fewer than one hundred employees, can offer their workers a way to stash away pre-tax dollars for retirement. Those dollars can then rack up gains that remain free of taxes until the money is withdrawn.

As with a SEP IRA, employees set up their own SIMPLE IRA accounts, but there are several important differences between the two plans. Workers can contribute to their own SIMPLE IRA accounts, up to a maximum of $9,000 in 2004 and $10,000 in 2005. The max then rises with inflation in 2006 and later years. If you're fifty or older, you can also make catch-up contributions to your SIMPLE IRA. Those contributions can be as much as $1,500 in 2004, $2,000 in 2005, and $2,500 in 2006, after which the max is adjusted for inflation.

Another major difference between a SEP IRA and a SIMPLE

IRA is that while the employer can choose not to make contributions to a SEP in a given year, employers who set up a SIMPLE IRA must contribute to employees' accounts each year in either of two ways: They can make a dollar-for-dollar match of up to 3 percent (but not less than 1 percent) of whatever the employee contributes to the plan, or the employer can contribute 2 percent of salary to each eligible employee whether or not the employee makes his or her own contributions. So it's possible that with a SIMPLE IRA you could end up with some retirement savings even if you don't put anything away on your own (not that I recommend doing so). Employer contributions, by the way, don't count toward the max that employees are allowed to contribute to their accounts.

The relatively low contribution limits make SIMPLE IRAs generally less attractive than 401(k) plans, especially if you're pulling down a high salary. Another downside: If you're under age fifty-nine and a half and you withdraw money before you've been in the plan two years, you'll face an early withdrawal penalty of 25 percent instead of the usual 10 percent. Ouch! After two years, the penalty reverts to the normal 10 percent. Despite these downsides, having access to a SIMPLE IRA is certainly better than having no retirement plan at all, and the fact that you can decide where to set up your account certainly gives you plenty of options when it comes to investing the money in your SIMPLE IRA.

Keoghs

A Keogh is a retirement plan that allows you to set aside pretax dollars for retirement if you're self-employed or you work for someone who is. Until a few years ago, getting the maximum benefit out of a Keogh was often a tricky affair that involved setting up two separate types of Keoghs, a money purchase plan that requires mandatory contributions each year, regardless of how the self-employed person's business fared, and a profit-sharing plan that allowed more flexibility with contributions. But with the passage of the 2001 tax bill, you can pretty much get by with a profit-sharing plan alone. Under this arrangement, you can set aside on a pretax basis up to 25 percent of your income to a maximum of $40,000, a big boost from the 20 percent max that had been in place prior to the 2001 law. (As with a SEP, the maximum percentage for the self-employed owner of a business as opposed to employees is based on income minus the contribution itself. That translates into a 20 percent maximum, which is still an increase from the earlier 15 percent for a self-employed person.)

Despite the increase in limits, Keoghs are a somewhat less attractive choice for self-employed individuals looking to set up a plan. The reason is that—again, as a result of the 2001 tax law—self-employed individuals can now save just as much for themselves and their employees by creating a SEP IRA, which is generally easier to set up and maintain than a Keogh. A SEP IRA is also more flexible in that you have until the tax filing deadline, plus extensions, to create and fund a SEP IRA. A Keogh, by contrast, must be set up by December 31 of the year for which you're making the contribution, although you do have until the tax filing deadline plus extensions to fund it.

There's another type of Keogh—a defined-benefit Keogh—that allows a self-employed person and the people employed by that person to stick away as much as 100 percent of their pretax income, subject to a dollar limit. This version is especially suited for people who have procrastinated about saving for retirement and are looking to put away big bucks in a relatively short period of time. Of course, there are several practical drawbacks. For one thing, it may be difficult to live day to day if you're sinking a huge percentage of your income into a retirement plan. What's more, setting up a defined-benefit Keogh can be quite complicated and definitely not something most self-employed people want to take on without the help of a retirement-planning expert or benefit consultant. Still, if you've got the bucks and you're behind in your savings plan, this type of plan can be an excellent way to make up for lost time.

Retirement Plan Resources

For more information about the ins and outs of IRAs, 403(b)s, and 457 plans as well as the entire smorgasbord of retirement savings plans for workers and owners of small businesses, here are some websites to visit.

CCH Financial Planning Toolkit (www.finance.cch.com): The Saving for Retirement link in the site's Retirement Planning section offers detailed information on virtually all the plans discussed in this chapter, including 403(b)s, 457s, SEP IRAs, SIMPLE IRAs, and Keoghs.

Fairmark Press (www.fairmark.com): Without a doubt the most comprehensive and detailed guide to Roth IRAs you'll find on the Web—or anywhere else.

MPower Cafe (www.mpowercafe.com): Primers as well as comprehensive information on IRAs, 403(b)s, and 457 plans.

403(b)wise (www.403bwise.com): Created by two former California teachers, this site provides news, calculators, and detailed information and advice about virtually all aspects of 403(b) plans, including how to calculate lucrative but daunting lifetime catch-up contributions.

457 Info (www2.icmarc.org/xp/vl/457info): This site, created by the Government Finance Officers Association and the ICMA Retirement Corporation, a company that specializes in retirement plans for public sector employees, tells you pretty much everything you need to know about 457 plans.

IRA Guide (www.quicken.com/retirement/IRA/basics): This section of the Quicken site offers everything from the nuts and bolts about opening an IRA to in-depth information about IRA rollovers.

Tax-Advantaged Savings via Annuities

With the exception of IRAs, all the retirement savings vehicles I've talked about so far are linked to employment—that is, you've either got to be an employee or the employer yourself to take advantage of them. But there's another type of savings vehicle that anyone, employed or not, has access to that also shelters investment gains from income taxes at least temporarily. That investment is an annuity, a hybrid that combines elements of the insurance world with the investment world.

The question, though, is whether an annuity is right for you. That can be difficult to determine for a number of reasons, one of which is that annuities are difficult to understand and even more difficult to evaluate. In the remainder of this chapter, I'll try to lift the veil from these often confounding investments.

Before we get into the nitty-gritty of annuities—and believe me, there's more than enough nitty and gritty to go around—I want to explain one important aspect of these investments that is crucial in deciding what role, if any, they should play in your retirement planning. Annuities are rather unique in that they can have two distinct phases. They can be used primarily as a tax-deferred investment to accumulate assets for retirement. In this phase, they are usually referred to as deferred annuities. But annuities can also be used primarily as a payout vehicle to convert assets you've already accumulated into a retirement income. When fulfilling this role, annuities are usually referred to as payout or income annuities, or even immediate annuities.

For a variety of reasons that will become clear shortly, I'm not a big fan of annuities for the accumulation stage of retirement. That's not to say they can never play a role. But I think that role is very limited for most people. In fact, I'd say you shouldn't even *think* of buying an annuity to build assets for retirement unless you've maxed out your contributions to all the other tax-sheltered plans I've described in this book (401(k)s, 403(b)s, IRAs, etc.). And even then they might not be a worthwhile investment. On the payout side, however, I believe annuities can and will play a significant role for many people in retirement. This chapter will focus only on the accumulation aspects of annuities. For a discussion of why you might consider payout annuities as a way to create a reliable income once you've retired, go to Chapter 9.

Basically, annuities come in two flavors—fixed and variable.

Since each type has its own peculiar characteristics and demands a different type of analysis, we'll take a look at each one separately.

Fixed Annuities: Security and Tax Deferral . . .
but Lots of Catches, Too

Fixed annuities are much like certificates of deposit, except that they're issued by insurance companies instead of by banks and they're not covered by federal deposit insurance. (There is a safety net of sorts in the form of state guaranty associations. That coverage varies by state but is typically limited to $100,000. For details of the coverage in your state, go to the National Organization of Life and Health Insurance Guaranty Associations site, www.nolhga.com.) Like CDs, fixed annuities provide security of principal in that they pay rates of interest that are guaranteed or fixed for a certain period (hence the term *fixed annuities*). Often their rates are comparable to or even a bit higher than what you might earn at the bank. Some insurers even offer attractive bonuses that can boost the initial rate well into double-digit territory. Unlike CDs, fixed annuities also have the advantage of tax deferral. The interest they pay escapes taxation until you withdraw your money. At that time, your earnings are taxed at ordinary income rates. If you're under age fifty-nine and a half when you withdraw money from a fixed annuity, you'll pay an additional 10 percent tax for early withdrawal.

But while fixed annuities may seem like an ideal way to get the security of a CD while earning a tax-deferred return, they come with a variety of strings attached that can seriously diminish their appeal.

Those guaranteed rates, for example, may be guaranteed all right but often for only one year. So if you sign up for an annuity with a rate of, say, 6 percent, you're typically sure of getting that rate for only the next twelve months. After that, all bets are usually off. That's also the case with the bonus rates. You get the bonus one year and then the insurer is free to set the rate wherever it wants, although many annuities do have a minimum guaranteed rate of return. Until recently, that minimum guarantee was about 3 percent, but when interest rates fell to forty-year lows in 2003, many insurers lowered their minimum guarantees, in some cases dropping them to 1.5 percent. In any case, aside from a minimum guarantee of 3 percent or less, you're pretty much at the insurer's mercy when it comes to renewal rates on your annuity.

This wouldn't be much of a problem if you could simply move your money to another annuity—or any other investment, for that matter—if you think the renewal rate the insurer is offering is too low. But you may be penalized heavily for doing so. Nearly all insurers impose surrender charges on their annuities, early withdrawal penalties that kick in if you withdraw more than 10 percent of your account value in any year. (These charges are separate from and in addition to the 10 percent tax penalty the government may levy on earnings withdrawn before age fifty-nine and a half.) Surrender charges usually begin at 7 to 10 percent and decline by a percentage point or so a year, usually disappearing after seven or eight years. In some cases, though, surrender charges may be as high as 12 percent and last ten years or longer. Some annuities charge an MVA, or market value adjustment, a feature that lowers the amount of money available for withdrawal in the event interest rates have risen since you bought your fixed annuity. And some annuities levy both a surrender charge and an MVA. It's possible that these charges could not only wipe out your earnings but also eat into your principal. If you earn a return, you would still owe taxes on that gain, of course, plus a 10 percent tax penalty if you're under age fifty-nine and a half.

One type of fixed annuity does allow you to lock in a fixed rate of return for a specific period. That version of a fixed annuity is known as a CD annuity, and it guarantees a rate of interest for a specified term, usually one to ten years. CD annuities have surrender charges, but they usually expire at the end of the annuity's term. So with a CD annuity you at least have the right to withdraw your money without paying a surrender charge if you don't like the renewal rate the insurer offers at the end of the CD's term. A market value adjustment could still apply, however.

Given all the possible hitches and penalties, I don't see fixed annuities as a very good way to accumulate savings for retirement. They could be used as a CD substitute for the conservative portion of your portfolio, but even then I'm not convinced they're worth the trouble of sorting through the contract and trying to understand the various charges and conditions. Once you're beyond age fifty-nine and a half, you might consider using a fixed annuity as a way to generate some current income, since the 10 percent tax penalty would no longer apply. But even then you must take care that surrender charges and market value adjustments don't do you in. To the extent you use a fixed annuity at all in the accumulation stage, I'd say you're better off sticking to CD annuities, which let you lock in a rate for a specific period of time, or going with an annuity that has low surrender charges that don't stretch out for many years. I know of only one fixed annuity that offers no surrender charge: the fixed account in the TIAA-CREF Personal Annuity. You can get details on that annuity by going to the TIAA-CREF website (www.tiaa-cref.org) and clicking on the After-Tax Annuities link.

Variable Annuities: A Shot at Capital Appreciation . . . but High Fees, Too

You can think of variable annuities as tax-deferred mutual funds. When you buy a variable annuity, you typically get to invest your money in anywhere from six to twenty or more subaccounts, which are essentially mutual fund portfolios. Indeed, these subaccounts typically come in the same varieties as mutual funds—growth, value, large-cap, small-cap, tech, and so on—and many are run by well-known managers in the mutual fund world. Some subaccounts may even carry the same name as mutual funds.

The tax treatment of variable annuities is similar to that of the fixed version in that gains in the variable annuities' subaccounts escape taxation until you withdraw those gains from your account, at which time you pay income tax plus a 10 percent penalty if you're under age fifty-nine and a half. But variables also come with a tax twist that undermines their tax-deferral advantage over mutual funds—namely, any long-term capital gains you earn in the variable annuity's stock and bond subaccounts are eventually taxed at ordinary income rates. That means that you are effectively converting capital gains to ordinary income. That's long been a disadvantage, since the tax rate on long-term capital gains has been lower than the tax rate on ordinary income. But this aspect of annuities has become even more of a disadvantage in the wake of the 2003 tax bill because that bill lowered the maximum capital-gains rate from 20 percent to 15 percent, and even lower for lower-income taxpayers. This means that capital gains that would be taxed at no higher than 15 percent can be taxed when withdrawn from a variable annuity at ordinary income tax rates as high as 35 percent. It takes many, many years of tax deferral to overcome this disadvantage.

On top of this tax disadvantage, variable annuities have a variety of fees that can further drag down returns. Like their fixed counterparts, most variables come with surrender charges that nick the value of your account for early withdrawals. But variables also have two additional layers of fees. There are management fees, which represent the expense of managing the subaccounts and typically range from 0.5 percent a year to more than 2 percent in the case of some subaccounts, usually international and small-stock portfolios. Then there are insurance charges. These average about 1.3 percent per year but can range as high as 1.6 percent or so. Combine the management expenses and the insurance charges, and it's not uncommon to see the total annual expenses on variable annuities come in at more than 2 percent and sometimes even close to 3 percent per year. It's possible to find variable annuities with slimmer expenses, such as those offered by Vanguard, TIAA-CREF, Ameritas, eAnnuity, and Schwab, to name a few. But low-cost annuities are still the exception rather than the rule.

It's the combination of lofty fees plus the unfavorable treatment of capital gains in variable annuities that, in my opinion, detracts from variable annuities' appeal as a way to accumulate assets for retirement. When you add the fees on top of the tax treatment of capital gains, you often need fifteen to twenty or more years of tax deferral before a variable annuity delivers a higher after-tax return than a plain old mutual fund. That would be fine if you were sure that the money you're investing in a variable annuity would stay there for *at least* fifteen years. But, really, how certain can you be of that? And if it turns out that you need to dip into that money within fifteen or twenty years, then the fees plus the extra taxes you pay on capital gains could very well leave you with less money than if you had simply invested in a mutual fund.

One final caveat: Many people buy variable annuities because of various bells and whistles insurers tack onto them to make them seem more appealing. One favorite is the death benefit. In its simplest form, this feature guarantees that when you die your beneficiary will receive the higher of the market value of your account or the amount you invested. But many annuities come with an enhanced version that, under certain conditions, guarantees that your beneficiary will receive the greater of your account balance or the value of your investment increased by, say, 6 percent per year.

Another popular feature is the guaranteed minimum income benefit, or GMIB. In this case, the insurer promises that as long as you hold your annuity at least ten years, you will receive a guaranteed level of income in the future, even if your subaccounts have performed so poorly that your annuity's account value has declined.

There's no doubt that these kinds of provisions have a certain emotional appeal. After all, the ability to lock in a retirement income in advance or protect your heirs against market downturns would appear to make financial sense. But these features add to the annuity's expenses. So the real question is whether these features are likely enough to pay off to make them worth the extra cost. For your beneficiary to collect on the death benefit, for example, not only does the market have to fall far enough so your account is worth less than your original investment, you've also got to die while your account value is down. That certainly could happen, but the odds are long.

Similarly, the guaranteed minimum income benefit sounds great on the surface. But if you check the fine print of the contract, you'll see that the size of the income you're being guaranteed is pretty small. Again, it's possible you could come out ahead by opting for this feature, but it's not very likely. So if you combine the low probability of collecting on bells and whistles such as the death benefit and the GMIB with the fact that they can boost an annuity's already substantial costs, I think it's hard to justify opting for these features. To protect yourself against a relatively small possibility, you're reducing the long-term buildup in your account value.

Given the various costs and complexities of annuities, I believe most people are better off forgoing them as a way of accumulating assets for retirement. (For the same reasons, I don't think it's a good idea to roll money from tax-deferred plans such as 401(k)s or IRAs into what are often called IRA annuities.) That said, however, I do think that once you're retired or about to retire, annuities deserve consideration as a way to convert assets you've accumulated in tax-deferred plans or other accounts into a retirement income. By taking this approach, you limit the number of years your capital gains are taxed at ordinary income rates and you pay annuities' extra fees. But you still get to take advantage of the one benefit that annuities offer that no other investment can: the guarantee of a lifetime income. That, it seems to me, is a trade-off that can make financial sense for many people.

Annuity Resources

If you'd like to learn more about how to evaluate annuities—and get details on fees and rates of return—here are a few sites you can check out.

Annuity.net (www.annuity.net): You'll find rates on fixed annuities and specifics on surrender charges and other penalties.

AnnuityNetAdvisor.com (client.annuitynetadvisor.com): This site's Education Center has good basic info on fixed and variable annuities, plus in-depth explanations of fees and expenses.

T. D. Waterhouse Annuities 101 (www.tdwaterhouse.com/ planning/retirement_center/annuities): Check out the fee calculator, which demonstrates how blimpish fees can erode your return.

The sites of the three major ratings companies provide financial strength ratings on insurance companies that issue annuities. Those companies and their site addresses are:

Standard & Poor's (www.standardandpoors.com)
Moody's Investors Service (www.moodys.com)
A. M. Best Company (www.ambest.com)

Chapter 5

CREATE A RETIREMENT PLAN THAT WORKS FOR *YOU*

Okay. At this point, you should have a good understanding of the new and still evolving retirement-planning landscape you're dealing with and the various challenges and opportunities it presents. Now it's time to get to the heart of the matter: creating your own personalized plan. Question is, how do you start? There's a scene at the beginning of *The Wizard of Oz* where Glinda, the Good Witch of the North, tells Dorothy that her only hope of getting back to Kansas is to visit the Wizard in faraway Emerald City. "But where do I begin?" Dorothy asks. Glinda tells her to "start at the beginning," at which point she directs Dorothy to the start of the yellow brick road.

Well, starting at the beginning may be good advice for getting to Oz. But, paradoxically enough, when it comes to the financial journey of retirement planning, you start not at the beginning but at the end. That's right—when creating a retirement plan, the best place to begin is by estimating the annual income you will need when you eventually retire. And it's from that starting point—or ending point, I suppose—that the rest of your plan will flow. For once you have a target of retirement income you wish to achieve—not a hazy, ambiguous sum but a specific dollar goal—you can then start working backward to figure out what you must do in the present to reach that goal.

Unfortunately, most of us don't have a very good sense of

how much income we'll need after we retire. Indeed, a 2003 survey of preretirees by the MetLife Mature Market Institute found that many people underestimate their retirement income needs by 30 to 40 percent. One reason is that few of us actually get around to assessing how much money we'll need after calling it a career. The Employee Benefit Research Institute's 2002 Retirement Confidence Survey found that only about a third of workers have actually tried to calculate how much they need to save by retirement. That's too bad, because people who go to the trouble to figure out how much they need to save during their career tend to accumulate more as well. According to the American Savings Education Council, Americans who have done a retirement calculation have nearly *five times* the savings of those who haven't bothered. I suspect that's because once most of us take a look at what we realistically will need to retire, we've got a lot more motivation to begin salting money away.

There are two different options for creating a plan. The first is the Low-Tech Approach, which provides a relatively quick and simple way of gauging how much money you need to begin saving today to retire comfortably. The second is the Computerized Approach, which involves online retirement-planning tools that make use of sophisticated statistical techniques and computerized simulations.

Which approach works best? I don't think there's any doubt that the online method gives you a more realistic sense of your likely success at achieving a certain level of retirement income. Indeed, one of the big advantages of these state-of-the-art online tools is that they make you think in terms of probabilities rather than certainties, which is important because probabilities are all we have in the real world. Even if we know for certain how much we'll save each and every month over the next twenty years, there's no way for us to know exactly what return we'll earn on every dollar we invest. The investment markets are too uncertain, too volatile for that. So while filling out the We're Not in Kansas Anymore worksheet that's the center of the Low-Tech Approach may seem to yield neat and clean projections, results in the real world aren't so certain. They're much more subject to variation. (You can get a sense of just how much results can vary by filling out the worksheet several times using different assumptions, which is something I recommend.) The best computerized retirement-planning tools, however, are able to factor volatility and uncertainty into their estimates far better than any paper worksheet. They're able to give you a sense of the range of possible outcomes you might experience, rather than suggesting that if you save a specific amount per month and earn an assumed rate of return, you will absolutely, positively end up with a specific amount of money.

On the other hand, I recognize that many people aren't going to put in the initial work of signing up for one of these online tools or go through the process of entering the data. Others may just not like working with computers. So for those people, the Low-Tech Approach with an easy-to-use worksheet will at least get them on the right track to a successful retirement, even if the estimates are less rigorous than those you would get from computerized forecasts. What's most important is that you create *some kind of plan,* that you go through some sort of reasonable process to figure out how much income you'll likely need once you retire and how you're going to get it. If you do that and monitor your progress, you will vastly increase the odds of being able to retire with a modicum of material comfort.

Even if you intend to take the Computerized Approach, I recommend that you read through the Low-Tech section below, if for no reason other than to gain a sense of what sort of issues and assumptions go into a retirement plan and the forecasting that such plans necessarily involve. The more you understand the dynamics of creating a retirement plan, the better the plan you'll be able to create, whether on paper or on a computer.

Creating Your Plan the Low-Tech Way

This six-step plan that will help you assess where you stand now in terms of preparing for your retirement, tell you where you need to get to by the time you're ready to retire, and show you what you've got to do between now and then to have a reasonable chance of retiring in the lifestyle you hope to achieve. I recommend that you enter your financial information on the We're Not in Kansas Anymore worksheet on pages 122–124 as you read along. One note before we begin: The dollar figures that you'll be inserting in the worksheet should be in *today's* dollars before taxes. In other words, when you estimate a target annual income for retirement, the figure should reflect the amount of money you would need before taxes if your future retirement were starting today. In reality, of course, the number of dollars you will need in retirement will be higher than the number you estimate today because of inflation. You will also likely owe taxes on that income. But things will get complicated fast if you have to estimate an inflation rate for the years ahead and then apply that rate to your current-dollar estimate to come up with a future-dollar estimate. The same goes for estimating the taxes you'll pay, not only because tax rates can be difficult to predict, but different types of income—Social Security, dividends, capital gains—can be taxed at different rates. Just thinking about it gives me a headache. So when estimating the income you'll need in retirement just use today's pretax dollars, and I'll make appropriate adjustments in the worksheet sections relating to the growth of your savings and investments so that all the figures are consistent and reflect what you'll have to start doing now to achieve the retirement lifestyle you desire.

Step 1: Determine How Much Income You'll Need in Retirement

Your target income figure—the amount you'll need to live comfortably in retirement—is the single most important figure in creating a retirement plan. Everything else is built around this goal—the amount you must save during your career, how you must invest your retirement savings, the way you'll draw down money from your portfolio once you retire.

Ideally, you don't want to rely on seat-of-the pants guesstimates and simplistic rules of thumb such as the 70 percent rule, which contends that because work-related expenses and the need to save disappear in retirement, you can maintain your present standard of living with less than your current income once you retire.

WE'RE NOT IN KANSAS ANYMORE
RETIREMENT WORKSHEET

Step 1. Estimate the annual income you would like to have in retirement. $_____

> If you're within ten years of retirement, fill out the Retirement Expenses worksheet on pages 127–129, or insert at least 75 to 80 percent of your current income.
>
> If retirement is further off, insert at least 80 to 90 percent of your current income.

Step 2. Estimate the annual income you expect to receive from the following sources:

> Social Security[1] $_____
> Company pension[2] $_____
> Part-time work $_____
> Other income (annuities, etc.) $_____
>
> Total $_____

Step 3. Estimate the income you must generate from your retirement investments. $_____

> Subtract the total in Step 2 from the figure in Step 1.

Step 4. Determine the amount you must accumulate by retirement to create the income in Step 3. $_____

> Multiply the figure in Step 3 by one of the factors below. Use the conservative factor if you plan to invest conservatively in retirement or

you want a high degree of assurance you won't run out of money while you're alive. Use the aggressive factor if you plan to invest aggressively or are willing to risk running short. Use the moderate factor if you fall between conservative and aggressive.

Conservative = 25   Moderate = 20   Aggressive = 15

Step 5. Total the market value of all the retirement savings you have now.

Include 401(k)s, IRAs, etc., plus any other savings and investments you have earmarked for retirement. $_____

Step 6. Figure out how much you must save each year between now and retirement.

To do that, follow a through c.

a. Multiply the amount in Step 5 by the appropriate factor below. Choose conservative, moderate, or aggressive, depending on your investing style. $_____

YEARS UNTIL RETIREMENT

	CONSERVATIVE	MODERATE	AGGRESSIVE
5	1.16	1.22	1.28
10	1.34	1.48	1.63
15	1.56	1.80	2.08
20	1.81	2.19	2.65
25	2.09	2.67	3.39
30	2.43	3.24	4.32
35	2.81	3.95	5.52
40	3.26	4.80	7.04

b. Subtract the figure you arrived at in a (above) from the figure in Step 4. The result is the additional savings you must accumulate by retirement. $_____

c. Multiply the figure from b (previous page) by the appropriate factor below. Again, choose conservative, moderate, or aggressive, depending on your investing style. **The result is the amount you must save this year to stay on track toward your retirement income goal. Redo this worksheet every year.**

$_____

YEARS UNTIL RETIREMENT

	CONSERVATIVE	MODERATE	AGGRESSIVE
5	0.1829	0.1776	0.1725
10	0.0847	0.0801	0.0758
15	0.0523	0.0481	0.0442
20	0.0361	0.0323	0.0289
25	0.0267	0.0231	0.0200
30	0.0205	0.0172	0.0144
35	0.0160	0.0131	0.0106
40	0.0129	0.0102	0.0079

[1]Be sure to use your Social Security benefit in today's dollars, not future dollars. If you plan to retire before receiving Social Security, multiply the Social Security figure you insert in Step 2 by the number of years until you'll receive Social Security and add it to the total in Step 4.

[2]The estimate you'll receive from your human resources department will most likely be in future dollars. To convert that figure to the current-dollar figure required by this worksheet, multiply the future-dollar figure by the conversion factor below that corresponds to the number of years you have until you will receive your company pension.

If you'll receive your pension in . . .	. . . multiply the figure by
5 years	0.86
10 years	0.74
15 years	0.64
20 years	0.55
25 years	0.48
30 years	0.41

There are several problems with the 70 percent rule. For one, the percentage of preretirement income one must replace in retirement can vary substantially depending on your level of preretirement income. In general, the higher your preretirement income, the higher a percentage of that income you will need to maintain the same lifestyle in retirement. The spending of higher-income people tends to drop less than that of those with lower incomes, no doubt because those earning higher wages have more ambitious plans for retirement that include lots of traveling and leisure activities. But there are other reasons as well. The Social Security benefits of higher-income retirees are taxed more than the benefits of those with lower incomes, which means higher-income retirees need a higher percentage of their gross preretirement income to maintain a given level of spending. Some researchers have calculated that, on average, people with incomes of $80,000 or more prior to retirement would likely need upward of 80 to 90 percent of their preretirement income to maintain their lifestyle.

There's also the fact that these "replacement ratios" or percentages are averages calculated from the spending habits of many, many people. Your spending could easily be well above or well below that average, depending on your financial situation and the lifestyle you plan to live in retirement. If your mortgage will be paid off by the time you stop working and you envision a relatively quiet and pensive retirement, you may be able to get by on a relatively small percentage of your preretirement income, say, 50 to 60 percent. On the other hand, if you're planning to circumnavigate the globe on cruise ships six months out of the year, then you may need 100 percent of your preretirement income, if not more.

Do your planning based on your particular needs, not percentages based on the averages of thousands of people you don't know and whose ideas of retirement living may vary dramatically from yours. If you're relatively close to retirement— say, within five to ten years—I recommend you fill out the Retirement Expenses worksheet on pages 127–129 and insert the final figure you arrive at in Step 1 of the We're Not in

Kansas Anymore worksheet. (You can also find interactive retirement expenses worksheets at various sites online.) This exercise provides a higher level of accuracy than you can get from estimating a target income figure based on a percentage of your current salary.

If, for whatever reason, you don't want to do the worksheet, then choose what you consider an appropriate percentage of your preretirement salary. Unless you have very good reasons to believe you can get by on less, I'd recommend 70 to 80 percent of your current income, more if you plan an active retirement with lots of travel and other recreational expenses.

If retirement is more than ten years off, however, then it will be tough to accurately estimate your actual retirement expenses. So you'll probably want to apply a percentage of your current income. Generally, I'd recommend at least 80 to 90 percent in order to allow for the growth in your income between now and the time you retire. In fact, if you're relatively early in your career or you still have many prime earning years ahead of you, then you may want to consider inserting 100 percent of your current income in Step 1 just for an added margin of safety.

HOW MUCH RETIREMENT INCOME WILL YOU NEED?

One way to estimate the annual income you'll require in retirement is to take a percentage of your preretirement income, usually 70 to 80 percent. You'll get a more accurate sense of how much income you'll need, however, by filling out the Retirement Expenses worksheet on the next page and estimating your retirement expenses category by category. When you're finished, you can insert the estimate you come up with into the main We're Not in Kansas Anymore worksheet on page 122. You should repeat this process periodically to track your progress toward your retirement income goal.

RETIREMENT EXPENSES WORKSHEET

EXPENSE	ESTIMATE OF ANNUAL COST IN RETIREMENT
Basics	
Groceries	$_____
Eating out	$_____
Clothing	$_____
Laundry/dry cleaning	$_____
Newspapers, magazines, Internet	$_____
Grooming/personal hygiene	$_____
Auto expenses (gas, insurance, loan or lease payments)	$_____
Other basic expenses	$_____
1. TOTAL BASICS	$_____
Housing	
Mortgage payment or rent	$_____
Property taxes	$_____
Homeowners'/renters' insurance	$_____
Utilities	$_____
Home repairs and maintenance	$_____
Other housing expenses	
2. TOTAL HOUSING	$_____
Health	
Health insurance	$_____
Medicare premiums (go to www.medicare.gov for an estimate)	$_____
Long-term-care insurance premiums	$_____
Life insurance	$_____
Dental care	$_____
Eye care/glasses	$_____
Medications	$_____
Other health expenses	$_____
3. TOTAL HEALTH	$_____

(continued on page 128)

RETIREMENT EXPENSES WORKSHEET *(continued)*

EXPENSE	ESTIMATE OF ANNUAL COST IN RETIREMENT
Leisure	
Travel and vacations	$_____
Entertaining	$_____
Hobbies	$_____
Athletic and social club memberships	$_____
Other leisure expenses	$_____
4. TOTAL LEISURE	$_____
Miscellaneous	
Charitable donations	$_____
Gifts	$_____
Assistance to family (siblings, children, grandchildren)	$_____
Other miscellaneous expenses	$_____
5. TOTAL MISCELLANEOUS	$_____
TOTAL EXPENSES	$_____
(Add lines 1 through 5 above)	

Convert Expenses to Estimated Retirement Income

The total figure above excludes one expense you will face in retirement: income taxes. Your income tax tab will vary depending on a number of factors: your total income, how much of that income comes from 401(k)s and IRA rollover accounts (where all or most of the withdrawals will be taxed) versus tax-free sources such as Roth IRAs and municipal bonds, and whether withdrawals from taxable investment accounts are taxed at ordinary income or capital gains rates. Your tax liability will also depend, of course, on where Congress sets tax rates during your retirement. You can't know for certain how much income taxes will add to your retirement expenses, but you can make a reasonable estimate. To do that, go to the line on the next page.

Annual Income You'll Need at Retirement

Multiply the total expenses figure on the previous page by one of the factors below and insert the result at right. **Use this figure in Step 1 of the We're Not in Kansas worksheet on page 122.** $_____

INCOME EXPECTED DURING RETIREMENT	FACTOR
Less than $20,000	1.08
$20,000 to $30,000	1.10
$30,000 to $50,000	1.11
$50,000 to $100,000	1.18
$100,000 to $200,000	1.25
$200,000 and up	1.33

Step 2: Estimate the Income You'll Receive from Social Security, Pensions, Part-time Work, and Other Sources

The next step in creating your retirement plan is to see how much of your targeted annual income you can get before having to dip into your retirement savings. For many, the single most important source of regular income during retirement will be Social Security. You can get an estimate of how much you'll collect by calling the Social Security Administration at 800-772-1213 or by going to the Social Security Online Benefits Calculator (www.ssa.gov/planners/calculators.htm). For the purposes of the worksheet, be sure to choose the option that gives your benefits in *today's* dollars. (Married couples should include benefits for both spouses. The one with lower earnings should use the benefit based on his or her own earnings record, or 50 percent of the higher-earning spouse's benefit, whichever is larger. Even someone who has never worked at a job covered by Social Security typically receives a benefit equal to half of his or her spouse's benefit.)

If you will be eligible for a corporate pension from one

or more employers after retirement, for example, you would include those payments here. (I'm talking about a traditional defined-benefit pension that pays you a monthly income at retirement. The amounts you have in 401(k)s and similar plans will be accounted for separately in Step 5.) The human resources department at whichever employers owe you a pension should be able to provide a figure for the benefit you'll receive.

Be careful, though. Companies often quote the monthly benefit you would receive based on your life alone, otherwise known as a single-life or straight-life option. If you want the pension to be paid not just as long as you live but for your spouse's lifetime as well, then the monthly payment will be smaller. To determine the amount the company will pay as long as you or your spouse are alive, ask for the monthly benefit under the "joint and survivor" option. Whichever option you choose, the benefits estimate you'll receive is usually quoted in future dollars, which is the number of dollars you'll receive when you retire. Since this worksheet is based on current dollars, you must convert that benefits estimate to its value in today's dollars (the amount those future dollars would be worth if you received them right now) before putting the figure into the worksheet. Failure to do that will overstate the value of your corporate pension and lead you to underestimate how much you must save for retirement. To convert your future company pension estimate to today's dollars, multiply it by the appropriate conversion factor in the footnote of the We're Not in Kansas Anymore worksheet. You can then insert the resulting figure into the worksheet. In some cases, companies will also provide the present value of your pension—that is, the lump-sum dollar value you would receive if the pension benefits you've accumulated to date were paid to you today. If your company provides such an estimate, you can use this figure instead of the monthly income amount, although you would enter the lump sum along with the value of your other investments in Step 5.

If you will be receiving income from an annuity, whether as

part of a retirement savings plan such as a 403(b) or an annuity that you've purchased on your own, include that amount in this section. Similarly, if you plan on working part-time in retirement, as many retirees do these days, include the income you expect to earn from employment.

Step 3: Estimate How Much Income You Must Get from Your Retirement Investments

If your income sources once you get to Step 3 are *higher* than your retirement income need, congratulations! You are in the distinct minority of people who won't have to rely on their savings and investments to provide income in retirement. (The other possibility, of course, is that you've set your retirement income target unrealistically low and you'll end up having to spend much more than you anticipate.)

For most people, however, there is a gap between the income you need for the retirement you want and the income you'll get from Social Security, pensions, and other sources listed in the previous step. You're going to have to rely on income from your savings and investments to bridge that gap. This is just another reminder that the lifestyle you will be able to afford in retirement depends on how much you manage to save during your career.

Step 4: Estimate How Large a Nest Egg You Need to Take Up the Slack

Now the challenge is to figure out how much money you will need to accumulate prior to retirement in accounts such as 401(k)s, IRAs, and other tax-advantaged savings plans as well as taxable accounts so that you can make annual withdrawals for the rest of your life that are large enough to bridge the gap you are facing from Step 3.

This is a thornier problem than it might seem. Many people tend to underestimate the amount of savings they'll need to carry them through retirement; put another way, they tend to overestimate how far whatever they have managed to save will carry them. That's because they forget several things. One is that the cost of living will likely rise tremendously during retirement, so the amount they'll have to pull out of their portfolio must be adjusted for the effects of inflation if they want to avoid having to lower their lifestyle. Another common pitfall retirees encounter is that they underestimate the length of time they'll spend in retirement. With life spans increasing virtually every year due to improvements in medical care, it's not uncommon for a sixty-five-year-old retiring today to spend twenty-five or thirty years in retirement, if not more. That means your retirement savings might have to support you for nearly as much time as you spent in your career.

Finally, there are investment considerations that must be factored in. If we lost sight of it during the booming '90s, the bear market that began in early 2000 reminded all of us just how much of a toll market setbacks can take on our investment portfolios. But most people probably still don't fully appreciate how dangerous such setbacks can be for retirees who are also relying on their portfolios for income during such setbacks. The problem is that retirees' portfolios experience a double-barreled effect. The portfolio's balance drops because of investment losses, but then it drops again because the retiree is pulling out money to live on. For most investors, a rebound in the market can restore the loss and then take the balance to new highs, usually within a few years. But a retiree's portfolio doesn't have the same resiliency. Why? There's not as much capital left to participate in the rebound because of the withdrawals for income. The result is that it's much easier than most people think to run through a portfolio in retirement, especially if you run into a bear market early on in retirement. All of which means that if you want a decent chance of being able to draw on your portfolio for the income you need for the rest of your life, you've got to accumulate a much larger stash than you probably think.

Ultimately, the amount of money you must accumulate in savings depends on the amount you wish to withdraw, how aggressively you invest your retirement stash, and what odds you are willing to accept that you might outlive your savings. The issue is too complicated to delve into here, which is why I devote the entire final chapter of this book to strategies that can increase the chances of your portfolio supporting you for the rest of your life. For the purposes of setting a target retirement portfolio for this step in your plan, however, what I've done is use the research and information discussed in the final chapter relating to withdrawal rates and the likelihood of portfolios lasting many years to give you three different options for estimating the size of portfolio you will need to make up for the shortfall in Step 3.

The conservative option requires that you accumulate the most assets, but it also gives you the biggest margin of safety—that is, if you accumulate this amount, you have the highest odds that your savings will be able to support you for the rest of your life. Choosing the moderate option means you don't have to accumulate the same level of assets as a retiree choosing the conservative course, but by accumulating fewer assets you are accepting a higher risk of your portfolio running dry during your lifetime. Finally, the aggressive option requires the smallest level of assets to support the withdrawals in Step 3, but the chances that your portfolio will not be able to support you throughout retirement are significantly higher than in the other two options.

You should also consider other factors before choosing one of the options. The younger the age at which you plan to retire, the longer you'll be depending on your retirement investments for income. That means you'll probably want a larger stash of savings going into retirement, which argues for the conservative option. Your estimate of your own life span is a factor, too. If you've got a family history of longevity, the conservative or moderate option would likely make sense. But if you truly doubt you'll beat the mortality statistics, then the aggressive option might be better for you. Your choice might also depend on how savvy an investor you consider yourself to be, since higher returns can support a given level of withdrawals for a longer time (although higher returns also come with higher up-and-down swings in the portfolio's value, which can lead to that double-barreled effect I talked about earlier).

Finally, as a practical matter, the option you choose may come down to what size portfolio you can realistically accumulate. Sure, we'd all like to have a nice, fat portfolio going into retirement that would ensure our comfort and security during our golden years. But given the other financial obligations we must meet, we simply might not be able to sock away the kinds of savings we need to create the level of savings we would like to have. Or for that matter, we might decide that achieving that level of savings would result in a preretirement lifestyle so grim that it's not worth living. So, as with most things, the target level of retirement savings you want to achieve is more often than not a judgment call, a balancing act between what you might prefer ideally and what is doable in the real world.

I recommend that you err on the side of caution—that is, shoot for a larger nest egg rather than a smaller one. But whichever option you choose, multiply the factor listed with that option times the shortfall you arrived at in Step 3. This will give you the target level of savings you need to achieve by the time you retire.

Step 5: Calculate How Much You Have Already Saved

Once you've set a target for how much you want to have accumulated in savings by the time you retire, you can see how close you are to that goal at the present time. Basically, you just total up the balances of all the savings that you have accumulated to this point for retirement, whether those savings are in accounts such as a 401(k), 403(b), or other employer-sponsored plan; a traditional IRA or Roth IRA; or savings you have in mutual funds or stocks or bonds that are held in taxable accounts but that you have earmarked for retirement. You do not want to include assets you have specifically set aside for other purposes, such as the money you might be holding in a money market fund or CDs as an emergency reserve or savings you may have in mutual funds or other investments for a house down payment or that you may be saving to buy a car or start a business.

There are two areas, however, that require a bit of discussion and a judgment call on your part. The first concerns a question that many families with children face: How much of your savings should go toward funding the future college education of a child versus your own retirement? Each family's response to this question must address its own financial circumstances, including factors such as the family's income, the portion of that income that can be devoted to savings of any kind, and the parents' eventual retirement income need. But at the risk of sounding heartless, I'd say that as a general rule, your first obligation is to yourself, then to your kids. In other words, you should first attend to whatever savings you need for retirement, and then move on to education expenses if you have money left over.

The reason is that when it comes to funding retirement, you've got relatively few options. You'll have Social Security and any pensions. But after that you're pretty much on your own. Your lifestyle will largely depend on how much money you've been able to stash away and invest. You've got much more flexibility on the college front with scholarships, grants and loans, and a broad range of colleges and universities to choose from with an equally broad range of costs.

The second issue is whether you should add the equity in your home to your other retirement assets to cover the shortfall in Step 3. The argument for including it is that your home is an asset that (you hope) is appreciating in value. And since it can be turned into income at retirement, some advisers feel it's appropriate to include it along with retirement funds and such. The argument against doing so is that many people prefer staying in their home once they retire. And if you don't end up selling, then you may be factoring in an asset you may not draw on when you retire, which means you may not have as much savings to actually draw on as you appear to have on paper. Even if you do end up selling your home to draw on its value, you're not going to be able to turn all the appreciation into retirement income. You'll have to live somewhere, so some of your money will still have to go to providing shelter. There are other reasons not to consider your home a retirement asset that have to do with the difficulty of managing it as an investment. I'll go into these issues in the next chapter, which deals with investing. For now, however, I recommend that you don't include your home's equity in this analysis. That's not to say your home can't play a role in your retirement plan. It can and does for many retirees. But I'd say that you should think of your home as a backup source of retirement income that you can tap if your investment accounts can't provide what you need. In keeping with that way of looking at your home, I'll address the ways you can incorporate it into your plan in Chapter 7, where I deal with a variety of strategies you can try if your main retirement plan doesn't get you where you need to be.

So for now at least, you should total the value of all the accounts whose assets you have earmarked for retirement, and then subtract that value from the target retirement savings figure you settled on at the end of Step 3. The resulting sum is the amount of savings you still have to accumulate in order for your savings to provide enough income that, combined with Social Security and the other sources you listed in Step 2, will give you the income you need to maintain the lifestyle you want in retirement.

Step 6: Determine How Much You Must Save Each Month or Year Between Now and the Time You Retire

In this step we'll figure out how much you've got to stick into savings and investments each year between now and the time you retire to bring your savings to the level needed to support you through retirement.

Aside from the number of years you have left until retirement, there are two major factors that determine whether you'll accumulate the savings target identified in Step 4: the dollar amount you save and the percentage return that you earn on those savings (as well as the return you earn on the money you already have saved). Those factors work hand in hand. The higher the return you earn, the less you have to put away each month or year to build the retirement stash you need. Conversely, the lower the return you expect to earn, the more you have to put away each month or year to build the amount you need. This makes perfect sense in that the investment return on your savings represents a form of saving itself. So the higher that return, the more your investments themselves are taking up a part of the burden of saving, while a lower return leaves more of that burden to you.

Given that relationship—the higher the return, the less savings needed from you—you might figure the simple answer to accumulating the retirement savings you need is to simply commit yourself to earning a high rate of return on your savings. After all, why not let your investments and the financial markets do some of the work for you? And indeed, that's how many people do their retirement planning. They forecast a high rate of return on their savings because by doing so it makes it appear that they will be able to achieve the retirement security they need without unduly cutting back on the spending they do today.

But notice I said that this strategy "makes it appear" that they'll be able to accumulate the retirement assets they'll need. The problem is that assuming a high rate of return and then actually earning it are two different things. The bear market that began in 2000 reminded us that periods of outsize gains like the 1990s are not sustainable. In figuring out how much you need to save from your current income to accumulate the retirement pot you'll need, *plan on the basis of realistic returns.* Toward that end, I've provided three rate-of-return options you can choose from in calculating the amount of regular savings you must undertake to hit your target level of retirement assets. The conservative option assumes an annual rate of return of 3 percent *net of inflation and investing expenses.* So, for example, if inflation averages 3 percent per year and you incur annual investing expenses of 1 percent or so on investments such as mutual funds, that 3 percent return would amount to a gross return of about 7 percent on your portfolio. The moderate option pushes the return assumption net of inflation and expenses up one percentage point, to 4 percent, and the aggressive option assumes a return of 5 percent net of inflation and expenses. Again, if inflation averages 3 percent a year and investment expenses are 1 percent, that would translate to an 8 percent gross return on the moderate option and a 9 percent gross return on the aggressive option. (For guidance on how you should invest to earn conservative, moderate, or aggressive returns, see the model portfolios in Chapter 6.)

These returns may strike you as quite low compared with the long-term returns you often hear quoted in the financial press. But remember, the market returns bandied about often do not take expenses into account, so that alone would tend to make them larger. It's also important to remember that our return expenses overall became inflated during the 1980s and 1990s. Many investment experts, including myself, think those periods distorted the long-term averages and that in the years ahead we'll see more modest returns that are essentially in line with what I've discussed above. That's not to say I'm predicting that these are the exact returns you or any other investor will achieve. Actual returns could come in higher or lower, depending on how the economy does and how investors react. And your individual returns will also depend on your expenses; many investors may incur expenses well above 1 percent per year. But these return assumptions are reasonable for the purposes of planning. The main idea is that you don't want to err too much on the high side (and thus not save enough to reach your target) or too much on the low side (and thus save so much that you diminish your lifestyle prior to retirement). Of course, if you believe these returns are too low, you do have the option of picking the aggressive option or, for that matter, assuming even higher rates of return.

In any case, assuming you do go with one of the three options I've given, move on to Step 6 in the We're Not in Kansas

Anymore worksheet on page 123. In part a you choose the number of years you have left before you retire, then select the appropriate factor for whichever of the three return assumptions you prefer (conservative, moderate, or aggressive), and then multiply that factor times the value of the retirement savings you have already accumulated (the amount in Step 5). The figure you get tells you how much your present retirement savings are likely to be worth in today's dollars by the time you retire. In part b of Step 6, you then subtract this amount from the total amount of retirement savings you need (the figure in Step 4). The result is the amount of savings you still must accumulate between now and the time you retire.

Finally, to translate this figure into an amount you must save each year, you move on to part c. Again, you choose the number of years you have until retirement, select the appropriate factor based on whether you've chosen the conservative, moderate, or aggressive return option, and then multiply that factor times the total amount you must accumulate between now and the time you retire. The result will be the amount in today's dollars that you must save this year to achieve the retirement income goal you set in Step 1.

Once you've completed this process, you essentially have a road map that gives you a decent sense of where you stand now, where you need to get to in the future, and what you have to do to get there. There are a lot of complications I've left out—such as the effect that taxes will have on the different types of accounts and investments that you own—because the purpose of the Low-Tech Approach is to give you a reasonable plan that you can actually put to work, as opposed to a far more complicated plan that may overwhelm you and paralyze you into inaction. I also recommend that you repeat this process once a year. One reason you must do periodic updates is that the We're Not in Kansas Anymore worksheet is designed to tell you what you must save in current dollars to meet a retirement goal based on your current income and assuming your savings earn their forecasted returns. But your retirement income goal will change as the result of inflation and the growth in your income, so you want to be sure your annual savings target is still adequate. Similarly, if returns come in lower than anticipated, for example, you'll have to increase your savings to meet your goal. Besides, occasionally recrunching the numbers with a fresh look at your assumptions and updated information about your earnings and retirement savings can tell you whether you're on track toward your retirement goal—and provide the opportunity to make adjustments if you're not.

The Computerized Approach to Retirement Planning

You'll be able to develop a more accurate retirement plan if you're willing to employ one of the several sophisticated retirement planning tools available on the Web. These tools rely on techniques that factor the real-life complexities of the financial markets into their projections. What's more, they allow you to develop a basic plan and then easily revise it to see how different assumptions about everything from investment returns to the number of years you will work until you retire affect your likelihood of achieving your targeted retirement income. But the advantage of the online approach is that it avoids some of the pitfalls of the Low-Tech method, the biggest of which is forecasting that your money will grow at a specific rate of return between now and the time you retire and assuming you will get that return year after year after year.

A growing number of online calculators use what are known as "Monte Carlo" forecasting techniques that, essentially, generate thousands of simulations, or possible scenarios, that take into account how inflation, interest rates, and the returns of different types of investments might vary based on their historical volatility. You plug in some basic financial information—the amount you've already saved for retirement, how much you still plan to invest on a regular basis in the years until you retire, the types of investments in your portfolio, and how much income you'll need in retirement. And within minutes these calculators can tell you the probability that you will meet your target retirement income goal. Don't like the odds? Then you can see how much you can improve the odds by varying such factors as the amount you'll save, the makeup of your portfolio, and the number of years you'll work before retiring. The beauty of this approach is that by couching its forecast in terms of probabilities rather than a false sense of precision, it gives you a much better sense of the inherent uncertainty in these types of projections. Knowing that, you can then adjust your plans depending on how much uncertainty you think you can handle.

Online Calculators That Are Worth a Look

Just because you find a retirement calculator online or as part of a software package doesn't automatically mean it uses Monte Carlo analysis or similar simulation techniques to make its projections. In fact, the retirement calculators at many online sites are nothing more than interactive electronic versions of the We're Not in Kansas Anymore worksheet. So while they may be easier to work with than a paper worksheet, the projections they spit out won't be any more accurate than if you do the same thing on paper.

But a growing number of retirement calculators are incorporating a variety of technically sophisticated forecasting techniques into their forecasts. The six sites listed on page 142 all offer far more detailed and sophisticated retirement projections than you can do on your own with a paper worksheet (and sometimes better than what some financial advisers offer). Typically, the sites that charge for their services provide more planning options and more advice geared toward specific investing options. But even the free services can give you a good sense of whether you're on track toward a secure retirement—and tell you what to do to improve your chances. I suggest you give a few a test spin. One of these services or a comparable one may also be available through your 401(k) plan.

SERVICE	ONLINE ADDRESS	COST
Financial Engines	www.financialengines.com	$39.95 per quarter for tax-deferred accounts only; $300 per year for taxable and tax-deferred accounts
ClearFuture	www.clearfuture.com	$11.95 per month or $109 per year as part of the premium service on Morningstar.com's website
Fidelity's Portfolio Planner	www.fidelity.com	Free to Fidelity customers
Financeware	www.financeware.com	$19.95 per month
CNNMoney's Retirement Planner	money.cnn.com	Free
mPower	money.msn.com/retire/planner.asp	$20 per year

Although these services differ somewhat in methodology and scope, the basic approach is pretty similar for all of them. You begin by entering such information as your earnings, the percentage of salary you contribute to your 401(k) or other retirement plans and your employer match, if any; the amount you've already accumulated in retirement savings and how you have that money invested; when you plan to retire; and the income you'd like to have at retirement. The sites then typically do two things. First, they assess the odds that you'll be able to hit your income goal given your current savings regimen and investments. Second, and more important, they show you how you can improve your odds by changing various aspects of your strategy—boosting your savings, changing your mix of investments, delaying retirement, et cetera.

To give you a better sense of what these services can do, let's take a hypothetical forty-year-old couple—call them Sam and Jane—and see what they can learn about their future retirement prospects by going through the retirement-planning process with the Financial Engines online service. We'll assume that Sam and Jane earn a combined $90,000 a year and that their retirement savings at this point consist of the $200,000 they have tucked away in their 401(k) accounts. The couple's 401(k)s allow them to contribute up to 10 percent of their salary to their respective plans and get an employer match of 50 cents on each dollar. But for now they each contribute 6 percent of salary. We'll further assume the couple invests 50 percent of their 401(k) stash (both existing balances and new contributions) in large-company stock mutual funds and the other 50 percent in bond mutual funds, although they also have access to a broad array of other funds. Finally, Sam and Jane would like to retire at age sixty with an income of $80,000 per year (including Social Security benefits) that keeps pace with inflation. They have no corporate pension. So the question is, how likely are they to reach their retirement goal if they continue along their current path?

After I entered this information about the couple and made a few other reasonable assumptions (such as a 3 percent annual salary growth for the couple during the remainder of their careers), the program calculated that based on what they're doing now, the couple had only a 20 percent chance of accumulating a nest egg that, combined with their Social Security benefits, would be large enough to provide the $80,000 inflation-adjusted income they desire. Not very good odds. So what can the couple do to improve their situation?

Well, by going to the section of the Financial Engines program that allows them to change various aspects of their strategy, Sam and Jane can see how specific moves can help them increase the odds of hitting their goal. For example, if Sam and Jane increase their 401(k) contributions to 10 percent of their salaries and continue to get the 50 percent match, their chances of achieving their $80,000 income goal more than double, rising to 41 percent. They could also accept more investing risk and invest more aggressively. Right now, with half their money in stocks and half in bonds, they've got a pretty conservative strategy for a young couple with twenty or more years until retirement. By investing in a portfolio that has less in bonds (say, only 20 percent instead of 50 percent) and by diversifying their stock fund holdings to include not just large-company stocks but also some funds that own small- and medium-size companies as well as some that own shares of foreign stocks, the couple can boost the chances of hitting their income target from 20 percent to 35 percent.

They can also consider delaying their retirement age, a move that would give their retirement portfolio more time to build in value. If instead of retiring at sixty they waited till sixty-five, that move alone would have a huge effect on their chances of getting the income they need, boosting their chances from 20 percent to 72 percent.

And, of course, they could also scale back their income target and decide to live a little less lavishly in retirement. For example, if Sam and Jane were willing to settle for a retirement income of $70,000 a year adjusted for inflation instead of $80,000, their odds of achieving that lower income would double from 20 percent to 40 percent.

Notice that the move that is likely to produce the smallest improvement in the odds of reaching their goal is the one that most people probably think of first—investing more aggressively. That's because you can increase investment returns only so far. After a point, you take on more and more risk, but you get very little, if any, extra return.

Increasing your saving, on the other hand, improves your odds more than tinkering with your investment strategy, as does cutting back on the amount of income you require in retirement. But the best way to boost your chances of hitting your goal is usually by delaying retirement. That's because your retirement savings have more of a chance to build if you leave them untouched for a few more years.

Of course, the couple isn't relegated to making just any one of these moves. They could alter their strategy to adopt several of these moves simultaneously. So, for example, if Sam and Jane increased their 401(k) contributions to the maximum 10 percent of salary allowed in their plan and also invested more aggressively as I described above, that combination of moves would boost the odds of achieving their $80,000 target income to 50 percent. If on top of that they extended their retirement age from sixty to sixty-five, their chance of success would jump to 89 percent. And if they also were willing to settle for an inflation-adjusted income of $70,000 rather than $80,000, they would have about a 94 percent chance of achieving their goal.

And that, basically, is the advantage to doing your retirement planning with an interactive online tool rather than a paper worksheet. You can easily vary one or more factors and get immediate feedback on how much you improve your odds of achieving your target income.

Again, I want to stress that no program, no matter how sophisticated, can tell you with pinpoint accuracy what the odds are that your strategy will lead to the income you want. The figures are still forecasts. Rather, the idea is to give you a better sense of what steps will increase your chances of accumulating the assets you will need and to demonstrate the importance of saving regularly, diversifying your assets, and taking enough risk to allow your savings to grow but not so much risk that you hurt your chances. And that is valuable information to have. So I think it's certainly worth your while to at least visit the sites of several of these online calculators, check out some of their materials, and consider giving them a test run (which you can do in some cases at no charge). If nothing else, you should come away with some insights into what it takes to create a successful retirement plan and learn about the variety of steps you can take to improve your future retirement prospects.

One more note: After going through the exercise of creating a plan either on paper or on a computer, you may find that the amount you need to save is well beyond what you can actually afford to put away given your financial circumstances. Indeed, that's not uncommon, especially if you've put off retirement planning until relatively late in life. If you find yourself in this position, the first thing you should do is review your assumptions. Perhaps you're being unrealistic and need to scale back your retirement income target a bit. Or maybe your target is fine, but you're going to have to delay your retirement, or factor in a part-time retirement job, or both. But even if after some fine-tuning you find that the required savings are beyond your current means, the worst thing you can do is throw up your hands in despair and do nothing. You are always better off if you begin saving *something* on a regular basis. So settle on an amount you can put away and start there. Then, try to increase that amount each year, and monitor your progress by re-crunching the numbers on your plan annually. And just to be sure you're not overlooking something, you'll probably also want to check out the catch-up strategies in Chapter 7.

Staying on Track

A retirement plan isn't something you can create and then put on autopilot. A lot of things can happen between now and the time you retire. Market setbacks, job layoffs, changes in your personal circumstances, unexpected expenses—all of these things can dramatically alter the arc of your retirement plan. Which means that once you've taken the effort to create a retirement plan, you want to be able to monitor your progress regularly with the following steps so that you stay on track toward your goal.

Review Your Overall Plan at Least Once a Year

Go through the process of creating a plan again, updating your balances and taking into account any new investments you've made or savings you've accumulated to see whether you are moving closer toward achieving the retirement income you'll need. Clearly, this process will be a lot easier if you've chosen to create your original plan with one of the online retirement programs.

It's also less of a burden if your employer provides decent access to your retirement account balances and other information online. Some provide annual checkups or reviews for participants in their retirement savings plans that allow employees to gauge their progress. In 2003, for example, companies that hired Fidelity Investments to oversee their 401(k) or other retirement plan could opt to have Fidelity mail an annual statement to participants showing how much monthly income a person might expect to receive at retirement based on that person's current investment strategy and how much that individual was currently saving. Better yet, the report also shows how much that income might be increased if the person adopts a different investment strategy or boosts his or her saving. I would hope that eventually this sort of report would become a staple of company retirement savings plans.

Reassess Your Investing Strategy

Examine your investment choices periodically—preferably once a quarter or certainly at least once a year—to make sure they're performing as expected and giving you the returns you need in order to accumulate a large enough retirement investment stash. This doesn't mean you should be changing your investments every time you do this review. If you own a growth fund that loses, say, 10 percent, it might seem like a sell candidate at first. But if most other growth funds are losing 20 percent, then perhaps your fund isn't doing so badly. The idea, though, is to compare the performance of your various investment options to an appropriate benchmark to see how they're performing. A brief period of subpar performance isn't something to worry about. Even the best mutual fund managers have periods where they lag competitors. But if a fund has subpar returns for, say, two years or longer, then you'll probably want to consider a replacement. While you're at it, you'll also want to reexamine how your portfolio is divvied up between stocks and bonds. Again, the idea is to ensure that your mix of stocks and bonds is doing the job of getting you the returns you require. In the next chapter I'll go into detail about how to choose investments for your retirement portfolio and how to set an appropriate mix of stocks, bonds, and other assets.

Reevaluate Your Savings Effort

At least once a year you should ask yourself: "Can I save more because of, say, a raise or paying down debt?" Go to your 401(k) or other company savings plan and see if you are taking full advantage of the company match and contributing the maximum the plan allows. If you can afford to save even more, look to other tax-advantaged plans or save outside such accounts.

Of course, there's always the chance that despite our best efforts, we regress on the savings front. In that case, you want to use this reevaluation exercise as a chance to get yourself back on a plan of disciplined savings.

Make Adjustments as Necessary

One of the advantages of regular monitoring is that you will be more likely to detect any backsliding early on. In turn, that gives you more leeway for making adjustments and getting back on track. So, for example, if you find that you're not making sufficient progress toward your goal, you may have to crank up your savings a bit. Or if the 50–50 mix of stocks and bonds that you had decided on for your portfolio just isn't delivering high enough returns given the savings you can realistically come up with, then maybe you need to accept more investing risk and increase your stock exposure. Or you may find that your retirement target date is just too ambitious and that you should plan on delaying it a few years. The last thing you want is to find out when you're sixty-five that your nest egg didn't grow nearly as much as you'd anticipated and your only hope for a comfy retirement is working till you're eighty or finding a rich relative with a kind heart who will take you in. In short, the best way to avoid a nasty retirement surprise is to plan early, review your plan often, and make adjustments as you go.

Should You Hire a Pro?

While I'm a staunch advocate of people doing as much of their investing and retirement planning as possible, there are times when even the most confident and resourceful among us may want a little help. You want to be sure, however, that you get competent advice in a way that's most helpful to you. Here's a rundown on your main choices, followed by a listing of sources that can help you choose and evaluate an adviser.

Hire an Adviser on an Ongoing Basis

You hire a financial planner or other adviser to assess your finances, create a retirement plan, and help you carry out that plan—that is, set savings goals, create a diversified investment portfolio, and recommend specific investments both within your company savings plans and other accounts. Typically, you would meet with the adviser periodically to assess your progress and make adjustments to the plan. The advantage is that you get assistance on an ongoing basis, which reduces the chances that your plan will career off track. The disadvantage is that it can be costly. Some planners charge an annual retainer for their services that may run several thousand dollars a year and then levy a per-hour charge if you require extra services. Some calculate their fee as a percentage of the assets they oversee, usually 1 to 2 percent per year. Others collect a commission on the investments you purchase through them. Before entering into a relationship with any planner or other adviser, make sure you understand exactly how you'll be paying and what the fees for specific investments and services will be.

Hire an Adviser to Create a Basic Retirement Road Map You Can Put into Action on Your Own

Typically, the adviser would assess your finances, figure out how much income you'll need at retirement and how much you must save to meet that target, and recommend how to structure your retirement investment portfolio to generate the returns you'll need to reach your goal. You would then choose the investments, monitor the progress of your plan, and make adjustments. Depending on the complexity of your situation, a planner could easily charge several thousand dollars for a comprehensive plan. Some planners may not charge for the plan itself but would expect you to buy investments or insurance that would generate commissions for them.

A less expensive version of this arrangement is to go to one of the growing number of investment or brokerage firms that offer planning services. Schwab, for example, offers a personal financial plan for $1,500 through its investment consultants, while Vanguard, the mutual fund giant, offers plans in areas such as retirement, investing, and estate planning for $500 each. You won't get the same customized advice in one of these prepackaged plans as you would hiring a planner to create a plan designed specifically for you. But if you mainly want to be sure your underlying strategy is sound, these cheaper plans should work just fine.

Hire an Adviser on an As-Needed Basis

Even the most self-confident investors sometimes find themselves in a situation where they'd like to consult a pro. Maybe you want a second opinion about how to handle that six-figure rollover from your 401(k). Or perhaps you're unsure whether to take your company pension as a lump sum or in the form of an annuity that makes lifetime payments. Or maybe you just want a second opinion to be sure there are no gaping holes in your retirement-planning strategy. In such cases, the solution may be to hire an adviser to work with you on a short-term basis, essentially just long enough to solve whatever problem or issue you face.

As a practical matter, it can be difficult to find an adviser willing to work on this basis, particularly if there's little chance of developing a long-term relationship. But there is a small but growing number of advisers willing to do so, usually for rates that range from $100 to $200 per hour. The advantage to this approach is that you pay only for the advice you need when you need it. The disadvantage is that if you keep going back with dozens of problems or queries, you could end up paying as much or more than if you'd hired an adviser on an ongoing basis.

If you decide you would like to have an adviser help you with your retirement planning, check out the resources below.

For Help Finding an Adviser

The Financial Planning Association (www.fpanet.org).
Searchable database of more than five thousand
certified financial planners.

National Association of Personal Financial Advisors
(www.napfa.org). Access to some seven hundred fee-only
planners.

Garrett Planning Network (www.garrettplanning
network.com). Lists more than a hundred planners
who will work for an hourly fee, typically $100 to
$200 an hour.

For Help Checking Out an Adviser

CFP Board of Standards (www.cfp-board.org). Database of
planners with valid Certified Financial Planner
credentials.

National Association of Securities Dealers (www.nasdr.
com). Employment and regulatory history on brokers.

North American Securities Administration Association
(www.nasaa.org). List of state regulators that oversee
smaller advisers (those with less than $25 million under
management).

Securities and Exchange Commission (www.sec.gov/
investor/brokers.htm). Fee schedules and disciplinary
history on registered investment advisers.

Chapter 6

INVEST WITH YOUR HEAD, NOT YOUR GUT

LIKE IT OR NOT, YOU ARE A PENSION FUND MANAGER

Since *you* are responsible for investment decisions, you must operate as your own pension fund manager. Understandably, this responsibility can be somewhat daunting, especially considering how the stock market has behaved in recent years. But it's important to keep in mind that occasional market meltdowns, however unsettling they may be, are a normal part of investing. If you want the long-term growth that stocks can offer, you can't completely avoid the market's turmoil. It *is* possible, however, to create an investing strategy that can help you take advantage of the long-term growth the investment markets have to offer while at least minimizing the damage that the market's jarring setbacks can cause.

Let's begin by talking about the way you should be investing for retirement.

Don't Let the "Experts" on Wall Street Dictate Your Investing Strategy

Based on my nearly twenty years of experience in covering the world of investing, I'm not at all convinced that what works well for Wall Street is what works best for individuals investing for their own retirement. In fact, I believe you'll increase your chances of accumulating the money you need for retirement by not following Wall Street's lead.

Here's why. Remember that wonderful scene toward the end of *The Wizard of Oz* when little Toto pulls back the curtain to reveal the true identity of the Wizard of Oz? The mighty and powerful wizard turned out to be nothing more than a little man pushing buttons and pulling levers to generate smoke, fire, and a bellowing voice that created the *illusion* of a mighty and powerful wizard. Well, that's how I think of Wall Street: more illusion of superior investing knowledge and performance than reality. That's not to say I think all of Wall Street is a fraud (although the various shenanigans of recent years involving security analysts as well as some mutual fund firms definitely put a big dent in the Street's credibility). And I certainly don't think that the people on Wall Street are stupid. Quite the contrary; some of our best and brightest work there. But the problem is that the business methods that are good for the people and the firms on Wall Street aren't necessarily the things that are best for you when you're investing for your retirement. Here are a few examples.

Wall Street Loves Fads . . . but Fads Are Dangerous for Us

Initial public offerings (IPOs), Internet mutual funds, glitzy tech stocks, and the like are good for Wall Street because they generate investment banking fees and sales commissions and get individuals excited about investing. But while the latest fad may seem like a good investment initially, the sizzle eventually fizzles and investors can get stuck with big losses.

Wall Street Likes to Make Things Complicated . . . but Complications Divert Attention from What's Important

Listen to the analysts and investment pundits, and you get the impression that successful investing involves following every wiggle in the financial markets. Sure, it pays to stay informed about the current state of the economy and the markets. But when you're investing for retirement, it's more important to set a long-term strategy than try to react on a nanosecond-to-nanosecond basis.

Wall Street Likes Lots of Action . . .
but More Action Means Lower Returns for Us

The prevailing investment philosophy on Wall Street is that you've got to jump from one investment or sector to another to capitalize on fleeting opportunities. Problem is, it's impossible to predict in advance which sectors will soar. When University of California finance professor Terrance Odean studied the results for sixty thousand households with discount brokerage accounts, he found that investors who traded the most earned annualized net returns 35 percent *lower* than the average for the households overall. In other words, less is more.

Okay, so if Wall Street shouldn't be your role model for setting a retirement investing strategy, what *should* your strategy be based on? The answer is simple: Your strategy should reflect *your* needs—that is, what's likely to yield the best results for you.

Keep It Simple

Just because your 401(k) plan has a smorgasbord of fifteen different investment options and the fund company you have your IRA with offers mutual funds that invest in everything from the best-known growth stocks to micro-caps you've never heard of, doesn't mean you've got to try to find a place for all these investment alternatives in your portfolio. You're better off focusing on a handful of solid, decent performing plain-vanilla choices—a large-company stock fund, a small-cap fund, a basic bond fund, perhaps a diversified international fund—than trying to stock your portfolio with investments of every conceivable type and style. The more complicated you make things, the harder it will be to keep track of your far-flung investments and the more potential you have for creating confusion and havoc that can derail your plan.

Think Portfolio, Not Individual Investments

Yes, we all want to choose investments that perform well relative to their peers. But your asset allocation—that is, how you choose to diversify your money among different types of assets such as stocks (and stock funds), bonds (and bond funds), and cash (money market funds, CDs, etc.)—has a much bigger impact on your investment returns than picking the right stock, bond, or mutual fund. And while you certainly don't want to let tax considerations drive your investing decisions, changes in the tax treatment of different types of investments such as those resulting from the 2003 tax law may have an effect on whether you decide to hold certain investments in taxable accounts or in tax-advantaged accounts such as your 401(k) or IRA. In the final section of this chapter I'll go into detail about how you can take advantage of the new tax law to maximize your gains.

Don't Overlook the Impact of Costs

An extra percentage point in fees here, another percentage point in expenses there, and pretty soon you're talking about a significant drag on your returns. How big a drag? Consider this: When *Money* magazine examined the effect of fees on the performance of mutual funds a few years ago, it found that high-cost funds underperformed their low-cost counterparts by roughly two percentage points a year over long periods. On a $50,000 investment, earning 10 percent annually instead of 8 percent would mean ending up with almost $22,000 extra before taxes after ten years.

Resist the Urge to Tinker

The vast amount of up-to-the-minute investment information available on the Internet and cable TV combined with the speed and convenience of online trading caters to an understandable urge to make changes in our investment portfolios. But remember, other investors have access to this information as well, which means that far from snapping up a bargain in the stock of the company just lionized on TV, you're more likely to end up buying in at inflated prices that have been bid up by other investors following the news just like you.

Don't Be Swayed by Market Euphoria—or Pessimism

Back in the late 1990s, many investors became so convinced that the good times would roll on and on that they invested large portions of their assets in tech and Net stocks. And when the market plummeted from early 2000 through 2002, investors went to the opposite extreme, dumping their stocks for losses and concentrating their money in "safe" investments such as bonds, money market funds, and CDs. They were wrong in both cases. If you remember nothing else at all from this chapter, remember this: Periodic upheavals are a normal part of investing. The best way to deal with these occasional convulsions is to avoid giving in to emotion and keeping a dispassionate long-term view.

Your Menu of Investment Choices

Stocks and Stock Funds: The Engine Room of Your Portfolio

ANNUALIZED STOCK RETURNS 1926–2003				
Annualized Return for the Entire Period: 10.4%				
1 YEAR	5 YEARS	10 YEARS	20 YEARS	30 YEARS
High return 54.0%	28.6%	20.1%	17.9%	13.7%
Low return −43.3%	−12.5%	−0.9%	3.1%	8.5%

Source: Ibbotson Associates

More than any other single investment, stocks and stock mutual funds are the ones that are going to power the savings you stash into your 401(k) and other vehicles on a regular basis into a tidy retirement nest egg that can help support you in retirement. What makes stocks so ideal for retirement investing, of course, are their solid long-term returns. Since 1926, stocks have earned a compounded annual return of 10.4 percent, or nearly twice the return of bonds. The reason stocks have been able to deliver such impressive long-term results is that when you buy stocks or shares of funds that own stocks, you are essentially buying a piece of the future profits of a company. And when you invest in a diversified group of stocks culled from various industries, what you're really doing is getting a share of the U.S. economy overall. As long as that economy keeps growing over the long term—as it has over the past three hundred or more years—then the value of your retirement savings should grow right along with it.

But while stocks are clearly your best shot for superior long-term gains, the road en route to those gains can be quite bumpy over the short term. Take a look at the table on page 156, which shows stock returns for very short to very long holding periods. Notice how huge the range of returns is if you hold stocks for just one year. You could have earned a return as high as 54 percent or as low as –43.3 percent. That's a gigantic range—nearly 100 percentage points—and certainly not the kind of discrepancy that would make most investors feel confident about owning stocks. There's just too much uncertainty.

But look what happens as you hold stocks for longer periods of time. First, the range between the high and the low return shrinks. Second, your chances of losing money decline the longer you hold onto stocks. And third, you have a greater chance of earning higher returns than you would have in less volatile assets such as bonds and Treasury bills. For twenty-year holding periods, for example, the *worst* annualized return for stocks is 3.1 percent. That's much better than the worst annualized returns for intermediate-term government bonds, 1.6 percent, and Treasury bills, 0.4 percent. (See the tables on pages 163 and 166.)

What's more, the upside is much, much better in stocks over longer holding periods. Over thirty-year holding periods, for example, the best annualized gain for stocks was 13.7 percent, more than double the best thirty-year period for Treasury bills (6.8 percent) and almost 60 percent higher than the highest thirty-year annualized gain for intermediate-term government bonds (8.7 percent). In fact, the *best* thirty-year annu-alized gains for intermediate-term government bonds was only marginally better than the *worst* thirty-year annualized gain for stocks (8.5 percent).

Past history guarantees nothing about the future, of course. But I think these figures demonstrate that if you are investing money for long periods of time—which is exactly what we're doing when we're investing for retirement—then stocks offer you the best shot at the kind of gains you need to make your re-tirement nest egg grow.

It's also important to keep in mind that I've been talking about stocks in general here. In reality, there are more than nine thousand individual stocks that fall into many differ-ent categories, several of which would be represented in a well-diversified retirement portfolio. There are any number of methods to slice and dice the stock market, but the way most in-vestment advisers divvy up the market is by size (small-cap, mid-cap, and large-cap), style (growth or value), and sector (the industry the company is in).

Size. By size, I mean a company's market value (also known as its market capitalization, or market cap), which is the total num-ber of shares outstanding times the current share price. There are no official rules for determining what market value consti-tutes a large-cap versus a mid-cap versus a small-cap stock. But the chart below shows generally accepted ranges within the in-vestment community.

SIZE	MARKET VALUE
Mega-cap stocks	$100 billion or more
Large-cap stocks	$10 billion to $100 billion
Mid-cap stocks	$2 billion to $10 billion
Small-cap stocks	$500 million to $2 billion
Micro-cap stocks	Less than $500 million

Source: CNNMoney.com

The fact that investors go to the trouble of categorizing stocks by size leads to an obvious question: Does size matter? The answer is yes, in that a company's size can play a role in the type of returns the stock might deliver and the risk, or volatility, you should expect from the stock. Larger companies tend to be more stable since they are more established and have deeper resources to draw on when the economy turns down. But they also have less growth potential if for no other reason than as the scope of a company's operations increases, it's harder for managers to increase profits at the same rate the company did in its fledgling stage.

Small companies, on the other hand, are usually able to grow their profits much more quickly than large companies, although they can also run into trouble more easily and experience greater setbacks. Which means that you are taking on more risk when you invest in small-cap firms. In return, for that extra risk, investors expect a higher payoff, and indeed, small stocks have tended to reward investors with somewhat higher returns than large companies over time. That margin of additional return can vary substantially at different times—or even disappear, for that matter, as was the case in the 1990s, when large-cap stocks provided the highest returns. But over long stretches, small-cap stocks can potentially increase annual returns by about two percentage points or so.

Style. In addition to size, investors also divide companies into two style camps—growth and value. Growth companies are those that are able to increase their profits faster than profits are growing in the stock market overall. Usually that translates to annual earnings increases of 15 percent a year or more over periods of five or more years. That potential for growth in profit is what makes many investors flock to growth stocks, bidding up the price of their shares in the process. The phenomenal earnings growth of companies such as Cisco pushed up their stock prices to stratospheric levels in the late 1990s, for example, which created huge profits for investors smart or lucky enough to buy into such companies before they became all the rage. The flip side to growth investing, however, is an equally large potential for losses. When the rapid earnings investors expect from growth companies don't materialize—which is what happened to many high-flying tech stocks in early 2000—growth stocks can get absolutely hammered, as Cisco did during the last bear market, falling more than 50 percent from its high point in early 2000.

Value stocks are virtually the exact opposite of growth shares. Investors have little regard for their growth potential, and in many cases value stocks are downright reviled, often because the company is experiencing business problems and its share price has been falling. So why would investors buy such stocks? Well, value investors are a bit like people who sift through piles of kitsch at flea markets hoping to find antiques that have been inadvertently mixed in with the junk. In fact, many value stocks have been so beaten down that they're selling for less than the true value of their earnings power or assets. Value investors try to buy these value stocks on the cheap in hopes of making big profits when other investors realize that the stock is worth much more than its price reflects. Value stocks usually, though not always, hold up better than growth stocks during market downturns for the simple reason that they're already selling at low prices that reflect bad news and low expectations.

Sector. The final way to look at stocks is by the industry or sector the company is in. Again, there's no official arbiter of how many different sectors there are or which companies fall into which sector. But two well-known investment research firms, Standard & Poor's and Morgan Stanley Capital International, break down the stock market into the following ten sector groups: consumer discretionary, consumer staples, energy, financials, health care, industrials, information technology, materials, telecommunication services, and utilities. Some of these sectors are pretty straightforward. The financials sector, for example, would obviously include banks, brokerage firms, and other financial services firms, while health care would include everything from hospitals and medical service providers to pharmaceutical companies. Others are a bit more opaque: Standard & Poor's defines the consumer discretionary sector as being the one most sensitive to the ups and downs of the economy, including such diverse companies as auto makers, textile and apparel makers, and hotels and restaurants. (You can find definitions of all the sectors at the Standard & Poor's website, www.standardandpoors.com.) But the basic rationale for divvying up stocks this way is that the various sectors don't all react the same way to changes in the economy and thus don't all grow at the same rate or move in unison with one another.

About Dividend-Paying Stocks

In the late 1990s, when dot-com and tech stocks were all the rage, the notion shareholders investing in companies that paid a regular cash dividend had become almost an anachronism. But when President Bush signed the Jobs and Growth Tax Relief Reconciliation Act of 2003 into law, dividend-paying stocks were suddenly hot. After all, dividends, which had been subject to ordinary income tax rates as high as 38.6 percent, were now taxed at long-term capital-gains rates no higher than 15 percent. Lower-income investors would face dividend tax rates of just 5 percent. The law even provides for that 5 percent rate to drop to 0 percent—no tax—in 2008 (although just for that one year). As a result, investment pundits began recommending dividend-paying stocks and mutual funds with almost the same alacrity that they had recommended tech and dot-com stocks during the 1990s bubble days, suggesting they were the best route to certain high gains.

Not so fast. Dividend-paying stocks certainly deserve a role in the portfolios of the overwhelming majority of retirement investors. But you would be making a big mistake to simply begin loading up on dividend-paying shares. For one thing, not all dividends qualify for the new lower tax rates. Unlike most dividends, dividends paid by real estate investment trusts (REITs) and most preferred securities are not paid out of funds that have already been taxed at the corporate level, so they are typically taxed not at the new lower dividend rates but at the higher rates that apply to ordinary income.

There are also some complications when it comes to mutual funds. When a mutual fund passes along to its shareholders dividend payments it has received from the shares of stocks in its portfolio, those dividends would qualify for the lower dividend rate. But not all payments labeled by mutual funds as dividends qualify for the new lower dividend tax rates. Most bond and money market mutual funds call their interest payments dividends. But dividends that are really nothing more than interest payments are taxed as ordinary income, just the same as any interest payments you receive from bank accounts or individual bonds you may hold outside of mutual funds. Mutual funds also refer to the short-term capital gains they pass along to shareholders as dividends. But, again, since these are short-term capital gains, they don't qualify for the new lower rates accorded to dividends and long-term capital gains. So these "dividends" are also taxed at ordinary income rates.

But even once you've identified stocks whose dividends are taxed at the more advantageous rate, that doesn't mean that pouring all, or even most, of your money into them is a smart strategy. Why? The market isn't a static place where one investment always retains an edge over competitors. The advantage dividend-paying stocks might have over other types of investments at any given time will narrow or widen as investors shift their money around. As more cash flows into dividend-paying stocks, their prices rise, which decreases their dividend yield and generally erodes their future return potential. In short, by becoming too popular, dividend-paying stocks could become overpriced and less likely than other investments to generate superior long-term gains (which is essentially what happened to growth stocks during the late 1990s). Meanwhile, the securities that people are selling or ignoring in order to buy dividend-paying stocks would become relatively better deals. All of which is to say that you can't assume that any one type of investment, whatever its tax treatment, is automatically the best deal at any given moment. So by all means I suggest that you include dividend-paying stocks as part of your overall portfolio mix. But don't limit yourself only to dividend-paying stocks in a misguided attempt to cash in on tax savings. At the end of this chapter I'll talk more about this issue, particularly as it relates to how to allocate your holdings of dividend-paying stocks (as well as other types of securities) between taxable and tax-advantaged accounts in order to maximize your returns.

Bonds and Bond Funds: Stability and Income

ANNUALIZED BOND RETURNS 1926–2003				
Annualized Return for the Entire Period: 5.4%				
1 YEAR	5 YEARS	10 YEARS	20 YEARS	30 YEARS
High return 29.1%	17.0%	13.1%	10.0%	8.7%
Low return −5.1%	1.0%	1.3%	1.6%	2.2%

Source: Ibbotson Associates

The long-term returns on bonds don't come anywhere close to those on stocks, but bonds or bond funds should still play a role in your retirement portfolio because their regular interest payments can provide a bit of ballast for your portfolio when the stock market gets turbulent. Look at the table of bond returns above. Notice how the downside in bonds is much, much lower than the downside in stocks, particularly over the short term? Stocks have lost as much as 43.3 percent in a calendar year. Intermediate-term bonds, on the other hand, have never lost more than 5.1 percent in a calendar year to date, and they have *never* posted a loss over a period of five or more calendar years. That's not to say it isn't possible that bonds couldn't manage a loss over some long period in the future. It's possible. But it's not very likely. Overall, bonds are simply a lot less volatile than stocks, but there are two risks you've got to be aware of: credit (or default) risk and interest-rate risk.

Credit risk. Credit or default risk is the risk that the bond issuer won't make the bond's interest payments when they're due (usually semiannually) or won't repay the bond's face value, or principal, when the bond matures. This risk isn't a concern if you invest in Treasury securities because Uncle Sam pays his debts (or, more accurately, makes sure U.S. taxpayers do). The danger of defaults is also relatively low for investment-grade corporate bonds. One study by Standard & Poor's showed that only about 2 percent or so of investment-grade corporate bonds defaulted within fifteen years of being issued. Default rates are even lower on municipal bonds, or munis—the tax-free bonds issued by state and local governments. On the other hand, the default rates on non-investment-grade corporate bonds—bonds known as high-yield or junk bonds—can be dramatically higher, ten times those of investment-grade corporates. I should add, however, that the mere fact that a bond defaults doesn't mean bondholders lose their entire investment. Bondholders often have claims on a company's assets and income, so even after a default a bond may still sell for upwards of 50 to 60 percent of its face value.

Interest-rate risk. This is more likely to cause trouble for bond investors because it's more prevalent than credit risk and it affects virtually the entire spectrum of bonds, from Treasuries to corporates to munis.

The best way to understand interest-rate risk is to think of a seesaw: When interest rates go up, bond prices go down, and vice versa. The logic behind this relationship is simple. Let's say I buy a $1,000 ten-year Treasury bond that has a 5 percent coupon rate. (The coupon rate is the rate the bond issuer promises to pay.) That means that each year for ten years Uncle Sam will pay me $50 in interest. When the bond matures in ten years, Uncle Sam will also repay me the $1,000 face value of the bond. And let's also assume that interest rates start climbing, so that ten-year Treasury bonds issued after the one I bought have a coupon rate of 6 percent.

At this point, I'm stuck with a bond paying 5 percent a year.

I can't change the coupon rate. That rate is fixed (which is why you sometimes hear bonds referred to as fixed-income investments). But I could sell my 5 percent bond and use the proceeds to buy a new 6 percent bond. Question is, though, would anyone be willing to pay me the $1,000 face value for my bond? The answer is no. Who in their right mind would want to give me $1,000 for a bond paying $50 a year if he or she can buy a new ten-year Treasury bond paying $60 a year? So the only way I would be able to unload my bond would be to accept a lower price for it, a price low enough to compensate the buyer for the lower interest payments relative to the new 6 percent bonds. In this case that would mean my ten-year Treasury would sell for roughly $930, or about 7 percent less than I paid for it. Had interest rates risen more than one percentage point, the price of my bond would have had to drop even further to entice someone to buy it.

Falling rates have the opposite effect on bond prices. If interest rates on new ten-year Treasury bonds had dropped to, say, 4 percent, my $1,000 bond with its $50 income payments would have become more valuable, and I would be able to sell it for more than its face value of $1,000. And if rates dropped by more than one percentage point, my bond would have become even more valuable.

There's one more thing about this interest rate–bond price seesaw you need to know. The longer the bond's maturity—that is, the more years until its principal is repaid—the more its price will move up or down with interest rates. When you think about it, this makes perfect sense. If you buy a three-year bond and rates go up, you're stuck with below-market interest payments for just three years. If you buy a ten-year bond and rates rise, you're locked into subpar payments more than three times as long. So, clearly, you would have to lower the price of the ten-year bond much more than the price of a three-year bond to compensate a buyer for being stuck with below-average payments for a much longer time.

That pretty much sums up interest-rate risk: bond prices on one side of the seesaw, interest rates on the other. As one goes up, the other goes down. And the farther out you go on

the seesaw—that is, the longer the maturity of the bond—
the bigger the swing up or down. For more about the risks
of investing in bonds, as well as for more information about
how they work, you can check out the Bond Market Association site (www.investinginbonds.com), the bond investing section of Money 101 (money.cnn.com/pf/101/lessons/7), the
Credit Ratings section of Standard & Poor's (www.standardand
poors.com), and, for information about government bonds,
the Bureau of the Public Debt (www.publicdebt.treas.gov/sec/
sec.htm).

Cash Equivalents: Preserving Your Capital

ANNUALIZED CASH EQUIVALENT RETURNS 1926–2003
Annualized Return for the Entire Period: 3.8%*

	1 YEAR	5 YEARS	10 YEARS	20 YEARS	30 YEARS
High return	14.7.1%	11.1%	9.2%	7.7%	6.8%
Low return	0.0%	0.1%	0.2%	0.4%	0.9%

Source: Ibbotson Associates
*Returns are for Treasury bills

While stocks and stock funds are providing long-term growth to
make your retirement stash grow and bonds and bond funds
are generating regular income that can mitigate some of the
ups and downs in the value of your portfolio, there's another
broad class of investments that are designed primarily to preserve your capital. These are known as cash equivalents, a name
they get because they are so liquid and so secure that they're almost the same as holding actual cash. This category includes investments such as money market funds, certificates of deposit,
and stable value funds.

Of course, in the investment world the flip side to security is
a low return, which is evident in the table above. So while these
types of investments may provide a safe harbor in times of mar-

ket turmoil, they're not the type of investments you should look toward to build your retirement nest egg and to prevent the purchasing power of your money from being eroded by inflation. For that reason, you probably don't want to put very much of your money in these type of investments when your main goal is still accumulating assets for retirement. Later on, after you've accumulated a sizable nest egg and are beginning to consider how you're going to start drawing income from your retirement stash, these investments can begin to play a larger role, although even then you don't want to overdo it.

Other Investment Choices

The investments I've outlined above are the ones you're most likely to use in your retirement portfolio. They're hardly the only ones you have to choose from, however. There are good arguments for putting some of your retirement portfolio in international stock funds, for example, because foreign stocks don't always move in sync with the U.S. market and can thus actually help lower the volatility of your portfolio. That said, I don't think you'd inflict harm on your portfolio by excluding international stock funds, and if you do choose to diversify into them, I'd recommend limiting them to between 10 and 15 percent of your overall stock holdings.

Real estate securities, such as REITs or funds that invest in REITs or companies that invest in real-estate-related companies, are another possibility to consider. They can offer solid long-term returns and, since real estate securities don't always go up and down with the overall market, they can provide a bit of ballast when the stock market is flagging. I wouldn't consider my personal residence as part of the real estate portion of my portfolio, however, in large part because it doesn't fit in well with a securities portfolio. Even though your home may represent the bulk of your wealth, it's unlikely you're going to sell it and plow some of the profits into other parts of your portfolio when home prices are rising or buy a larger house when prices are declining. So I recommend that any real estate you acquire for investing purposes be in the form of REITs, real estate funds. And as with foreign stocks, you shouldn't invest more than, say, 10 to 20 percent of your portfolio.

While many mutual fund companies, as well as 401(k) and other retirement plans, offer sector funds that allow you to invest in a particular industry or sector of the economy, I'd caution against doing so. In theory, the notion of plowing your savings into a sector that's just about to explode for humongous gains works fine. In reality, this strategy is risky and can backfire, as it did for many tech investors in the 1990s. If you want to take a modest stake in a particular sector or industry beyond your core portfolio holdings, fine. But your overall goal should be to maintain a broadly diversified portfolio, not one with big bets on specific industries or sectors.

Think Index Funds!

Index funds are an excellent way to harness the long-term growth potential of the stock market that is simpler and more likely to lead to higher returns than picking stocks and mutual funds on your own. These funds have become increasingly popular in 401(k) plans the past few years, although if you don't have access to them through your 401(k), you can certainly invest in them through an IRA or other retirement account.

The premise behind index funds is simple. Instead of frenetically buying and selling stocks as fund managers do in conventional actively managed mutual funds, index fund managers take a passive approach—that is, they hold all or nearly all of the stocks in whatever benchmark they're tracking. Most investors probably think of index funds as funds that track the Standard & Poor's 500, a widely followed benchmark made up of large-company stocks that account for roughly 80 percent of the value of all publicly traded U.S. stocks. But in fact, you can find funds that mirror dozens of indexes. If you want to track small-cap stocks, for example, there's the Russell 2000, which consists of two thousand small-company stocks. Or if you want to buy the entire U.S. market in one fund, you can invest in a fund that tracks the Wilshire 5000, an index made up of virtually every publicly traded stock in the United States. Here's a quick rundown on their advantages.

They're cheap. Annual expenses for stock mutual funds run about 1.4 percent of assets on average, which means a $100,000 account is being nicked for about $1,400 a year. Most index funds charge less than half that amount, and some charge as little as 0.2 percent. Those savings can boost your retirement account's value over time. This cost advantage is especially valuable in bond funds, where returns are lower and, thus, expenses tend to eat up a higher percentage of returns.

They're tax-efficient. Buying and selling by fund managers creates gains on which you must pay taxes, which lowers your after-tax return. Because index funds rarely trade securities, they generate far fewer taxable gains. This isn't a big plus for tax-advantaged accounts, but tax efficiency can significantly boost your returns in the investing you do outside tax-advantaged accounts such as 401(k)s and IRAs.

They're more predictable. When you buy an actively managed mutual fund, you may do better than the overall market in some years, far worse in others. You're never really sure. With an index fund, your return will pretty much mirror the return of whatever market or index you're tracking. Of course, that also means that when the market goes down, index funds tied to the S&P 500 and other indexes that track the broad market will go right down with it.

They outperform most other funds. Largely because of their lower fees and lower transaction costs, index funds tend to outperform the majority of actively managed funds over long periods.

I wouldn't go so far as to say you should *never* own actively managed funds. But I do think that most investors should consider making one or more index funds a core holding in their portfolio. If you're interested in learning more about the fundamentals of indexing strategies, I suggest you check out the Index Funds site at www.indexfunds.com.

Should You Invest by the Stars?

With so many different investment choices available today, it's not surprising that overwhelmed investors would gravitate toward rating systems that would appear to take the work—and the guesswork—out of choosing investments. And the most popular rating system of all is the star system created by the mutual fund research firm Morningstar. On the surface it's simplicity itself: Morningstar awards funds anywhere from one to five stars based on their past risk-adjusted performance, with the best funds getting five stars and the worst just one star.

But does following the stars lead to superior returns? To answer that question, we've got to take a look at how Morningstar arrives at its star ratings.

When Morningstar launched its star ratings back in 1985, it originally ranked funds based on how they fared versus very broad categories of similar funds. But this led to problems. If large-company growth stocks happened to be hot, then funds that invested in those types of stocks tended to garner more stars than funds that invested in, say, small-company value funds. The ratings in such cases weren't so much a reflection of manager skill as of what types of stocks were in vogue at the time.

So Morningstar revised its system in the summer of 2000, granting stars based on how funds in similar categories— large-cap growth, small-cap value, short-term government bond, et cetera—compare against one another. Basically, Morningstar scores funds based on the returns they earned and the risks they took over the past three years (and past five and ten years if the funds were around that long). The 10 percent of funds with the highest score in each category receive five stars, the next 22.5 percent get four stars, the following 35 percent earn three stars, the next 22.5 percent get two stars, and the bottom 10 percent get one star. The result is more an apples-to-apples comparison that has a better chance of reflecting managers' skill rather than market trends. Even if small-company funds are doing horribly compared with large-company funds, a small-cap manager could still earn high grades by outperforming his or her peers.

I don't think there's any doubt the revised system is an improvement. But it still doesn't get around the fact that past performance isn't a very reliable predictor of future performance for a variety of reasons. Sometimes funds that outperform funds in the same category in one period lag their peers in other periods. There's also the possibility that superior performance over a given stretch of time is due not to skill but to dumb luck. Finally, fund managers tend to move around a lot. So even if skill was behind a fund's past record, it's possible that the manager responsible for that record has moved on to another fund.

You may want to take the Morningstar ratings into account in sizing up a fund, perhaps even use it as something to narrow down your search to a manageable number of candidates. The ratings can also provide a quick way to gauge the performance of funds you already own. But in choosing investments for your retirement portfolio, you need to go beyond the rating and check out other issues such as whether the fees the fund charges are reasonable, whether its results have been consistent, whether you're comfortable with level of risk the fund takes, and, most important, whether the fund fits into your portfolio's asset allocation. Bottom line: You should *never* choose your funds by stargazing alone.

Allocation Is All

Wouldn't it be great if there were some foolproof way of knowing when to jump into stocks just as they were about to soar and then bail out into bonds just before the stock market tanked? Or, better yet, wouldn't it be neat if we could move from sector to sector, jumping from tech to financials to health care to utilities, catching each one just as it was skyrocketing to gains and exiting just in time to sidestep the losses? The problem, of course, is that there isn't. We don't know in advance which assets or sectors or individual stocks are going to give the highest returns over a specific period. And basing your investment strategy on such a guessing game is self-defeating, a recipe not for success but for failure, even disaster.

So what's the alternative? Two words: asset allocation. It sounds like a mouthful, but it's one of the simplest and most effective investing strategies around. Basically, it boils down to spreading your money among a variety of investments that don't all move in the same direction at the same time. By diversifying your portfolio this way, you do two things: first, you are able to take advantage of the higher returns that assets with high volatility, such as stocks, offer while dampening the short-term ups and downs that go with riskier assets; and second, you increase the odds of having some money in at least one asset class that does well, and you eliminate the chances of having all your dough in an asset class that gets absolutely clobbered.

For example, let's say that, emboldened by the incredible 28.9 percent a year run that stocks had from 1995 through 1999, you had decided to put your entire retirement savings into stocks. Which, of course, is exactly what many people did. To their utter dismay, however, they found that the past isn't always a prologue to the future. From the beginning of 2000 through early 2003, stocks actually lost 36.5 percent. But what if instead of making an all-or-nothing-bet in stocks, you had slipped a portion of your money—say, 30 percent—into bonds? How would you have fared? Well, over that same period from the beginning of 2000 through early 2003, bonds gained nearly 40 percent. So having a small stake in bonds would have spared you a little of the pain and loss of an all-stock portfolio.

Of course, by diversifying you do give up some potential return. You will never have all your money in the asset class that hits a home run. That's probably why many people abandoned the whole notion of diversification in the go-go 1990s. With stocks such as AOL and Cisco doubling every six months, the idea of asset allocation seemed absurd, outdated, not New Era enough. But when the crash came, people realized that by ignoring asset allocation they missed out on its biggest benefit: it prevents you from striking out, from losing big. In effect, then, asset allocation works as a type of insurance for your portfolio. It gives you a chance to get long-term returns high enough to make your savings grow, yet at the same time provides some protection from the inherent uncertainty of the investment markets.

Mixing It Up

How, then, do you arrive at an asset-allocation strategy that makes sense for you? Basically, creating your own portfolio mix involves a three-step process.

Play the Zigzags

The main principle behind asset allocation is that all assets don't march in lockstep with one another. Which is to say that while some assets zig, others zag. I already mentioned how bonds prospered while stocks got hammered in the bear market that began in early 2000. But this zigzag effect goes beyond just stocks and bonds. Even different types of stocks sometimes march to distinctly different beats. While many tech stocks soared to gains of more than 100 percent in 1999, for example, financial stocks lost 1 percent on average. And when tech stocks got hammered for losses of more than 30 percent on average in 2000, health care stocks gained more than 50 percent overall. Of course, by the time the bear market really settled in, virtually all stocks were suffering losses. But they didn't suffer them equally. Tech stocks led the way, with average losses of nearly 40 percent, while financials lost a bit over 3 percent.

To measure this zigzag effect, securities analysts use a statistic known as correlation (more technically, the coefficient of correlation). The mathematics that goes into calculating the correlation between two assets is too complicated and boring to go into here, but the main idea boils down to this: If two investments move exactly in sync with each other, their correlation is 1; if they move exactly in sync but in opposite directions, they have a correlation of −1. And if their movements are not related at all, their correlation is 0.

Now here's where things get interesting. You might think that if you threw together a bunch of very volatile assets you would have a very volatile portfolio. But that's not necessarily true. If those assets have low correlations to one another, then the ups and downs of one can effectively cancel out much of the ups and downs of another, lowering the volatility of your portfolio overall. In short, by taking advantage of this zigzag effect, you can build a portfolio whose risk, or volatility, is less than the sum of the riskiness of its parts. Even better, by taking into account different assets' returns as well as their correlations, you can create a mix of assets that, theoretically at least, will provide the best return for whatever level of risk you're willing to take. I say "theoretically" because factors such as returns and correlations can change, so there's no guarantee you'll be able to cook up an ideal mix. Still, by thinking in terms of building a portfolio of assets that don't all move at once, you have a much better shot at getting solid long-term returns than you would by engaging in the guessing game of trying to pick the best stocks or funds.

Determine Your Time Horizon

The single most important thing in setting your asset allocation is your investing time horizon, or the number of years you have until you reach your investing goal. If you know you'll have only a few years before you will need to convert your portfolio to cash—perhaps you want to make a down payment on a home— then stability of principal should be your major concern. In such a case, you would want to tilt your portfolio mix more toward investments like bonds and money market funds and away from stocks. Why? Because stock prices are highly volatile and you wouldn't want to have to unload them during a bear market like the one that began in early 2000, where stock prices sank roughly 49 percent from their bull market peak. Yes, stocks do eventually recover. But if you don't have the luxury of being able to wait for that rebound, the best policy is to limit your exposure to stocks.

On the other hand, if you're still in your career and investing for a retirement that is years off in the future, then you don't have to concern yourself as much with short-term ups and downs in the market. You've got plenty of time to recover from stock market losses. So you want to focus on making sure your retirement nest egg grows, which means that the bulk of your retirement portfolio should be in stocks and stock funds.

One mistake many investors make is that, as they get closer to retirement, they think of themselves as having a short investing horizon. As a result, they often begin moving much of their money out of stocks and into bonds. That's usually not a good move. It's true, of course, if you're sixty and planning on retiring at age sixty-five, your time horizon obviously isn't as long as that of a forty-year-old who won't be calling it a career for another twenty to twenty-five years. That said, however, it's not as if your investing comes to an abrupt halt when you retire. You'll be relying on your portfolio for income during a retirement that can easily stretch for thirty or more years. When you're looking at that sort of time frame, you still want to make sure your investments overall grow faster than inflation, and to achieve that goal you've got to tilt your allocation toward stocks. Indeed, even *after* you're retired, you still need to have a significant portion of your portfolio in stocks to ensure that your portfolio doesn't run down before you do. Investing during retirement raises a whole set of other issues that are a bit off the point here, so I'll address those separately in Chapter 9 when I discuss the right way to set a withdrawal strategy after you've retired.

Do a Gut Check

It's one thing to say you ought to keep most of your retirement portfolio in stocks because you need the growth. It's another thing to be able to stick to that allocation when the stock market is going through one of its periodic convulsions. So when you're setting your asset allocation, you've also got to take your emotions into account—that is, how are you going to react if stock prices take a dive of 20 percent or more?

Coming up with an allocation that realistically reflects your investing needs as well as your emotional ones isn't as simple a chore as it may sound. Back in 1998, for example, when the bull market was still in full swing, Oppenheimer Funds polled investors and asked how they would react if the stock market dropped dramatically. Only 8 percent of those polled said they would sell stocks, and fully 37 percent said they would buy more. Now, one could interpret this survey as proof that many investors have a rather high risk tolerance and are quite willing to hold on during short-term turmoil to reap stocks' enticing long-term gains. I have another interpretation. I think it shows that in the euphoria of a bull market investors *think* they're much bigger risk takers than they really are. The pain isn't so bad when losses are theoretical. When the market actually dives 30 percent or more, however, losses take on new meaning, and you see investors fleeing stocks for the security of bonds and money market funds, as many did after the market began melting down in early 2002. But remember that if you keep changing your allocation every time the market makes a big move up or down, you undermine the whole purpose of asset allocation. So set an allocation that is aggressive enough to give you the returns you need, but not so aggressive that your stomach will start churning every time you hear the Dow went down a hundred points.

Setting Your Portfolio Allocation

When it comes to actually setting the percentage of your portfolio that will go into various types of assets, you have two basic approaches: You can take a very scientific, technical approach, or you can go by the seat of your pants. I think either approach can work, as long as you don't make drastic changes to your allocation in response to the prevailing euphoria or pessimism in the market.

The Scientific Approach to Asset Allocation

This approach to asset allocation traces its roots back to the early 1950s, when a young Ph.D. student at the University of Chicago named Harry Markowitz came up with the remarkable insight that combining highly volatile assets with low correlations to one another could create a portfolio less risky than the sum of the riskiness of its parts. Even better, Markowitz showed that if you knew an asset's standard deviation (essentially the volatility of its returns), its correlation to other assets (how much it zigs and zags in relation to other assets), and its expected return (the gain you would expect to receive in the future), you could figure out which specific mix of securities would give you the highest return for whatever level of risk you wanted to take. He called this process portfolio optimization because it creates a portfolio with an optimal balance of risk and return.

Markowitz won a Nobel prize for this work, plus his theories spawned a major growth industry in "optimizer" programs, basically software programs designed to help investors allocate their assets. But no matter how technically advanced these programs get, they still have to grapple with one hard reality: We can't foresee the future, which means they can't *guarantee* you the highest return for the least risk. That said, however, these programs can certainly help you arrive at a reasonable asset-allocation strategy for your retirement portfolio. If you want to use this approach to allocating your assets, you can work with a financial adviser who knows his or her way around such programs. Or you can check out sites, such as those I mentioned in Chapter 5, that incorporate sophisticated asset-allocation programs into their retirement-planning advice.

The Seat-of-the-Pants Approach to Asset Allocation

I'm not talking about winging it here. Rather, the idea is that by using some knowledge of how different types of securities work, how they've performed in the past and how they're likely to perform in the future, and by realistically gauging your risk tolerance, you can arrive at a reasonable asset allocation. Below I'll outline the thought process you should go through if you prefer to take this approach. And to help you turn this process into a specific asset mix, I'll also provide three model portfolios that you can use as a guide to creating your own allocation.

One more thing: The key to setting an asset allocation is

to know how your assets are invested now. One way to do that is to go to the Morningstar Portfolio X-Ray tool in the Investment and Planning Tools section of the T. Rowe Price website (www.troweprice.com; choose Individual Investors, then Investment Planning and Tools, then Tools and Calculators, and look for this tool). You simply plug in the ticker symbols of the stocks and mutual funds you own, and it instantly tells you how your portfolio overall is divided up among broad asset classes such as stocks, bonds, and cash as well as how your portfolio breaks down by small versus large stocks, by growth versus value, and by industry sectors.

Stocks versus bonds. The first step in creating your asset allocation is figuring out how much of your portfolio should be in stocks and how much in bonds. This breakdown, more than any other single factor, will determine what size returns you earn over the long run and how much the value of your portfolio jumps around on a short-term basis. The earlier you are in your career and the more time you have before you start drawing on your portfolio for income, the more you should devote to stocks and the less to bonds. Some advisers may recommend that people just starting out in their careers actually put 100 percent of their money in stocks or stock funds on the theory that stocks offer the highest long-term returns and that someone with an investing horizon several decades long has plenty of time to recover from market setbacks.

But I would be reluctant to put all my money in stocks—or, for that matter, any single asset class—no matter what my age. There's no guarantee stocks will do as well in the future as they have in the past. So it makes sense to hedge a bit and keep some money in bonds. How much? If you're in your twenties to early forties, then having somewhere between 70 and 80 percent of your portfolio in stocks or stock funds is a reasonable place to start. You could adjust that percentage up or down, say, five percentage points, depending on your tolerance for risk. As you get older, you can scale back your stocks-bonds mix a bit, perhaps getting down to, say, 60 to 65 percent in stocks or stock funds by your mid-fifties and then 55 percent or so by the time you're ready to retire. But you don't want to pull too much of your money out of stocks because even after you've retired, you still need the growth potential of stocks to keep the value of your portfolio from being eroded by inflation.

Large stocks versus small stocks. Over the long term, small stocks can generate returns roughly two percentage points a year higher than large stocks can. So having them in your portfolio can give you a shot at higher long-term gains. On the other hand, small stocks are much more volatile than big stocks. The key to investing in small shares, therefore, is to invest enough to take advantage of small stocks' return potential without making your portfolio too risky. There's no magical percentage that works for everyone, but generally you should keep your small-stock holdings roughly in line with the percentage that small stocks represent in the overall stock market, about 10 to 15 percent of all your stock holdings.

Growth stocks versus value stocks. The returns of growth and value stocks tend to seesaw, with growth generating higher returns over a period of, say, three to five years only to fall behind as value takes the lead for a comparable period. Value stocks, for example, ruled in the early 1990s as the U.S. economy was coming out of a recession, but as investors became infatuated with the potential for rapid earnings increases, growth shares, and technology stocks in particular, took the lead in the late 1990s. Then the bubble burst and value took the lead again. Since the timing of these seesaw swings is difficult if not impossible to predict, you want to have both styles represented in your portfolio in roughly equal proportions.

Your bond stake. When it comes to the bond holdings in your retirement portfolio, you have two main concerns: maturity and credit quality. On the maturity front, I think it makes the most sense to stick to bonds or bond funds in the short to intermediate range—that is, maturities of two to seven years or so. You may be giving up a bit of interest income, since longer-maturity bonds usually do pay the highest interest rates, but shorter-maturity bonds are much less volatile. Since you're looking to bonds more to provide steady income and stability than explosive gains, it makes sense to err a bit on the safe side in the bond portion of your portfolio.

As for credit quality, I also think you should tilt toward safety. That means sticking to funds that invest in U.S. Treasury securities or other government bonds and/or highly rated corporates. (If your 401(k) plan offers stable value funds, you can put those squarely in the high-quality and short to intermediate-maturity camp for asset-allocation purposes.) For investing you do *outside* a 401(k) or other tax-advantaged retirement plan, like a Keogh or IRA, you may also want to consider high-quality tax-free municipal bonds or bond funds. That decision largely comes down to which tax bracket you're in and what interest rate munis are paying relative to taxable bonds such as Treasuries and corporates. The Bond Market Association website (www.investinginbonds.com) has a calculator that can help you determine whether you're better off in taxable or tax-exempt issues given current rates and your tax situation.

You may be able to eke a bit more return out of the bond portion of your portfolio by investing in high-yield bond funds, better known as junk bonds. But you are also opening up yourself to a higher possibility of defaults, especially during recessions and other periods of economic turmoil. So if you decide to own these types of bond funds at all, I'd recommend you make them no more than 5 to 10 percent of your portfolio, and even less if bonds are a very small portion of your overall holdings.

Three Model Portfolios

On pages 181–183 are three model portfolios that can help you arrive at the right mix for your retirement portfolio. I'm not suggesting you should adopt any one of these exactly as is. Rather, think of them as guidelines you can fine-tune for your own circumstances.

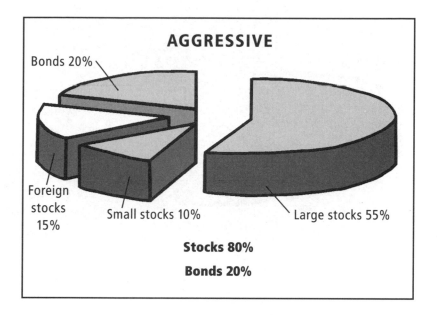

AGGRESSIVE

Bonds 20%

Foreign stocks 15%

Small stocks 10%

Large stocks 55%

Stocks 80%

Bonds 20%

Best for: People early in their careers, most likely those in their twenties to mid-forties, or anyone willing to take above-average risks in hopes of generating higher returns.

Advantages of this portfolio: Its high stock component makes it the most likely of these three portfolios to deliver the highest long-term gains and create the largest nest egg.

Disadvantages of this portfolio: Its low bond component makes it the most volatile of the three portfolios. During bear markets and other market downturns, this portfolio is going to suffer the most.

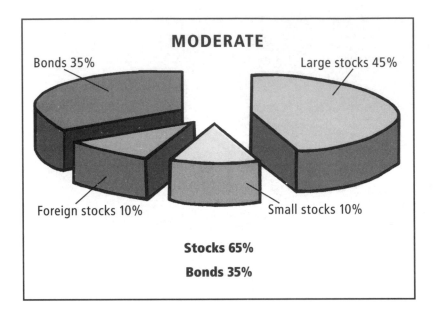

MODERATE

Bonds 35%

Large stocks 45%

Foreign stocks 10%

Small stocks 10%

Stocks 65%

Bonds 35%

Best for: People in the mid to late career stages, most likely those in their late forties to late fifties, who will be retiring in a decade or so. Also a possibility for older investors who are willing to take on a bit of risk to increase the chances that their portfolio won't run down before they do.

Advantages of this portfolio: It has a stock component large enough to generate moderate, if not spectacular, long-term returns and a bond component large enough to offer relatively decent protection during periods of market turmoil.

Disadvantages of this portfolio: It may not provide the returns young investors need to build a sizable nest egg, nor may it offer enough downside protection to satisfy older investors or those with truly low risk tolerances.

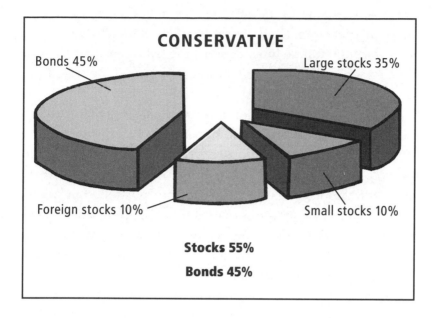

CONSERVATIVE

Bonds 45%

Large stocks 35%

Foreign stocks 10%

Small stocks 10%

Stocks 55%

Bonds 45%

Best for: People in their late fifties or older who expect to retire soon.

Advantages of this portfolio: A 55–45 blend of stocks and bonds provides some growth potential while also offering good protection even during periods of severe market stress.

Disadvantages of this portfolio: Because of its relatively small stock component, this portfolio may not provide high-enough returns to generate an adequate inflation-adjusted income for a retirement that lasts thirty years or more.

Rebalancing Act

Once you've gone to the trouble of setting a portfolio allocation, you don't want to let it get too far out of whack. Otherwise, your portfolio will no longer reflect the balance you worked so hard to achieve between your risk tolerance and the size of the returns you need to reach your retirement goals.

A quick example will demonstrate what I'm talking about. Let's say that in the beginning of 1995 you had decided that a mix of 80 percent stocks and 20 percent bonds was appropriate for you. And let's further assume that over the next five years you hadn't added any new money to your portfolio but simply let your gains ride in both stocks and bonds. Well, since stocks returned roughly three times as much as bonds over that period (24 percent a year versus 8 percent), the gains in the stock portion of your portfolio would have caused your portfolio allocation to tilt more heavily toward stocks. In fact, at the end of the five-year period, you would have had a much more volatile portfolio mix of 90 percent stocks and 10 percent bonds. Which means that going into the bear market of 2000, you would have had a much smaller buffer of bonds than you had started out with in 1995. In short, whether you knew it or not, you would have been taking more risk in your investment portfolio than you set out to take when you set your allocations.

So to keep your portfolio on track, you need to rebalance your holdings to bring the various asset classes of your portfolio back to their proper proportions. Basically, this amounts to nothing more than either putting new money into the areas of your portfolio that have lagged (bonds, in the example above) to increase their weighting within the portfolio, or selling off some assets in areas that have grown in value (stocks, in the case above) and reinvesting the proceeds in areas that have lagged, or both.

This simple act of rebalancing does two things. First, it maintains the risk-reward profile of your portfolio. This is important because it prevents you from inadvertently taking on too risk much when stocks are doing well, thus making you much more prone to steep downturns when stocks suffer a set-back, or too little risk when stocks aren't doing well, making it less likely you'll get the gains you need for future growth. And second, since rebalancing usually involves selling some assets that have gained in value and buying others that have dropped in value, it also forces you to practice the oft-recommended but little-followed technique of selling high and buying low.

There are a variety of ways you can pull off this rebalancing act, but most investors rely on one of three methods: calendar rebalancing, setting ranges, or tactical rebalancing.

Calendar Rebalancing

The premise here is simple. You set a specific time period—say, at the end of the quarter or end of the year—and then check your allocations. If they're off by more than, say, five percentage points or so, you bring them back to their original proportions. I like this method the best because it's neat and simple, which means you're more likely to actually do it. I also think that for most people annual rebalancing will work just fine. If you feel ambitious enough to go through this routine quarterly, more power to you, although, frankly, I don't see much benefit in doing it more frequently than that.

Setting Ranges

This method is more popular among money managers and large institutional investors. Basically, you set an allocation range for each asset class and then rebalance only if your holdings move outside that range. So, for example, you might set a range of 55 to 65 percent for stocks. If your stock holdings remain within that ten-percentage-point band, you do nothing. But if they fall outside that range, you either add new money or sell assets to bring them back within their appropriate range. Institutions do this because it allows them to track their portfolio allocations more closely, which means the portfolio never strays very far from its risk-reward profile. I don't like this method as much as calendar rebalancing for two reasons. First, it requires you to keep constant tabs on your portfolio, so as a practical matter, I don't believe many people will stick to this strategy. Second, it can lead to lots of trading, which can drive up costs and lead to higher tax bills in the case of taxable portfolios.

Tactical Rebalancing

This method involves resetting your allocation depending on your outlook for different asset classes. So, for example, if gains in the stock market have swelled the stock portion of your portfolio, you might decide to let that higher weighting ride if you believe the prospects for stocks are still bright, or you might bring your allocation back toward its original setting if you feel stock prices are likely to stagnate or fall. In truth, I don't really consider this a rebalancing strategy. To me this is really more than guessing at which asset class will perform better in the future. Of course, the whole premise behind asset allocation and rebalancing is that we don't *know* which asset classes will outperform in the short run (or the long run, for that matter, but at least there we can make educated guesstimates). In my opinion, tactical rebalancing basically undermines the whole concept of asset allocation and rebalancing, so I don't recommend this method.

You want to be mindful when rebalancing, however, that you could be generating trading costs and tax consequences that could drag down your returns. If you are rebalancing a portfolio other than a 401(k), IRA, or other tax-advantaged account, you probably want to try to bring your allocations in line by directing new money into asset classes that have become underweighted rather than selling assets. This way you won't incur income taxes on the sales or generate trading costs. But if your allocations have gotten so out of whack that it would take you more than, say, a year's worth of new additions to bring them back in line, then I'd say you should probably just go ahead and sell assets and rebalance. Yes, that may result in some taxes, but you can minimize the bite by selling securities with the highest cost (to reduce your gain), by unloading ones that you've held more than a year so you qualify for the lower capital-gains tax rates, or perhaps even by selling some securities in which you have a loss.

When you're dealing with tax-advantaged accounts such as your 401(k) or IRA, however, then taxes aren't an issue. So you can feel free to sell assets from overweighted categories and move the money into underweighted ones. In fact, some 401(k) plans offer rebalancing programs that allow you to bring your portfolio back to its proper proportions with the click of a mouse.

Whatever rebalancing method you choose, stick with it. Otherwise, your portfolio will veer off track, taking your investing strategy and chances of a comfortable retirement with it.

Factoring the 2003 Tax Law Into
Your Retirement Investing Strategy

If you kept abreast of the investing coverage in the financial press in the wake of the 2003 tax law, you could easily come away with the impression that the new tax rules required investors to totally revamp their investing strategies. But that would be a mistake. Yes, several aspects of the law do make some investments relatively more attractive than others in certain circumstances, and it does make sense for investors to consider ways to gain whatever advantage they can from the new tax laws, particularly when it comes to deciding whether to hold particular investments in a taxable versus a tax-advantaged account such as a 401(k). But the chances that such an assessment would lead most investors to radically revise their portfolio are remote. Indeed, a reassessment followed by some marginal changes is the most likely response, not a radical restructuring. Here, then, is how I recommend you consider incorporating the provisions of the new tax law into your retirement investing.

Your Asset Allocation Is Still the
Starting Point for Your Investing Strategy

Tax changes or no, the way you divvy up your assets among stocks and bonds is still the most important investing decision you will make and will largely determine your returns and how large a retirement fund you accumulate. And taxes are not a key driver in determining your asset allocation. Rather, as I pointed out in the previous section, your time horizon, investing goals, and tolerance for risk are the key factors. Thus, taxes shouldn't have much of an effect on your overall asset allocation, which means the mix of stocks and bonds that was right for you before the tax bill was signed is likely to be pretty much the same mix that's right for you today. Sure, you might tinker around the edges a bit. The fact that dividend payments are taxed at a much lower rate than interest payments on bonds might make you slightly more apt to invest in dividend-paying stocks or funds. But remember: Stocks are much more volatile than bonds, and dividend payments are much more iffy than bond interest payments. So you don't want to make any radical shift in the amount you devote to bonds versus stocks, even if you're shifting money to dividend-paying stocks.

Holding for the Long Term Makes Even More Sense than Before

Throughout this chapter I've harped on the need for investors to think in terms of holding their investments for the long term. A short-term focus leads to more trading and the possibility of more mistakes, and it generally drives costs up and returns down. If anything, the new tax law reemphasizes the virtues of long-term investing. Why? Simple. Now that the new law has widened the gap between the maximum tax rate on short-term gains (which can be taxed at rates as high as 35 percent) and the maximum tax rate on long-term gains (15 percent), it makes even more sense to focus on long-term gains. That's not to say there aren't ever instances in which you may want to take short-term gains or invest in mutual funds that generate short-term gains. But you must be very selective about it and, when possible, try to restrict short-term gains to tax-advantaged accounts.

Your 401(k), IRA, and Other Tax-Advantaged Retirement Savings Plans Are Still Likely Your Best Shot at Accumulating a Sizable Retirement Nest Egg

After the new tax bill was signed, many articles pointed out that 401(k)s and similar accounts had become relatively less attractive. The reason is that all gains, including long-term capital gains and dividends, in these accounts are taxed at generally higher ordinary income rates, while long-term capital gains and dividends earned outside these accounts qualify for lower long-term capital-gains treatment. But that doesn't mean you should stop participating in a 401(k) or stop funding an IRA or similar account. For one thing, 401(k)s and IRAs still offer an initial tax break plus tax deferral on the account's gains (tax exclusion in the case of a Roth IRA). Those are still very valuable features, particularly for long-term investors. What's more, most 401(k) plans also offer matching funds, the equivalent of free money that automatically boosts your return. Finally, in the case of the 401(k) at least, the fact that your contributions are automatically deducted from your paycheck makes regular saving easy and relatively painless. Which means most of us are much more likely to save regularly than we would be if we had to sit down and write out a check every two weeks or each month. So don't let the pursuit of tax savings lure you away from your 401(k) and other tax-advantaged accounts.

With those guidelines in mind, however, you may want to consider making some moderate adjustments to your investing strategy, particularly in the area of deciding where to hold specific types of investments. Here is a rundown of how you generally want to spread out your portfolio in light of the tax treatment for different types of investments.

Investments that generate long-term capital gains or pay dividends. In general, you'll want to hold these types of investments in taxable accounts so that you can take advantage of the 2003 tax bill's more advantageous rates for long-term capital gains. So, for example, individual stocks that you plan to hold longer than a year and which would therefore qualify for long-term capital-gains treatment would generally be good candidates to hold in taxable accounts outside your 401(k). The same goes for mutual funds that pay most of their gains in the form of long-term capital gain distributions. Such funds would include not only actively managed funds whose managers tend to hold for the long term and thus generate mostly long-term capital gains, but also other tax-efficient funds, such as low-turnover index funds and tax-managed funds, or portfolios whose managers actively try to minimize taxable gains by, among other things, using losses in some stocks to offset gains in others.

Similarly, as much as possible you want to hold stocks and stock mutual funds that pay dividends in your taxable accounts in order to take advantage of the more favorable rates afforded dividend payments under the 2003 tax bill. There are exceptions, of course. REITs, for example, pay dividends that typically do not qualify for long-term capital-gains treatment, so you would ideally want to keep REITs and REIT mutual funds in a tax-advantaged retirement account.

Investments that generate short-term capital gains. You're generally better off holding investments that provide most of their return in the form of short-term capital gains in tax-advantaged retirement accounts such as a 401(k) or IRA. The reason is that *all* gains within tax-advantaged accounts, regardless of whether they're short- or long-term or interest or dividend payments, are taxed at ordinary income tax rates anyway. So to the extent you hold such investments, you might as well keep them in your tax-advantaged accounts, allowing you to take advantage of lower long-term capital-gains rates with the cash you have available to invest in taxable accounts. What's more, you'll at least get to postpone paying taxes on any short-term gains until you withdraw the money from your account.

So, for example, mutual funds whose managers frequently buy and sell securities and thus generate lots of short-term capital gains would generally be good candidates for your 401(k) or IRA. If you like to actively trade stocks or mutual funds, you should also ideally restrict this to your tax-advantaged retirement accounts since frequent trading can lead to short-term gains that are taxed at the highest rates. By the way, I don't recommend that you engage in frequent trading. As I noted in the beginning of the chapter, I think there's good evidence that frequent trading leads to lower returns than holding for the longer term. But if you're going to trade anyway, try to restrict it to your tax-advantaged retirement accounts.

Bonds and other investments that pay regular interest. Since bond interest payments are taxed at less favorable ordinary income tax rates, you want to hold them as much as possible in tax-advantaged retirement accounts as well. Again, the idea is that since the payments will be taxed at ordinary income rates anyway, you might as well hold them in tax-advantaged accounts so that you can at least postpone the taxes you'll owe on those interest payments. By dong this, you'll also be able to earn interest on the money that you didn't have to shell out to the feds in taxes.

But there's one other issue to consider in bonds—namely, whether you're better off in tax-exempt munis rather than taxable corporate or government issues. The higher the income tax bracket you're in, the more likely you'll earn a higher after-tax return by investing in municipal rather than taxable bonds. If munis are a better deal for you, then invest in munis (or, more likely, muni bond funds) and hold them in your taxable account.

The theory that interest-paying investments fit best in tax-advantaged retirement accounts suggests that you should also keep investments such as CDs and money market funds in tax-advantaged accounts. But whether that makes sense varies depending on your circumstances. For example, if you see your money market funds and CDs as stashes you can dip into for emergencies or to meet unexpected expenses, then you'll probably want to hold them in taxable accounts. Otherwise, you may be hit with the 10 percent tax penalty that typically applies to early withdrawals from tax-advantaged retirement accounts. Of course, if you're over age fifty-nine and a half, then such penalties aren't an issue, and it may make sense to hold short-term interest-paying investments in your retirement accounts.

You don't want to get too wrapped up, however, in trying to squeeze every possible advantage out of the tax laws. And you've also got to exercise some common sense. Let's say that virtually all of your retirement nest egg is in your 401(k) and that you do very little investing in taxable accounts. That doesn't mean that you should limit yourself to bonds and mutual funds that generate short-term capital gains. Similarly, if you have virtually all your investable assets in taxable accounts, that doesn't mean you should avoid bonds or bond funds because their payments are taxed at ordinary income tax rates. The single most important thing you can do when investing for retirement is to build a diversified portfolio. If you can do that while taking advantage of the tax laws, fine. But don't let tax considerations interfere with your goal of building a diversified portfolio along the lines I described earlier in this chapter. Besides, tax laws can and do change at the whim of Congress. (Indeed, the current tax rates on capital gains and dividends are set to expire after 2008 unless Congress extends them.) If you go to extreme lengths to restructure your portfolio so that it jibes with whatever tax rules are in effect at any given moment, you may find yourself having to go to extreme lengths again to restructure it when the law changes, which could mean lots of transaction costs (and tax payments) that could drive your returns down. So make taxes a consideration in your investing, but keep diversity as your number one goal.

Take a Holistic Portfolio Approach

Throughout this chapter—indeed, throughout this book—I've been talking about "your portfolio" as if you keep all your retirement investments in one pot. But for many of us, that's not the case, or at least not maybe the way we think of it. Many of us think of our investments as being in multiple discrete portfolios: our 401(k) portfolio at work, our IRA rollover portfolio, perhaps a Roth IRA portfolio. And, of course, many of us also have retirement assets in taxable accounts, regular mutual fund and brokerage accounts.

For the purposes of retirement planning, however, it's important that you think of all the investments you've earmarked for retirement as part of one all-inclusive pot. This is especially true for asset-allocation purposes. Let's say you've decided that for your return needs and tolerance for risk, you've decided on an asset allocation of 45 percent large-cap stock funds, 10 percent small-cap, 15 percent foreign funds, and 30 percent bonds. Well, that asset mix should apply to *all* your retirement assets. In other words, when you total the value of all your retirement accounts, they should break down at least pretty close to those percentages. If they don't, then you don't have a true overall retirement investing strategy. What you've got is a bunch of disparate accounts, some working at cross-purposes with others.

Taking this holistic approach doesn't mean that every single account has to break down into the exact percentages you've chosen for the various asset classes. What's important is that the portfolio as a whole follows your asset-allocation plan. In fact, you should look for ways of taking advantage of the various different accounts to come up with a better overall portfolio. If, for example, your 401(k) offers a terrific large-cap fund but doesn't offer a particularly good small-cap or foreign fund, you can put more money in the 401(k) large-cap account and do your small-cap and foreign investing in accounts outside your 401(k). You're still shooting for the same overall asset mix, but you're making the best use of the various choices available to you. Similarly, as I explain at the end of this chapter, you may want to hold certain assets in taxable accounts and others in tax-advantaged accounts for tax reasons.

You can also make your various portfolios work to your advantage when it comes time to rebalance your portfolio. Let's say that the growth portion of your taxable mutual fund portfolio has swelled in value, requiring you to sell some of your growth shares and reinvest the proceeds in value funds. If you do that in your taxable account, you'll generate taxable gains and have to give up some of your stash to taxes. You may be able to rebalance without paying the taxes, however, by selling growth holdings in your 401(k), where there are no tax consequences, and then putting the proceeds into value funds within your 401(k).

Of course, making sure you've got the right asset mix can be a bit unwieldy if you're dealing with multiple accounts held in a variety of different places. The solution: Log all your retirement holdings into a program such as the Morningstar Portfolio X-Ray tool. By doing so, you'll see how all your holdings combined break down by asset class, investing style, and market sector, making it relatively simple to see whether your retirement assets as a whole still reflect the asset-allocation strategy you've set.

Chapter 7

IF PLAN A ISN'T WORKING,
GO TO PLAN B

A retirement plan should be like a yellow brick road that lays out a clear path that starts during your career and wends its way throughout your life. And ideally, once you start out on this road, you should stick to it until you retire, and indeed even during retirement.

But let's face it. In the real world, yellow brick roads can get pretty bumpy. Even in the unreal world of Oz, Dorothy and her friends ran into several detours in their journey along the yellow brick road. Perhaps we don't get the early jump on saving that we'd hoped for. Or maybe we embark on a savings program, but unexpected expenses interfere with our discipline to save. Or perhaps we don't earn the returns we thought we would on our investments, or our employer's matching contribution to our 401(k) is in the form of company stock that's now virtually worthless. There are any number of ways that reality can intrude on our well-laid plans or, for that matter, prevent us from even making plans, well-laid or not. Suffice it to say that, for a variety of reasons, many of us find ourselves at age forty-five, fifty, or even older, yet we still haven't accumulated nearly enough assets to allow us to retire anywhere close to our current lifestyle.

Granted, this is not a position you want to be in—financially unprepared and retirement looming. But if you are, it is not a time for panic. It is a time to become more determined and more resourceful, a time to look for options you may have over-looked before, a time to focus all your effort and energy on using whatever time you still have to prepare for retirement. In short, it's time to go to Plan B.

These strategies will require discipline and effort—which you will have to provide. You're effectively trying to compress what should have been a career's worth of saving and investing into a much smaller span of time, which means you're going to have to concentrate and work hard to get results. You should also know that no strategy can make up for a lifetime of neglect. That would be unrealistic. So don't expect that within the space of five, ten, or even fifteen years that you can be in the same po-sition you would have been in had you saved and invested for retirement during your entire career.

On the other hand, doing *something*, no matter how late you start or how little you're able to do, is always better than doing nothing. And if you embark on one or more of the strategies I lay out in this chapter, you should be able to make an apprecia-ble improvement in your standard of living during retirement. So no matter how far you've fallen behind in your retirement planning—even if you haven't done any retirement planning at all to date—I recommend that you consider following one or more of the strategies below. It could mean the difference between a grim retirement and a golden one.

Strategy 1: Rev Up Your Savings

If you're approaching the big five-oh—or even the big six-oh—and you realize you haven't accumulated nearly enough to pro-vide a decent retirement for yourself, the single most effective thing you can do to salvage the situation is to begin saving as much as you possibly can. Let me be clear: I'm not talking about *thinking* of starting to save or *considering* a savings pro-gram. I'm talking about *doing* it. In fact, I'm talking about doing it to the max, an immediate crash course in saving in which you commit to making retirement saving your number one financial priority.

Changing your savings habits late in life won't be easy. But at least you'll likely have a menu of tax-advantaged savings plans you can take advantage of to help you squeeze the most out of however much you manage to salt away. I'm talking, of course, about such plans as 401(k)s, 403(b)s, IRAs, Keoghs, SEP IRAs, and so on. Such plans' tax benefits, higher contribution limits, and even catch-up provisions for people fifty and older make them ideal ways to rack up a significant pool of retirement assets over a relatively short period of time. So if you're planning to launch an all-out savings sprint to retirement, these plans should be the place to start your run.

Obviously, the amount of money you can accumulate will depend on such factors as how much you manage to put away, how many years you have until retirement, and the rate of return you earn on your investments. But to give you an idea of how large a nest egg it's possible to build even if you're starting late in life, let's take a look at a hypothetical scenario. Assume you're fifty years old, you earn $50,000 a year, and you have accumulated *nada,* zip, nothing for retirement to date. Assume further that you work for a company that allows its employees to contribute 6 percent of salary to its 401(k) plan and that you're eligible to contribute to an IRA. So, from your starting point of zero savings, how much might you be able to accumulate by, say, age sixty-five?

Let's start with the 401(k). If you make the 6 percent annual contribution each and every year until you retire and earn an 8 percent annual return on your investments, that move alone could net you more than $100,000 by the time you call it a career at sixty-five. If your employer is generous enough to offer a 50 percent match on your contributions—as many are these days—the combo of your contributions, the employer's match, and the 8 percent return on your savings could leave you with a nest egg of over $150,000 by the time you retire.

Save more in your 401(k) and you can do even better. Remember those catch-up contributions I mentioned in Chapter 3 and Chapter 4? Well, if you managed to make the maximum 401(k) catch-up contribution each year (starting at $3,000 in 2004 and rising to $5,000 by 2006) on top of your regular 6 percent, you could increase the value of your nest egg by more than $135,000, bringing its value to just under $300,000.

The possibilities don't end there, however. Let's say that your will to save is so strong that you also manage to make the maximum contribution to an IRA each year, starting with the $3,000 max in 2004 and rising to $5,000 by 2008. Assuming the same rate of return as your 401(k), that would give you an additional pot of savings that could total more than $130,000 by the time you're sixty-five. And for the coup de grâce, let's finally assume that you also stash away the maximum annual IRA catch-up contribution ($500 in 2004, doubling to $1,000 in 2006). That would give you another $26,000 or so, bringing your overall IRA pot alone to more than $150,000.

So how much might you possibly end up with by saving like a fiend for fifteen years? Well, the table on page 199 shows how much each of the moves I've described above could individually add to your retirement nest egg. And it also shows that if you carried out each and every one of these moves faithfully for fifteen years, you could end up with a grand total of just over $450,000—that's right, almost half a million. Not bad for someone who didn't even begin saving for retirement until age fifty.

Now, as I've been going through this hypothetical scenario I've been careful each step of the way to say that you *could* end up with a certain amount of money, as opposed to you *would* or *will* end up with that amount. I've done that because I don't want to create the impression that any of these sums is somehow guaranteed. For one thing, this hypothetical scenario assumes you earn 8 percent on your money year in and year out. Fact is, when you're investing in things such as mutual funds, stocks, and bonds, you don't know exactly what your return will be. You could end up with a higher return, or you could get a lower return. What's more, even if the investments you chose generated an annualized return of 8 percent, you won't get that

BUILDING A NEST EGG AT AGE FIFTY

Even if you have no retirement savings at age fifty, it's still possible to build a tidy little nest egg by the time you're sixty-five—provided you're willing to do some heavy-duty saving and take full advantage of options such as 401(k)s and IRAs.

IF YOU DO THIS STARTING AT AGE FIFTY . . .	. . . YOU COULD END UP WITH THIS AMOUNT AT AGE SIXTY-FIVE*
Contribute 6 percent of $50,000 salary to a 401(k) each year	$105,000
Get a 50 percent employer match on your contributions	$52,000
Make the maximum annual 401(k) catch-up contribution	$137,000
Contribute the annual maximum to an IRA	$132,000
Make the maximum annual IRA catch-up contribution	$26,000
All of these moves together	$452,000

*Example assumes 3 percent salary growth per year and an 8 percent annual return on savings. Figures are rounded to the nearest thousand.

8 percent like clockwork every year. Your returns will bounce around. And as I explained in Chapter 5, when you're adding money to a portfolio over time, the order of the returns you get will determine the amount you end up with. Which means that even if your investments earned 8 percent on average over fifteen years, you could end up with less than the amounts in the table above, or you could end up with more.

There's also the question of whether you or anyone else would be able to pull off the level of savings described in this scenario. To contribute the max to both the 401(k) and the IRA and do the maximum catch-up contributions would require an enormous feat of will. And even if you had the will, siphoning off this much for saving might not leave you enough to live on.

But the point of this example isn't to suggest that you can

guarantee yourself a nest egg of a precise size by making specific moves. The point is to show that even if you're getting a late start on your retirement planning, you can still accumulate a sizable chunk of assets *if you're willing to do some diligent saving*. I don't expect that many people would be able to pull off all the moves I listed above. But if you can manage a couple of them, or for that matter just one, even contributing the maximum amount to an IRA each year, you can build a retirement nest egg that can make your retirement more comfortable than it would otherwise be.

Strategy 2: Delay Retirement for a Few Years

Many of us have a specific timetable in mind when it comes to retirement. We want to retire at a certain age, or we plan to call it quits after a certain number of years on the job. But sometimes that plan may not be financially feasible. Perhaps we didn't begin saving early enough in our career to accumulate a nest egg large enough to support us. Or maybe we saved plenty, but devastating market losses such as those many retirees and wannabe retirees sustained during the bear market of 2000 seriously depleted our nest egg. Whatever the case, sometimes you've got to reassess your situation and realize that, at least for now, retirement is not the best option. You're better off putting in a few more years on the job.

And, in fact, working longer is a choice many more people are considering. For example, a survey of high-income investors conducted by Quicken.com after the onset of the 2000 bear market found that 13 percent of those polled said they were planning to retire later than they had originally thought they would, and more than a third of this group said they would work an extra five years or more. A similar Gallup survey conducted for the financial services firm UBS found that roughly 20 percent of those surveyed said they expected to postpone retirement by four years on average.

This delaying tactic can make a lot of sense. The mere act of postponing the time you'll begin dipping into your retirement assets allows your portfolio more time to grow. And if you manage to continue making contributions to your retirement savings plans during the time you stay at work, you're also throwing into the pot new money that, along with whatever return it earns, can boost the value of your nest egg even more. The combined effect of these two factors can be quite dramatic.

Let's say, for example, you had hoped to retire at age sixty but felt that your retirement nest egg of $200,000 wasn't quite enough to generate the level of income combined with Social Security that would allow you to maintain your present lifestyle. Well, if you postpone retirement for five years and during that time earn an annual 8 percent rate of return, the growth in your portfolio alone could add almost $95,000 to its value by the time you're sixty-five. And if you also managed to contribute, say, $5,000 a year to your retirement savings for those five years through your 401(k) or other retirement savings, your retirement nest egg could grow almost another $32,000. In short, by holding off five years, you might be able to increase the value of your retirement assets by more than $125,000, or more than 60 percent—enough to make an appreciable difference in the way you live during retirement.

Finally, there's a less obvious benefit to delaying retirement. Since you will be starting your retirement at a later age, you will be drawing on your portfolio for fewer years. As a practical matter, that reduces the odds that your savings will expire before you do, which means you can draw from your portfolio with greater confidence that your savings will be able to see you through your retirement. I don't want to minimize the emotional adjustment that may be involved in having to stay at work for several more years when you thought you would be relaxing at home or pursuing the interests you didn't have time for during your career. But when you consider the extra margin of financial security a few extra years of work might bring—and how that additional financial security can translate into greater peace of mind during your later years—postponing retirement can be one of the smartest retirement-planning decisions you'll make.

Strategy 3: Think Rehire Instead of Retire

If you're on the verge of retirement but feel you don't have quite as large a stash of retirement savings as you would like, another option to consider is taking a part-time job. In fact, the idea of part-time work during retirement is becoming so commonplace that soon we may think of it not as a backup but as a normal option for retirees. According to AIG/SunAmerica's 2002 Re-Visioning Retirement survey, for example, 95 percent of those who had not yet retired said they expect to work in some capacity during retirement. Indeed, nearly half said they would work in retirement if they were paid little or nothing at all. A poll of workers over age forty-five in 2002 by the American Association of Retired Persons (AARP) found similar sentiments: 69 percent of those polled said they plan to continue to work in retirement, and 84 percent of that group said they would continue to hold jobs even if they were financially set for life, the idea being that working during retirement keeps one vital and engaged in life.

Regardless of the motivation, holding a part-time job in retirement can dramatically improve your financial well-being. The main reason is that to the extent part-time earnings can help pay living expenses, you can reduce withdrawals from your portfolio and give it more of a chance to grow and support you in later years.

Let's say, for example, that you retire at age sixty-two and take a part-time job during the first ten years of retirement that allows you to lower the annual draws from your IRA by $10,000 a year. In effect, that allows $10,000 per year that you would have withdrawn to remain in your portfolio and compound without the drag of taxes. Assuming an 8 percent annual rate of return, that means by the time you're seventy-two you could have more than $150,000 that you wouldn't have had if you hadn't worked. The result: you've given yourself a lot more financial wiggle room that could easily come in handy later in retirement when you might not be as disposed, or for that matter physically able, to work.

One more thing: Retirees who want to work will find it's now easier to do so without seeing their Social Security benefits reduced because of their extra income. Prior to 2000, seniors who worked beyond normal retirement age saw their Social Security benefits lowered by $1 for every $3 they earned above $17,000 a year. But the Senior Citizens' Freedom to Work Act of 2000 ushered in rules that are more work-friendly. Today, once you reach full retirement age (which ranges from age sixty-five to sixty-seven, depending on your year of birth), you can receive full Social Security benefits no matter how much money you earn—although, depending on your income, those benefits may still be taxed. Alas, if you receive Social Security benefits and work while you are *below* full retirement age, you will lose $1 in benefits for every $2 you earn above an annual ceiling, which was $11,520 in 2003. So if you plan to start taking Social Security before full retirement age and think you might also hold a job, it's a good idea to see in advance how much of your benefits you might have to give up. You can find that out by calling your local Social Security office or by going to the Retirement Earnings Test calculator on Social Security's website (www.ssa.gov/OACT/COLA/RTeffect.html).

Strategy 4: Scale Back Your Portfolio Withdrawals

If your retirement stash isn't as large as you would like it to be but you're not willing or able to postpone retirement or even take a part-time job after your retire, there is another way to make the retirement assets you do have last longer—namely, reduce the amount that you withdraw from your portfolio each year. Financially, the effect of this tactic is much like that of working during retirement. Cutting back on your withdrawals leaves more money in your portfolio than you would have had without scaling back. This extra sum can then earn a return and grow, thus giving you a larger portfolio to tap in the future than you would have had if you had not cut back.

Let's say, for example, that instead of drawing $25,000 a year from your retirement portfolio, as you had originally planned, you cut back your withdrawals to $15,000 a year for the first five years of retirement. And let's further assume that the $10,000 that remained in your portfolio each of those years earned an 8 percent annual rate of return. This would mean that at the end of five years, your portfolio could have roughly $63,000 more than if you had withdrawn that ten grand each year as originally planned. That's right—by toughing it out with smaller withdrawals for just five years, you could have access to more than $60,000 that you otherwise wouldn't have had. Effectively, you have accumulated sixty grand while you're retired. That kind of "addition" to your retirement portfolio can dramatically improve your prospects in your later retirement years.

Now, I don't want to suggest that this strategy is something that you can pull off effortlessly. Clearly, lowering the amount you withdraw from your portfolio means you'll also have to lower the amount you can *spend* in retirement. (That's why I think this strategy is somewhat less attractive than working part-time in retirement, a move that actually gives you more spendable income.) So unless you've got a fair amount of wiggle room in your budget—lavish vacations you can turn into merely comfortable ones, renting a vacation home each year instead of buying one, and the like—you may not be able to get by on much lower withdrawals than you had planned on.

Still, if you manage to downsize your withdrawals only by a small amount, you can still improve your prospects for later in retirement. Again, the idea is that any change for the positive is better than doing nothing at all. Generally, the cutbacks you make in the early years of retirement will produce the biggest impact for the simple reason that your savings will have more time to grow. That said, however, you may find yourself in a position where you start out with a level of withdrawals that seems comfortable but later seems to be draining your portfolio too quickly. In such cases, scaling back withdrawals can give your portfolio a chance to regenerate itself and reduce the chances of it running dry when you may need it most, that is, in your later years of retirement. For more on the crucial issue of how to manage withdrawals from your portfolio after you retire, see Chapter 9.

Strategy 5: Get Money from Your Home

While many of us might not have accumulated as large a nest egg as we would like in the form of stocks, bonds, and mutual funds in our retirement portfolio, we may have another substantial source of wealth that could be tapped during retirement—the value of our homes. In fact, for most Americans, their home is still their single largest asset, bigger even than the amount they've racked up in company savings plans and other retirement accounts. Indeed, home prices, which had already climbed substantially during the 1990s, continued to rise sharply even as stock prices fell and languished in the bear market between 2000 and 2003. As a result, by 2003, the median price of a home in the United States—that is, the midpoint, or the price at which half the homes in the United States sold for more and half sold for less—had risen to just under $162,000. And in many high-priced areas, such San Diego and Anaheim, California, and Long Island, New York, the median price was more than double that amount. This means that many people who bought homes at relatively modest prices decades earlier may now be sitting on a substantial amount of home equity, in many cases several hundred thousand dollars.

The question, though, is how does one draw on that built-up equity? For that matter, should one tap it at all? Many financial advisers are wary of viewing a personal residence as an asset to be tapped during retirement for the simple reason that many older people don't want to pack up and leave their home after retiring. For example, a 1996 survey by the American Association of Retired Persons (AARP) found that eight out of ten seniors said they prefer to stay in their own home and never move. Similarly, some people see the old homestead as a legacy they can leave to their heirs, a way to provide for children, grandchildren, or others. Obviously, the decision of what, if anything, one ought to do with the value of one's home during retirement is a personal one. That said, however, if you don't have other assets that can provide a decent level of income in retirement, it would be foolish not to consider using the one large asset you do have to make your retirement more comfortable. The issue then becomes the best way of doing this.

One option is to sell your current house and then use some of the proceeds to pay cash for a less expensive home, either a smaller one in your area or a less expensive one elsewhere, leaving you with a tidy sum to live on. Let's say, for example, that you paid $50,000 for your home many years ago, have since paid off the mortgage, and then sold it for $250,000. Ignoring for simplicity's sake real estate commissions and other transaction costs, the sale would leave you with $200,000 in profit, tax free. (Under current tax law, married couples pay no tax on up to $500,000 in home sale gains, while single taxpayers get a pass on up to $250,000 in gains. There are a few other strings attached to this break. So before selling your home, I suggest you check out IRS Publication 523, "Selling Your Home," which is available on the IRS website, www.irs.gov.)

Of course, the amount you would have left over to live on would depend on how much you've got to shell out for new digs. If you live in an area where house prices have been rising at a good clip in recent years, you may have trouble finding something you consider habitable that's selling at a price low enough to leave you a substantial amount to live on. You could conserve some of your profit stash by applying only part of it to the purchase price and taking out a mortgage. But if you do that, you will also be taking on a new expense in the form of monthly mortgage payments. In short, this option typically makes sense only if you're able to trade down to a much less expensive home than the one you're selling, or if you're willing to live in an apartment or rental home where the rent would be affordable given your retirement income.

A second option is to tap the equity in your home by borrowing against it. Assuming the same scenario as above, for example, you might refinance your home with a new first mortgage equal to 80 percent of your home's value, which in this case would give you $200,000 in cash. Or you could probably come away with the same amount of cash by taking out a home equity line of credit against the value of your home.

But this option also has its downsides. For one thing, some lenders may not even want to give you a mortgage if you are retired and generating no regular salary income—or if they do make the loan, they may demand a higher rate. Even if you qualify for a mortgage, you would now have monthly loan payments to worry about in addition to other expenses. A home equity line may offer more flexibility in terms of making payments. Many home equity lines, for example, allow you to make only interest payments for several years or longer or even make no payments at all. Still, all the while the loan is outstanding, the interest meter is running, and eventually you will have to begin repaying the loan. The last thing you want is to find yourself in a situation late in retirement where you're forced to sell your home because you just can't make the loan payments.

There's a third option, however, that allows you to get at your home's equity without selling the old homestead and without taking on the burden of ongoing loan payments: a reverse mortgage. Basically, a reverse mortgage is the mirror image of a conventional home loan—instead of you making payments to the bank each month, the mortgage lender makes payments to you. That payment could be in a lump sum, but most reverse mortgages are set up to provide you a credit line that you can draw against as you wish or have a specific amount sent to you each month. The amount of a reverse mortgage you qualify for depends on factors such as your age, the prevailing level of interest rates, the amount of equity you have in your home, and borrowing ceilings set by lenders. The ceilings vary depending on house values in the areas where you live, but the limit in high-cost areas under the Federal Housing Authority's Home Equity Conversion Mortgage program stood at just under

$281,000 in 2003 (although even higher limits apply in Alaska and Hawaii), while the ceiling under the Federal National Mortgage Association's HomeKeeper plan was just under $323,000. You may be able to find even higher mortgage ceilings with other lenders.

You must be at least sixty-two to take out a reverse mortgage, and the older you are, the higher the amount you can borrow given the same amount of equity in your home. With the FHA's Home Equity Conversion Mortgage, for example, a sixty-five-year-old homeowner who owns a house free and clear that's worth $200,000 could qualify for a loan of about $116,000, which could be taken in a lump sum or in payments of about $650 a month for life. A seventy-five-year-old person in the same position could qualify for a lump sum of about $132,000 and monthly payments of roughly $840.

The money you get from a reverse mortgage isn't taxed, since it isn't actually income but proceeds from a loan. You or your heirs do eventually have to repay the loan, plus interest and fees. But typically that doesn't happen until you die, sell your residence, or move out permanently (say, to enter a nursing home). Of course, since you are not making payments on the loan, the amount you owe is growing larger over time. The amount you must repay, however, can never exceed the home's value, even if home prices sag after you sign the deal or if your borrowings plus interest exceed the value of the home. Nonetheless, repaying the reverse mortgage could very well eat up all the equity in your home, leaving nothing for your heirs. If that's a problem, a reverse mortgage may not be the right move for you.

While a reverse mortgage can be a godsend for retirees who haven't accumulated enough other assets to generate sufficient income, it does have some drawbacks. For one thing, the closing costs and other fees can total many thousands of dollars, pushing up the effective interest rate in the early years of the loan. If you sell your house within a few years of taking out the loan, you would have given up a good portion of your equity in fees. So, generally, the longer you plan on remaining in your house, the better a reverse mortgage is as an option. You should also know that sifting through the terms of the various reverse mortgage plans available can be daunting. Generally, most homeowners get the largest cash advances through the FHA's Home Equity Conversion Mortgage program, although I would recommend comparing the deal offered by several lenders before making a decision.

Before you even think of talking to lenders, however, I recommend you first bone up on reverse mortgages on your own. You can start that process by going to the Reverse Mortgages section of the AARP website (www.aarp.org/revmort). Once there, you'll find plenty of material explaining how reverse mortgages work, what the various fees are, and how to compare offerings by different lenders. AARP also offers a counseling service if you're considering an FHA Home Equity Conversion Mortgage. You can reach a counselor by e-mailing your request to RMcounsel@aarp.org (include your name, state, telephone number, and the best weekday time for a counselor to call) or by calling AARP's counseling referral request line at 202-434-6082.

Strategy 6: Relocate to a Less Expensive Area

Another way to stretch the purchasing power of your retirement income is to move to an area of the country that has lower living costs than where you're now living. Admittedly, this is a somewhat radical strategy for squeezing more out of your retirement savings and resources. After all, such a move would likely entail disrupting family ties and the entire network of social relationships that typically play a central role in our lives. On the other hand, many people seem willing to at least contemplate such a change. For example, when *BusinessWeek* and America Online polled people forty-five years of age or older with incomes of $75,000 or more several years ago, 45 percent of those surveyed said they would consider moving to another region of the country after retiring. Who knows, perhaps they see relocation as a welcome bit of adventure—a chance to experience new activities and people, a move that can add an exciting new dimension to a new stage in life. Or perhaps they feel that a little distance from family members and old friends (or at least some of them) may not be such a bad thing, and that keeping in touch by telephone or through occasional visits is all the proximity they need.

In any case, if you're willing to consider making such a move, relocating can often lower your living expenses by 15 to 20 percent or even more, depending on where you're moving from and moving to. (Obviously, if you're already living in a place that's at the lower end of the range in living expenses, the potential savings from relocating are limited.) What's more, since relocating would likely involve selling your current home, you may be able to simultaneously lower your living expenses *and* trade down to a less expensive home, thus freeing up some cash that can bolster the value of your retirement portfolio and generate future income to boot.

Gauging living costs in different cities around the country is no easy task, but you can at least get a sense of how much further relocating might stretch your income by checking out the Salary Calculator at Homefair.com, a site that compares cost-of-living data from hundreds of cities around the United States. The process is simple. After clicking on the calculator, you select the state and city you now live in and then the state and city you're thinking of moving to. You then plug in your present salary or, if you're already retired, the annual income you expect to receive during retirement. The calculator then tells you how much income you would need at your new location to maintain the same standard of living you have in your present area. So, according to the Homefair site, someone living in Boston on an income of $50,000 a year would need only $38,000 or so a year to maintain a similar standard of living in Charlotte, North Carolina. Clearly, the kinds of savings you might realize will depend a lot on your particular situation. Still, if you can reap savings anywhere close to the area of 10 to 20 percent a year, you will see a major improvement in your financial circumstances during retirement.

Of course, you're not going to choose a place to live solely on the basis of living expenses. After all, retirement is a time when you want to enjoy yourself, have some fun, and do things you didn't have time for during your career. Which means if you're thinking of relocating, you'll also want to be sure you're moving to an area that has weather that suits you, plenty of recreational and cultural facilities, perhaps a college or university nearby, decent medical care, low crime, acceptable taxes, affordable housing—in short, all the things that make a town, a city, or a suburb truly livable. And if you're thinking you might want to earn a little extra income during retirement—or you want to work just to keep from getting too bored—you'll also want to find an area that's economically vibrant enough to offer employment opportunities that might interest you.

So, how do you identify such places? Well, one place to start is with the Lifestyle Optimizer, also available at the Homefair site. With this tool you can screen for cities nationally or state by state using a variety of criteria ranging from home prices to crime rates, weather, and population. You can also check out other sources for retirement places that might offer you a combination of affordable living costs and an enjoyable quality of life. The Retirement Havens website (www.retirementhavens.com), for example, offers a broad range of resources that can help you find and evaluate possible retirement spots both in the United States and abroad. And each year, for example, *Money* magazine publishes a story that lists the editors' choices for Best Retirement Places, a roundup of living spots with a variety of climates and terrains that tend to have clean air, low crime, reasonable taxes, and populations large enough to ensure a high level of recreational and cultural amenities. (You can also find this story on the CNNMoney website, money.cnn.com.) In short, by doing a little legwork you can easily come up with a short list of relocation candidates that you can then research more extensively to see if any of them is the right fit for you. Who knows, you may find you've not only managed to stretch your retirement assets but launched a new adventure that will rejuvenate you in the latter part of your life.

Strategy 7: Invest More Aggressively

Most people tend to think of this option first when they realize they're approaching retirement yet haven't accumulated as large a retirement nest egg as they'll need. Done carefully, restructuring your investment portfolio to earn a higher rate of return can significantly boost the value of your assets. For example, if you've got $100,000 saved and earn an 8 percent annual rate of return over the next ten years, your portfolio would grow to just under $216,000. If you can eke out a higher return from your portfolio—say, 10 percent instead of 8 percent—then your portfolio's value would grow to something more on the order of $259,000, letting you go into retirement with an extra $43,000. (Note that I've used *would* instead of *could*, as I did in Strategy 1. That's because we're dealing with the growth of a single sum of money—$100,000—as opposed to adding money to the portfolio over time, as was the case in Strategy 1. Of course, there's still the issue of whether or not you can actually earn the higher rate of return, which is hardly a certainty.)

I've saved this strategy for last, however, because it also carries the risk of backfiring and actually leaving you worse off than you were before. One pitfall is that many people go overboard in their quest for more attractive returns. Instead of trying to squeeze, say, 10 percent out of their portfolio rather than 8 percent (which is already a challenge), many people are more likely to shoot for something like 16 percent, figuring their $100,000 will grow to $441,000 over ten years, giving them an extra $225,000 over what they'd have with an 8 percent return. Their thinking goes like this: "Gee, if I can just be a smarter and more aggressive investor, I can make up for the savings I didn't accumulate when I was younger and create a far more comfortable retirement for myself." This kind of thinking is implicitly encouraged, in my opinion, by online retirement calculators that provide pull-down menus offering rates of return well north of 10 percent.

But such thinking can lead to disastrous results, which is why I don't believe that more-aggressive investing should be the first

strategy most people should turn to in order to build their retirement portfolio. And even in the cases where more aggressive
investing may be called for, it's a move that's got to be approached with caution and a full awareness of the risks involved.

The basic problem with the strategy of investing more
aggressively to build assets more quickly is that we can't just
choose the level of returns we earn on our investments. Yes, we
can shoot for a higher level of returns, and we can structure our
portfolio to try to achieve loftier gains. Typically, that means investing a larger portion of our savings in stocks and stock mutual funds, and even in especially volatile sectors of the stock
market, such as small-cap growth stocks and tech shares. But
there's no guarantee that tilting a portfolio toward a higher-
octane mix of investments will actually generate those higher
returns, at least not consistently over many years. There is one
thing we can be sure of, though: By investing more aggressively
we *definitely* take on more investment risk. Indeed, we actually
run the risk that we may make ourselves worse off than we
would be had we stuck to a more conservative investing plan.

To understand why that's the case, you've got to understand
a bit about the relationship between risk and reward in the investment world. Most people understand the basic premise that
the higher the reward, or return, you seek, the greater the risk
you've got to take with your investments. And many people also
understand that higher risk, in the investing world, is associ-
ated with higher volatility—that is, the more aggressive your
portfolio, the more its value will jump up and down. A portfolio
with, say, 90 percent stocks and 10 percent bonds will get hammered much more severely during market downturns than a
portfolio that is evenly mixed between stocks and bonds. And if
a good portion of that 90 percent in stocks is invested in small-
cap growth companies or tech stocks, then the value of that
portfolio will be even more prone to market setbacks.

But many people don't understand the full implications of
this volatility. The problem isn't just that your portfolio's value
will bounce around. If that were the case, then earning higher
returns would be just a matter of conditioning yourself to hold

on during downturns so that you earn higher returns over the long term. The problem is that higher volatility also introduces uncertainty about the level of return you'll actually achieve. Basically, the more volatile your mix of investments, the wider the potential range of returns you might receive. This results in a subtle sort of paradox: In shooting for higher returns, you actually open yourself up to the possibility of much *lower* returns than you would achieve by investing more conservatively. So if you invest more aggressively to raise your target level of returns from, say, 8 percent to 16 percent per year, the risk isn't just that you may fall slightly short of 16 percent. The risk is that you may fall *way* short of 16 percent. You might end up with 6 percent or 5 percent, or for that matter you could end up with losses, as did many people who jumped into tech stocks in the 1990s. By shooting for a more modest return target, however, you narrow the range of possible returns. Yes, that means less of an upside, but it also means less chance of really blowing it with subpar returns.

As a practical matter, therefore, I think you've got to be very careful about revamping your investing strategy in order to boost your returns and turbocharge the growth of your retirement assets. That's especially true late in life because you have less time to recover from setbacks in your portfolio and, unlike younger people, you probably don't have fresh savings coming into your portfolio that can help compensate for investment losses.

So if you want to boost the value of your retirement portfolio by raising your target rate of return, fine. But you've got to be realistic about it and consider the downside. Would you still be able to retire if your more aggressive stance led to a much lower rate of return than you anticipated? Would you be able to postpone retirement if your portfolio suffered a setback? If you're already retired and you intend to invest more aggressively, would you be able to scale back withdrawals from your portfolio to allow it to recover from a downturn in the market? All of these are things you should consider before taking on a more aggressive investment strategy.

And if you do decide to go ahead, proceed with caution. If I were within five to ten years of retirement, I would be extremely wary of creating an investment portfolio that would be more volatile than the aggressive model portfolio of 80 percent stocks and 20 percent bonds that appears in Chapter 6. And if I were closer to retirement or already retired, I would think hard about doing anything more aggressive than the moderate model portfolio of 65 percent stocks and 35 percent bonds. Whatever you do, don't try to boost your returns by taking big positions in specific sectors of the market, whether it's fast-growing small stocks, biotech shares, or whatever happens to be hot. The narrower your bet, the more risk you take on, and the more uncertain it is you'll hit your higher return target. Instead, if you want to take a shot at higher gains, do it by increasing your stock exposure overall while maintaining a broadly diversified group of stocks and funds, as I outline in Chapter 6. This way, you'll still have a chance at achieving higher returns. But if you fall short, at least you'll suffer less damage than you would with a less diversified portfolio.

Creativity and Resourcefulness Go a Long Way

Of course, you shouldn't feel limited to following just one of the seven strategies I've outlined above. You can try one, two, three—for that matter, mix and match as many as you think will help your situation and that you're able to pull off. But you should also feel free to develop other strategies besides the ones I've listed here. There may be any number of opportunities that present themselves if you look for them. Maybe instead of selling your present home, you'll find that you can raise some extra income by renting out a room or sharing living expenses with a friend or relative. Or perhaps as part of your relocation plan, you'll decide to buy a duplex or two-family home near a university so that you can rent space to local college students. Or maybe you'll launch a business that you can run part-time from home.

The key is to be resourceful. I wrote a story several years ago for *Money* magazine that showed that some retirees are able to get by on far less income in retirement than they had earned during their careers. In researching that article, I interviewed a man who had been a lawyer during his career days but had since retired to a small farm outside the city. He estimated that after retiring he was getting by on less than 50 percent of the income he'd required during his years as an attorney. Of course, if you aren't likely to retire to a farm and live off the fat of the land, you may think this man's story has little to do with you. But, in fact, most of his savings came not because he was able to grow his own fruits and vegetables or raise livestock. Rather, he was able to get by on much less because he streamlined and simplified his life. He spent less on eating out and fast food and eliminated his cell phone and other unnecessary expenses. And far from seeing these cutbacks as a privation, he saw them as a way to create a new, more satisfying and peaceful lifestyle.

I'm not suggesting that the answer lies in moving to the hinterlands and living like an ascetic, or in eliminating so many expenses that your golden years become a grim time of eking out a meager existence where you agonize over every expenditure. There's certainly no fun in that. Rather, when it comes to financial matters, to deciding how to spend and how to invest your money, I'm suggesting that you think broadly, think adventurously, think outside the box. If you approach your retirement finances with an intrepid spirit and the confidence to try new things, you'll be surprised at the abundance of opportunities that are there for the taking.

Chapter 8

CREATE A PERSONAL
SAFETY NET

THE RIGHT WAY TO THINK
ABOUT INSURANCE

You could be one of the most diligent savers for retirement that the world has ever known. And you could also be one of the world's savviest investors, a person whose skill at choosing investments and creating a diversified portfolio ranks up there with Wall Street's wisest and most experienced pros. But if you die, are forced to leave your job because you become disabled, or end up having to spend much of the assets you've accumulated for retirement on expensive care in a nursing home, then all your planning could be for naught. That's why insurance coverage has got to be an integral part of any reasonable retirement plan for you and your spouse.

In this chapter I'll go over three types of insurance you should consider as a component of your retirement strategy: life insurance, which pays your survivors if you die; disability insurance, which provides income if an injury or illness prevents you from working; and long-term-care insurance, which helps cover the cost of medical care in a nursing home, assisted-living facility, or even in your home. I have two goals in mind with this chapter. First, I want to outline the various options and choices you have in each of these types of insurance so that you can pick a policy that best suits your needs. Second, and equally important, I also want you to think carefully about the way you integrate insurance coverage into your financial life in general as well as in your retirement plan.

The main purpose of insurance is to provide a personal safety net of sorts, that is, to protect you from risks that could wipe you out financially or leave you or your family unable to cope with the financial aspects of life. In short, insurance helps shield you from risks that you don't have the financial resources to protect yourself from on your own. It's important to remember, however, that insurance protection itself also has a cost that affects your financial well-being. The more insurance coverage you buy, the more money you spend on premiums and the less you have available for current living expenses *and for retirement savings.* So when you're choosing insurance protection and buying a policy, you should think of it as a balancing act. You want to get enough protection so you or your survivors will be able to cope in the event something happens to you that results in a financial setback. But you don't want to overburden your budget with insurance premiums to the point where insurance costs interfere with your ability to carry out the rest of your retirement plan. The key is balancing the cost of insurance with the benefit. In some cases, particularly long-term-care insurance, that may mean forgoing the insurance entirely because the cost may simply be unaffordable for you or because there are other ways to guard against the risk of long-term health costs. So if you consider insurance in this light, I think you'll be far more likely to make better choices both in the specific policies you buy and in the types of protection you choose to buy or, as the case may be, not buy.

Life Insurance: The Foundation of Your Personal Safety Net

Life insurance is one of those things that most of us know we need but many of us never quite get around to buying. That's not surprising. After all, it's not something we're required to have, like auto insurance. And in a certain sense, paying life insurance premiums year after year may even seem like throwing money away. If you haven't died and the insurer hasn't had to pay a benefit to your beneficiaries, wouldn't you have been better off keeping the premiums and investing them in a retirement account? Throw in the fact that sifting through different types of coverage can be a daunting process that can lead to a major-league migraine, and it's not surprising that many of us put off the task of getting coverage.

The problem with procrastinating or casting about for reasons we don't really need insurance anyway is that if we depart this world without adequate coverage, we may leave behind a family that may have to deal with financial hardships and a spouse or other loved one whose retirement plans may have to be radically trimmed back. So if you don't have life insurance now, this is a good time to read on to see whether you need it and, if so, what kind. And if you do have coverage, you should take this as a chance to review your needs and see whether the policy you own fits them.

Do You Really Need Life Insurance?

The primary purpose of life insurance is to provide support for your dependents if you die prematurely. So if you're not married and don't have children, other relatives, or close friends who depend on your salary, then you probably don't need life insurance (although you may want to have a small policy to pay burial expenses, ensuring that you get a decent send-off when you die). But if you have a spouse, children, siblings, a parent, or others who rely on your salary for their living expenses, then life insurance is almost certainly a must. The idea is that when you die, the proceeds from your life insurance policy will replace enough of the income lost by your death so that your survivors can maintain something close to the standard of living they enjoyed while you were alive. If you would be leaving behind a spouse or other person who was depending on your income and assets for his or her retirement, then you want to be sure that your insurance coverage would provide enough ongoing income to allow that person to continue to save for retirement. If that person is close to retirement age, then you would want sufficient coverage to provide a large enough sum that, combined with Social Security and other pensions, would generate a reasonable retirement income.

Whether they sincerely believe it or it makes for a good sales pitch, some insurance agents and financial planners tout certain types of life insurance policies as terrific investments for building the value of your retirement nest egg. In extreme cases, they may even suggest that investing in an insurance policy is a way for you to build your own "private pension." Typically, an agent will suggest that you invest premiums of several hundred dollars a month or more into the policy, the attraction being that the earnings on the investment portion of your premium grow without the drag of taxes and, in theory, produce a tidy sum by the time you're ready to retire. And then comes the really attractive part of the pitch: you can pull out this money tax free, first by withdrawing the money you've paid in and then by borrowing against the policy's earnings via low- or no-cost loans that don't have to be repaid; they're simply deducted from the death benefit when you die.

The problem with this scenario is that it glosses over several possible pitfalls. For one, a good chunk of your initial premiums in a cash-value policy go to pay commissions and marketing fees. So if you don't stick with the policy for twenty to thirty years, you could end up with far less than if you had simply invested in a plain old mutual fund. But even if you stick it out for the long term, the cash value might not materialize as easily as it appears in the sales presentation. And that's not just because the market might not deliver the assumed returns. The insurer could raise its administrative and marketing charges or even boost the cost of the insurance protection, which would reduce the value of the policy.

Those tax-free loans could also prove problematic because borrowing could reduce the policy's cash value enough so that you would have to pay more premiums into the policy to keep it in force. If you can't afford those premiums—after all, you'll likely be retired by the time this might happen—the policy would lapse and all the loans in excess of the premiums you've paid plus any remaining cash value in the policy would become taxable. So instead of reaping tax-free income, you could be staring at a big tax bill. My advice: Buy insurance for protection against financial losses you can't absorb on your own and do your investing separately in tax-advantaged accounts such as 401(k)s and IRAs and in conventional investments such as stocks, bonds, and mutual funds.

How Much Is Enough?

You'll hear any number of rules of thumb for how much life insurance you ought to have. For example, the American Council of Life Insurers suggests you have coverage equal to five to seven times your annual earnings. But rules of thumb can be misleading. If you've paid off your mortgage, have no other debts, and have plenty of money tucked away in investments, you may be able to get by with much less than five times your salary. If you have no savings and a spouse and several kids depending on your income, seven times your salary might be inadequate.

The best way to arrive at a reasonably accurate fix on the amount of life insurance you need is to do what insurers refer to as a needs analysis—essentially a review of your income, expenses, assets, and debts with the aim of figuring out the amount of life insurance that will allow your survivors to meet their obligations and get on with their lives. To arrive at a realistic estimate, you should think hard about such issues as what type of lifestyle you would want your survivors to be able to enjoy after you're gone and what type of expectations you have for your spouse and children's future. Would your spouse be able to work while caring for the kids, and if so, how close could he or she come to replacing your income? How little would you be willing to see your survivors live on? Have you already accumulated enough retirement savings for your spouse to maintain a comfortable living standard in retirement without you? Does your spouse still have enough time to work and generate more savings, or would you need to provide a lump sum that could generate retirement income?

Once you've considered such questions, you can begin to crunch the numbers and arrive at an estimate. One way to do that is to complete the worksheet below. But I think an even better way to go is to check out one or more of the insurance needs calculators on the Web, such as the one at the life insurance sections of the TIAA-CREF site (www.tiaa-cref.org/lins/index.html) and Insurance.com (www.insurance.com). The advantage to doing this analysis online rather than on paper is that you can more easily try a variety of different scenarios using different assumptions.

How Much Life Insurance Do You Need?

Filling out the worksheet below will help you assess how much life insurance you need. If you're married, you should also have your spouse go through this exercise.

1. How much annual income will your survivors need for living expenses?

Estimate the amount of money your family would need to live on if you were to die. You can use your current budget to arrive at an estimate, but don't forget to deduct your personal expenses. You can include mortgage payments in this figure. Or you can leave out this expense if you decide to pay off your mortgage with insurance proceeds, in which case add your mortgage balance to line 4. Make sure your income estimate includes enough for a surviving spouse to save for retirement.

$_____

2. How much income will your survivors get from other sources?

Include survivors' earnings, pension benefits of yours if they'll be paid upon your death (if they're paid in a lump sum, add them to line 6), and Social Security benefits for dependent children (for an estimate, go to www.ssa. gov or call 800-772-1213).

$_____

3. Living expense shortfall.

Subtract the amount in line 2 from the amount on line 1.

$_____

4. How much money will you need to meet your survivors' income needs?

If your survivors will require income for only a short period—say, ten years or less—then you can multiply the number of years by the amount on line 3. If your survivors will require income over a longer period, however, then you'll want to estimate the amount you would need to invest to pay the annual shortfall (plus inflation) to your survivors. In that case, multiply the amount on line 3 by one of the three factors below. The conservative factor gives you the largest margin of error, the aggressive factor the smallest.

Conservative = 25   Moderate = 17   Aggressive = 13

$_____

5. Onetime expenses.

Include any obligations you'll want to pay immediately, such as funeral bills and estate settlement costs, if any. If you plan to pay off your home mortgage and other loans, include those balances here, too (if not, include the payments in line 1). Similarly, you can enter a figure for your children's college costs here, or you can estimate the amount you plan to save annually to meet that expense and add it to the other expenses in line 1.)

– $_____

6. What assets do you now own that your survivors can draw on?

Include the amounts your survivors would receive from any insurance policies you own or receive through work plus any investment assets they would receive. Do not include amounts in 401(k)s, IRAs, and assets earmarked for retirement, since a surviving spouse would be counting on these assets for retirement income. If your survivors would sell your home and trade down to a less expensive one, you can include any home equity that might be freed up in the process.

– $_____

7. Your insurance need.

Subtract the amounts in lines 5 and 6 from the amount in line 4.

$_____

As you go through this exercise, it's important to keep two things in mind. First, you may find that you simply can't afford to buy the amount of insurance recommended by a calculator or this worksheet, at least not without cutting back dramatically on your retirement savings or making other radical changes in your budget. In such cases, you'll have to scale back the amount of insurance to a level that's reasonable given your budget. Ultimately, you're better off taking on a level of coverage you can maintain rather than trying to buy too much and then having to trim your savings or let the policy lapse. You can always look into getting more coverage later on if your financial situation improves.

The second thing to remember is that for most people life insurance is a temporary need. As you accumulate more assets and savings and the kids leave home after graduating from college, the amount of income you would have to replace in the event of your death declines, as does the amount of insurance you need. By the time you're retired, you may not need any coverage at all, unless you think your heirs would need the insurance payout to cover estate taxes. (The Economic Growth and Tax Relief Reconciliation Act of 2001 raised the amount of an estate exempt from federal estate taxes to $1.5 million in 2004, a figure that climbs to $3.5 million in 2009. The tax then disappears entirely in 2010, only to resurface with a $1 million exemption amount in 2011 unless Congress extends the repeal. These limits are well above the amounts most people are likely to leave to their heirs. But given the uncertainty surrounding the future of this tax and Congress's penchant for making frequent and often contradictory changes to our tax laws, I think it's a good idea to check in with a financial planner who specializes in estate taxes if you think you may leave an estate large enough to get hit with this tax.)

What Type of Policy Is Best?

You have two basic choices. The first is term insurance, which provides bare-bones insurance protection in the form of a death benefit for a specific period of time. You pay an annual premium and your beneficiaries receive a death benefit or payout when you die. The most basic form is an annual renewable term, or ART, which in most cases guarantees that you can renew your contract each year without a medical exam. The premiums start low in ART but increase each year and can be several times their initial level later in life. People who prefer the certainty of knowing what their insurance premiums will be year to year often opt instead for a guaranteed level premium term policy, which locks in the premium for a specific period, usually ten to twenty years. At the end of that period you can usually renew, although you must pass a medical exam.

Your second choice is cash-value insurance. This comes in several different forms—whole life, universal life, and variable life, each of which works a bit differently—but what they all have in common is that they combine term insurance with an investment account that grows tax-deferred until you withdraw the money. For the vast majority of people term insurance is

225

the better way to go. And that's especially true if you're already having trouble saving enough money to fund the kind of retirement you would like to live.

The reason term is almost always the better option is because the annual premiums on term policies are substantially lower than cash-value premiums for the same amount of coverage. A forty-year-old man, for example, might pay anywhere from $300 to $600 a year for twenty years for $300,000 worth of term insurance coverage, depending on the company and his medical condition and family health history. The same amount of coverage in a cash-value policy could cost five to ten times that amount. As a practical matter, the fact that cash-value premiums are so much higher than term premiums means that most people simply can't afford to get the amount of coverage they need in a cash-value policy. And since your primary goal in buying insurance is to get as close as possible to the amount of coverage you need, term usually ends up as the only realistic option by default.

That said, there are a few situations where cash-value insurance could be the better choice. Most term policies are not renewable after a certain age, typically seventy-five or eighty-five. Cash-value policies, on the other hand, can remain in force for your entire life (which is why cash-value policies are often called permanent insurance and why the debate over whether term or cash value is the better choice is known as "term versus perm" in insurance circles). So if you want to keep a policy for the rest of your life as a way to leave a legacy for your heirs or to cover estate taxes, then you would have to buy a cash-value policy. Because cash-value policies have steep up-front costs, however, you should consider buying one only if you're sure you can keep the policy at least twenty years.

Since you'll be buying a policy for the long term, you'll want to be sure the company issuing the policy has the financial wherewithal to meet its obligations to policy holders. The best way to do that is to stick with companies that receive high financial strength grades from the three major insurance company ratings firms: A. M. Best (www.ambest.com), Standard &

Poor's (www.standardandpoors.com), and Moody's Investors Service (www.moodys.com). This is particularly important these days, as many insurers' portfolios are still recovering from the double whammy of losses they took in the stock market in recent years and in the bonds of companies such as Enron, Global Crossing, and WorldCom. The three ratings firms don't all employ the same rating scale, but you should try to limit yourself to insurers that receive ratings that fall at or near the top of the scales of the three firms. You can find ratings for specific insurers at each firm's website.

What's the Best Way to Buy a Policy?

If you decide on term coverage, you can start your search at one of the online insurance websites that offer dozens of quotes on various types of term policies. Among those you might try are AccuQuote (www.accuquote.com), Insure.com (www.insure.com), InstantQuote.com (www.instantquote.com), Insweb (www.insweb.com), and SelectQuote (www.selectquote.com). These services will certainly provide you with quotes from a broad range of companies, but just to be sure you're getting competitive prices, you may also want to get quotes from a few companies that have reputations as low-cost policy providers, such as Ameritas Life Insurance (www.ameritasdirect.com; 800-555-4655) and USAA (www.usaa.com; 800-365-8722. USAA caters primarily to members of the armed forces and their families, but the company's life insurance policies are available to the general public).

Be careful, though: the lowest quotes apply only to people who meet strict underwriting standards. If you're even slightly overweight, use tobacco, have even a relatively minor health problem, or have a family history of premature death due to heart disease or cancer, your premium can be significantly higher than the low quote you'll see on the screen.

If you feel you want more guidance in choosing a policy, then you'll have to work with an insurance agent or financial adviser who sells insurance. Remember, though, that there's a powerful incentive for agents to recommend cash-value coverage since the premiums, and thus the commissions, are much higher than for comparable amounts of term coverage. Ideally, you'll want to deal with an agent who has several years of experience and has completed the training necessary to attain the relevant professional credentials, such as a C.L.U. (Chartered Life Underwriter), C.F.P. (Certified Financial Planner), or Ch.F.C. (Chartered Financial Consultant). For help in finding such an adviser in your area, check the websites of such organizations as the Society of Financial Professionals (www.financial pro.org) and the Financial Planning Association (www.fpanet. org).

If you decide a cash-value policy is right for you, you may be able to save money on commissions by buying what's known as a low-load policy—that is, one with lower commission and marketing fees. These policies are usually sold through advisers who, rather than collecting commissions, charge a fee for their services. You can find out more about low-load policies by contacting the Fee Planners Network (www.feeplannersnetwork. com), Low Load Insurance Services (www.llis.com), and the National Association of Personal Financial Advisors (www.napfa. org), which is an organization of financial planners who accept only fees and not commissions for their work. Before you buy any policy, you may also want to check out the policy evaluation service offered by the Consumer Federation of America (www.consumerfed.org). The service will calculate a cash-value policy's rate of return and provide other information to help you evaluate the policy. The cost is $55 for one policy and $40 for a second policy submitted at the same time ($65 and $40 for variable policies).

Disability Insurance: Protecting Your Earning Power

While we may not like to think about it, the possibility of dying prematurely is a risk that most of us are at least well aware of. But there's a risk we tend to overlook that has an even greater chance of wreaking havoc with our finances and our retirement planning: the risk of losing our income for an extended period due to a disability. Indeed, Northwestern Mutual Insurance estimates that a thirty-year-old man has about a 25 percent chance of becoming disabled for ninety days or longer before age sixty-five, while the odds for a thirty-year-old woman are 31 percent. (If you'd like to calculate the odds based on your age and sex, check out the What Are the Odds? calculator at the Northwestern Mutual website, www.northwesternmutual.com.)

Disability insurance can protect you against this risk. Essentially, disability policies replace anywhere from 50 to 80 percent of your income if an illness, injury, or other condition seriously disrupts your earning ability. (Insurers typically won't write policies to replace more than 80 percent of your income because they don't want you to have an incentive to just sit around collecting benefits instead of going back to work.) But this coverage can be expensive. Annual premiums on disability policies typically run in the neighborhood of 2 to 5 percent of your income, which means that someone earning $50,000 a year might pay $1,000 to $2,500 a year and possibly more, depending on the policy's specific benefits. When you shop for a policy, you want to come away with a sufficient amount of coverage so that a long-term disruption in your career won't wipe you out financially and ruin your retirement prospects. But you don't want such so much coverage that paying the premiums prevents you from carrying out the rest of your retirement plan. Here's a rundown of the various questions and issues you should weigh when considering this coverage.

How Much Disability Coverage Do I Need?

As a rule of thumb, people buy a policy that would pay between 50 and 67 percent of their current salary. But the appropriate figure can vary widely depending on such factors as your age, your living expenses, what kind of assets you may be able to rely on in the event of a long absence from work due to disability, and whether there's someone else in your household who could step up to replace a significant share of your income. To get a better sense of how much coverage is right for you, I suggest you check out an online disability income calculator, such as the one at the website of the Life and Health Insurance Foundation for Education (www.life-line.org). This organization isn't exactly disinterested when it comes to disability insurance; it was formed, after all, by seven insurance groups representing about 160,000 insurance agents. But the calculator itself seems to be pretty straightforward and if nothing else is a good way to get an idea of how much, if any, disability insurance you need.

Do I Need This Coverage if I Get It at Work?

About 40 percent of people who work at companies with one hundred or more employees receive or have access to disability coverage at work, while for those who work at smaller companies about half that percentage get coverage. So there's a chance you may already have this coverage as an employee benefit. Employers don't typically pick up the full cost of the coverage. But even when they don't, it usually pays to sign up for this insurance if your employer offers it. The reason is that the premiums on individual policies can be five times or more what you'll pay on a group plan.

Even if you do get the coverage through your employer, it may not be enough or may have limitations you should be aware of. Some companies cap benefits at 50 percent of salary—usually salary before commissions and bonuses—although many firms will let you buy additional coverage. Keep in mind, too, that if your employer pays the premiums, the benefits from your policy are taxable. If you make the premium payments, the benefits are tax free. So you'll want to check with your human resources or personnel department to get the specifics on your coverage. Only then can you determine whether what you're getting through work is adequate. If you decide it's not, you may want to buy additional coverage on your own. Be prepared to take a medical exam to show that you're insurable.

What Kind of Disability Is Needed to Trigger Benefits?

Some policies—known as "own occupation" or "own occ" policies—will pay benefits if you're unable to perform the duties of your normal occupation. Others will pay only if you have a disability that prevents you from doing any work at all. "Own occ" policies are harder to come by and cost more because the insurer is taking a bigger risk that if you can't return to your regular job you won't take another for less pay. If, on the other hand, you have a policy that requires you to work at another job if you're able but pays residual benefits, then you have the option of returning to work in some capacity and receiving benefits to make up for the difference in income between your old job and the new one. One more thing: in the event you're able to return to your job but can work only reduced hours for a period of time—which is quite common for people recovering from severe illnesses or injuries—some policies pay partial benefits.

How Long Must I Be Disabled Before Benefits Kick In?

That's up to you, since most policies allow you to choose a waiting period of as little as sixty days or as long as a year before you begin receiving payments. (Actually, you should add thirty days to whatever waiting period you choose, since your first check won't arrive until thirty days after the waiting period expires.) The shorter the waiting period, the higher the premium on the policy, which makes sense since a shorter waiting period increases the odds you'll collect on the policy. While that may seem like a good reason for choosing a short waiting period, you're probably better off choosing a longer period, say, six months or more. Yes, that means you won't collect on your policy if you have short periods of disability. But the point of this coverage isn't to protect you from short absences from work. Rather, it's to protect you against the much more serious risk that a prolonged episode of illness or disability will undermine your financial security and possibly wipe out your retirement savings as well. Choosing a long waiting period will allow you to lower your premium—thus freeing up more money for retirement saving—while still protecting you against the potentially devastating consequence of a long-term disability.

How Long Can I Collect Benefits?

Here again, the choice is yours. Most companies let you choose to collect benefits for a specific number of years, such as two, five, or ten. Or you can opt to have benefits paid to age sixty-five, sixty-seven, or the rest of your life. As with a waiting period, longer is generally better because you should primarily look to protect yourself against long-term disruptions in your earning power. Since lifetime payments can be prohibitively expensive, however, most people choose to receive benefits until they begin collecting Social Security, which at this point is sixty-five or sixty-seven depending on when you were born.

How Do I Go About Getting Coverage?

You can certainly bone up on disability coverage on the Web and even apply for policy quotes at sites such as Disability Income.com (www.disabilityincome.com), Low Load Insurance Services (www.llis.com), and 4 Disability Insurance Quotes (www.4-disability-insurance-quotes.com), just to get an idea of what coverage might cost you. But given the complexity of this type of insurance and the variety of different issues that must be weighed even beyond the ones I've raised here, I think it makes sense to consult an adviser who not only is familiar with disability coverage but also understands how this coverage ought to fit in a retirement-planning strategy. In short, look for someone who can help you settle on a policy that provides a prudent level of protection against a major disruption in your earning power without jeopardizing your retirement savings strategy. For that kind of help, I recommend you get referrals from an organization of financial planners, such as the Society of Financial Professionals (www.financialpro.org), the Financial Planning Association (www.fpanet.org), or the National Association of Personal Financial Advisors (www.napfa.org).

Long-Term-Care Insurance:
Protecting Your Nest Egg in Retirement

Of the three types of insurance discussed in this chapter, long-term-care insurance is often the trickiest when it comes to deciding whether you really need it and, if so, what policy is appropriate. You'll come across plenty of statistics suggesting that the odds are very high that a prolonged illness during retirement or a stay in a nursing home late in life could wipe out your retirement nest egg and leave you unable to pay for care you desperately need. But as convincing a case as some of these stats may make for the need for long-term-care insurance, they may not make the case that *you* in particular ought to have this coverage. What's more, these policies can be very expensive and thus represent a significant drain on income and assets that otherwise could be used to build your retirement nest egg.

In the remaining pages of this chapter, I'll describe what this insurance is designed to cover and then outline the main factors you must consider to determine whether or not you should buy it. If you decide long-term-care insurance might be appropriate for you, you can then move on to the section that discusses the various features and options you may want to consider in a policy and gives advice on how to shop for a policy. Although only a relative handful of companies offer long-term-care insurance to their employees these days, it's worthwhile to check with your employer to see whether or not you receive such coverage or have the option of buying it through your employer. If your employer does over such coverage, that doesn't mean the policy is adequate for your needs. You'll have a better sense of whether that coverage is appropriate, however, after reading the rest of this chapter.

What Is Long-Term-Care Insurance Designed to Cover?

Basically, these policies are meant to cover the cost of an extended stay in a nursing home or assisted-living facility, care in an adult day care center, and even care and treatment in your own home. The best policies should cover not just skilled medical care that you would receive from a doctor, a nurse, or another medical practitioner but also the cost of assistance with daily activities you might have difficulty performing on your own if you become chronically ill, disabled, or mentally incapacitated because of a disease such as Alzheimer's. Indeed, in order to receive benefits from most policies, you must usually show that you are unable to perform at least two of a group of five or six activities of daily living, which typically include personal care and grooming activities such as eating, bathing, toileting, being able to get in and out of bed, and dressing yourself.

What Are the Chances I'll Require Long-Term Care?

You'll see all sorts of frightening statistics suggesting a high probability you'll need long-term care at some point as you grow old. One commonly cited stat based on a 1991 study of nursing home admissions published in the *New England Journal of Medicine* claims that you face roughly a one in two chance of entering a nursing home. Some experts put the odds at 55 to 65 percent that the elderly will require some form of long-term care.

But these stats need some qualification. The study published in the *New England Journal of Medicine* included short stays of just a few days or weeks as well as long-term stays in nursing homes. In fact, the study found that just over 20 percent of sixty-five-year-olds would spend a year or more in a nursing home, and less than 10 percent would spend five years or more. Obviously that's still a considerable risk but hardly a given that you'll require such care. It's also important to remember that figures in such studies are averages based on large groups of people. Your chances of having an extended stay in a nursing home or requiring long-term assistance at home will depend on your particular circumstances, ranging from your sex (women have higher odds than men) to how much exercise you get and how well you take care of yourself now, how active and engaged in life you'll be after retirement, and your family history of afflictions such as heart disease and dementia. So you'll want to take a dispassionate look at your own personal circumstances—ideally in consultation with your doctor—to see where you fall on the spectrum from a relatively small to a relatively high risk of needing expensive long-term care.

What's the Cost of Long-Term Care?

There's little doubt that an extended stay in a nursing home or similar facility or even prolonged care in your home can take a substantial chunk of your retirement savings, if it doesn't eat through them entirely. Recently, the average cost of a nursing home was upward of $56,000 a year, or a bit over $150 a day, although that cost can vary widely depending on where you live. In New York State, for example, daily rates can easily run 60 percent higher than that figure. And the cost of having a health care aide come to your home can be anywhere from $12 to $24 an hour, again depending on where you live and the type of care you require.

These figures, of course, are in today's dollars. Which means that, even assuming relatively modest inflation in the years ahead, people in their early fifties could be looking at annual costs two to three times higher than these figures, if not more, by the time they're in their eighties, when the odds are highest they'll be facing such costs.

Again, though, the toll such figures might take can vary tremendously depending on your particular situation. If you end up staying in a nursing home only briefly or require home care for only a short time, then the cost of yearlong stays will overstate the long-term-care costs you'll incur. On the other hand, if your family has a history of chronic illnesses and you end up spending several years in a facility that provides long-term medical care or assisted living, then the total cost could easily be in the high six or even seven figures.

Options for Meeting Long-Term-Care Expenses

Even if you believe it's likely you'll require expensive long-term care after you retire, it's not a given that you should buy a long-term care policy. Indeed, for many people who will need long-term care, buying a long-term-care policy would be a waste of money. Here's a quick rundown on your four basic options for dealing with this potential expense: relying on Medicare and then Medicaid, creating your own health care fund, paying for care from your retirement assets, and buying a long-term-care policy.

Medicare/Medicaid. Despite its major overhaul in 2003, Medicare, the government's health insurance program for people sixty-five and over (as well as certain disabled persons), still does not cover long-term care per se. It will, however, cover a portion of the first one hundred days of a nursing home stay, provided you meet certain conditions. You must have been hospitalized for at least three days before being admitted to the nursing home, and a doctor must say you require a skilled nursing or rehabilitation staff to manage, observe, and evaluate your care. Medicare does not pay for custodial care, which is nonskilled, personal care, such as helping you with activities like bathing, dressing, and eating. In some cases Medicare may also pay for skilled home care after you've been hospitalized. For details of the types of care Medicare will pay for and the conditions that apply, check out the government's official Medicare site at www.medicare.gov.

Once your Medicare benefits run out, Medicaid, the joint federal-state health insurance program for people with low incomes, will pay for long-term care. But Medicaid coverage kicks in only after you've run through most of your assets. Medicaid does allow you to hold on to certain assets, such as your primary residence and a car, but the amount of assets you're allowed to keep as well as income qualifications for Medicaid benefits vary by state. (For details on eligibility requirements for Medicaid, check out the Centers for Medicare & Medicaid Services site at cms.hhs.gov.) It's also possible to maintain your eligibility for Medicaid yet still keep assets in the family by gifting certain assets to family members or setting up trusts. This is a complicated process, however, so you should probably consult an elder-care attorney familiar with the ins and outs of Medicare and Medicaid before attempting to restructure your finances in an effort to remain eligible for Medicaid while shielding assets.

Given the dynamics of these government programs, many financial advisers recommend that you forget about long-term-care insurance unless you own investments and other assets (excluding your home) worth at least $100,000. If your assets are worth less than that amount, it's unlikely you can afford long-term-care premiums. And if it turns out you require long-term care, you're probably better off just running through whatever assets you have and then letting Medicaid pick up the tab.

On the other hand, if you have substantial investments and assets besides your home—say, in the neighborhood of $2 million or more—then you may be able to pay for long-term care by drawing on the value of your assets rather than spending premiums on a long-term-care policy (although you certainly want to be sure that your assets could generate enough income for needs beyond long-term-care expenses, especially if you have a spouse who'll also be depending on those assets).

Generally, though, it's the people in between these two extremes—assets too substantial to allow them to quickly qualify for Medicaid yet not substantial enough to pay the tab of long-term care for an extended period—who are the main candidates for long-term-care insurance.

Insure yourself. Another option is, in effect, to create your own long-term-care reserve by saving and investing today to meet potential long-term-care expenses in the future. The advantage to this approach is that if you don't end up incurring long-term-care costs or if those costs are relatively minor, then you haven't spent money on an insurance policy you didn't use and you still have use of the money you put away, plus any earnings it's generated.

The downside to this approach is that you would have to sock away quite a bit of money in order to cover even a year's stay in a nursing home. Let's say, for example, that a one-year

stint in a nursing home will cost $150,000 by the time you're re-
tired. Assuming you earn an 8 percent rate of return and begin
investing money each month starting now, you would have to
put aside roughly $265 a month for twenty years to fund just
one year's care and double that to pay for two years of care. And
that's on top of the regular savings you would have to accumulate for retirement. For most of us, this isn't a realistic option
and certainly not a good one if your family history suggests you
could spend considerable time in a nursing home.

Rely on your retirement savings and other assets. You may also be
able to pay for long-term care by spending down the mutual
funds, stocks, bonds, and other assets you have accumulated for
retirement. Another possible source of revenue is tapping into
the value of your home equity by selling your home or by taking
out a home equity line of credit or a reverse mortgage. (For
more on these options, see Chapter 7.)

But if you have a spouse or other family members who are
also relying on these assets, then spending your retirement assets on long-term care might not be a viable option. So before
you count on your nest egg or other assets you've accumulated
as a possible source of funds for long-term care, think through
how drawing down those assets will affect others in your family
and whether you would have enough money left to support you
(and a home to return to) if you recover enough to leave the
nursing home.

Buying a long-term-care policy. The final option, of course, is buying a long-term-care policy that will help pay for the cost of a
nursing home or other medical and custodial care. If you go
this route, however, you must be able to afford the premiums,
which can get quite pricey. For example, the annual premium
for a fifty-year-old man looking for a policy that would pay up to
$150 a day for long-term care for as long as five years could
easily run $1,300 to $1,600 a year or more, depending on the
insurer and what specific policy features are chosen. Premiums
for the same policy are higher if you buy at a later age. A seventy-

year-old, for example, might pay three times that amount for the same coverage.

You may hear language that suggests your premium cannot be raised. That's true in the sense that the insurer can't single you out individually for a rate increase. But insurers have the right to increase rates for an entire class of policy holders. So before you buy, consider whether you can afford to make current, and possibly higher, premium payments over many years. If you can't do that, then the policy will lapse and you'll have paid for protection that won't be there later in life, when you're most likely to need it.

What to Look for in a Policy

There are a variety of options you must consider if you're thinking of buying a long-term-care policy. Here's a rundown on some of the most important ones.

A reasonable daily benefit. You can find policies that will pay as little as $50 a day in benefits. That may be okay if you live in a very low-cost area and you have other resources you can fall back on. But if you'll be depending primarily on the policy to pay for care, you'll probably need a benefit in the $100- to $150-a-day range, and even more in high-cost areas. To gauge the daily benefit that's right for you, figure out roughly what you would have to spend for nursing home or similar care in your area and then subtract what you can afford to pay from your own assets. The amount left over is what you'll need a long-term-care policy to cover. (For a rough idea of nursing home costs in your state, check out the Needs Analysis section of the Long-Term Care Quote site at www.ltcq.net.) You'll also want to ensure that the benefit can be used to pay for a wide variety of services and for care you receive not just at a nursing home or assisted-living facility but also at home.

Duration of coverage. Most policies will pay benefits for one to six years or for your lifetime, whichever you choose. The longer the period, the higher the premium. In general, you want to pick the longest period you can afford, especially if you have a family history of Alzheimer's or other condition requiring years of care.

Elimination period. This is insurance jargon for how many days you must wait before your coverage kicks in. This period can typically range from 0 to 365 days. Most people choose a period of 90 to 100 days, but going with a longer waiting period can be a good way to lower your premium while maintaining coverage in other areas. Some policies require you to meet the waiting period only once, while others reset the waiting-period clock each time you receive benefits under the policy.

Inflation protection. Most policies allow you to increase the daily benefit level so it will cover the higher cost of care in the future. This feature increases your premium, but there's not much point in buying this coverage if the benefit will be whittled down to nothing by inflation when you need it. You usually have two choices: a 5 percent compounded inflation option or a 5 percent simple inflation option. The difference between these two options is significant. With the 5 percent compounded feature, a $150 benefit would increase to just under $400 after ten years. That's because not only is the benefit itself being increased by 5 percent annually, but each year's rise is also being increased by 5 percent, much the same as compound interest. The 5 percent simple feature, on the other hand, provides for a 5 percent per year increase times the number of years the policy has been in effect. Thus, at the end of twenty years the 5 percent simple option would boost a $150 daily benefit by 100 percent, or $150, bringing it to $300, or 25 percent less than the 5 percent compounded option. The younger you are when you buy the policy, the more you need the compounded option. If you're over sixty-five when you buy a policy, however, then the 5 percent simple option would likely provide enough protection.

Tax considerations. Long-term-care policies fall into two categories: tax-qualified and non-tax-qualified. With a tax-qualified policy—the version most people opt for—part of your premium is considered an unreimbursed medical expense, which can be a tax-deductible expense if your total unreimbursed medical expenses are greater than 7.5 percent of your adjusted gross income. (The portion of your premium that qualifies for this tax benefit depends on your age and inflation. The older you are, the bigger the deduction. Of course, if you don't itemize deductions, you can't claim the deduction.) Payouts from tax-qualified policies are tax free up to a federally mandated ceiling, which was $220 per day in 2003. Amounts above the ceiling may also be tax free if you can demonstrate the money was used to pay bona fide long-term-care expenses.

Tax-qualified policies usually have more restrictive triggers than nonqualified policies before benefits can be paid. For example, you must need "substantial assistance" with two activities of daily living, and a medical professional must certify you'll need care for at least ninety days.

It's typically easier to collect benefits under a nonqualified policy—you may be able to collect if you cannot perform just one activity of daily living—but the premiums aren't tax deductible, nor are the policy payments tax free. In light of this different treatment, you should weigh the advantage of the benefits in a nonqualified policy being easier to collect versus the disadvantage of the tax treatment of these policies. It's possible that the government may give nonqualified policies the same tax advantages as qualified ones in the future, but that's hardly certain. As a result, some policies may contain a provision allowing you to switch your nonqualified policy for a qualified one if your benefits are treated as taxable income.

When to Buy a Policy

If you've decided you need long-term coverage, the best time to buy is usually when you're in your fifties or sixties. Premiums are lower if you buy earlier than that, but other obligations such as paying off the house, sending the kids to college, and saving for retirement are probably soaking up the bulk of your disposable income. Postponing the decision to buy to an even older age would seem to make sense in that you'll have cut down the period during which you'll be shelling out premiums. But premiums rise steeply with age, so waiting may make the coverage unaffordable, plus an insurer might reject you on medical grounds. Whenever you decide to buy, however, be sure you'll be able to handle the premium payments in the long term. The last thing you want to do is pay premiums for many years and end up dropping the policy just about the time when you're most likely to need it.

How to Buy a Policy

As with disability insurance, I think the issues involved in choosing a long-term-care policy are complex (and confusing) enough that it pays to sit down with an adviser who knows the intricacies of these policies and how they relate to your particular situation. But again, as with disability, I think it's important that the adviser not be someone who is solely a long-term-care expert. Rather, you want counsel from someone who realizes that a long-term-care policy must fit in as part of an overall retirement plan—someone who can help you make the trade-off between the need for sufficient coverage and the need to meet your current financial obligations, including saving for retirement. To find such an adviser, I recommend you start with the sources I listed earlier in the section on disability insurance.

That said, it doesn't hurt for you to do some preliminary legwork on your own. A number of sites, including Mr. Long-Term Care (www.mrltc.com), ElderWeb (www.elderweb.com), and AARP (www.aarp.org), provide some good detailed information about the various issues surrounding long-term care—Medicare, Medicaid, tax considerations—as well as details on how long-term-care policies work. To get an idea of the cost of specific policies, you can even check out a few sites that offer online quotes. At Long-Term Care Quote (www.ltcq.net), for example, you can do a needs analysis that can help you determine what size benefit you'll need, then fill out a brief questionnaire that immediately yields quotes and details on the policy benefits from several companies. What's more, by clicking on the Design Your Own Policy button, you can see how changing various policy features—raising or lowering the daily benefit, increasing or decreasing the waiting period, and so on—affects your premium. That's not to say you can get coverage for the premiums you see quoted. Ultimately, the rate you pay will depend on the insurer's assessment of your health, your family's medical history, and factors such as what prescription drugs you may be taking. But at least you'll have a good idea of the general cost of coverage and how that cost can vary depending on the features you choose and the company selling the policy.

Chapter 9

PLAN YOUR EXIT STRATEGY

You've saved diligently and invested wisely. You've maxed out on every tax-advantaged retirement savings plan known to man and you've built a tidy retirement nest egg. In short, you've reached the end of the yellow brick road of retirement planning. The hard work, at least from a financial point of view, is pretty much over. Now it's just a matter of relaxing and living off the assets you worked so hard to accumulate. What could be simpler?

Not so fast. Yes, one phase of retirement planning has pretty much come to an end—the accumulation stage—but that's only half the equation. The other half is the drawdown phase, during which your goal is to tap your assets in such a way that you don't run out of money before you run out of time. For most of us, this is the part of retirement planning we think about the least and do virtually no advance planning for. Which is kind of ironic because in many ways the drawdown phase can be even more of a challenge than the accumulation stage. The main reason is that you've got a lot less wiggle room than when you're saving for retirement. Think about it. While you're building your nest egg, you've got plenty of time and opportunity to make up for mistakes or market setbacks. You can increase the amount you save, you can invest more aggressively, and, of course, you've got time on your side. You know that if you hang in long enough, rising stock prices can make up for bear market setbacks or lousy returns from poor investments.

But once you've retired and you start pulling money out of your portfolio, there's much less room for error. If the value of your portfolio sinks, you're not likely to have new savings that you can pour in to shore it up. And time is no longer your ally, at least not as much as it was when you were in your thirties or forties. To put it bluntly, your margin of error when managing your money during retirement is much smaller than during the accumulation stage. So you've got to be especially careful about the strategy you set and the specific decisions you make to carry out that strategy.

In this chapter, we're going to take a look at the various options and strategies you have for transforming your retirement stash into an income that will support you for the rest of your life. As in the accumulation stage of retirement planning, there's no single strategy that works best for everyone. The approach you take will depend on such factors as how much money you've accumulated, how much income you need to draw from your assets to live on, how much of that sum will come from Social Security and other pensions, how much you plan on leaving to your heirs (deserving and undeserving), your estimate of how long you'll live, and how concerned you are about outliving your money. As if that's not enough, you'll also have to deal with issues such as deciding whether to tap assets in 401(k)s, IRAs, and other tax-advantaged accounts or in taxable accounts first. And, of course, there are the government's required minimum distribution rules (or RMDs, as they're known in benefit circles), which whack you with onerous fines if you fail to withdraw certain amounts from your IRA and other savings plans by a certain age.

There are a lot of variables here, and I'll be the first to admit that things can get complicated in a hurry. But not to worry. The drawdown phase is entirely manageable if you're willing to set a thoughtful strategy, monitor it, and make appropriate adjustments along the way. And after reading this chapter you should have a good foundation for creating a sound strategy for this phase of retirement.

One more thing before we get into the nuts and bolts of this chapter. If you're under age fifty and retirement still seems more like a far-off mirage than a looming reality, you might be tempted to blow this chapter off. I mean, why worry about converting assets to income when your main focus is still trying to accumulate assets and invest them for the future? First things first, right? Think again. Fact is, the accumulation and withdrawal phases of retirement planning are inextricably linked. The sooner you come to grips with the fact that living off retirement savings for a span of three decades or more may be more difficult and require a larger stash than you think, the more incentive you'll have to save now. If nothing else, I hope that reading this chapter will give you a more realistic sense of just how much money you need to support a retirement that can easily stretch for thirty years or more. It's a rude awakening on the eve of retirement to find that the 401(k) balance that seemed so huge—$500,000—won't go nearly as far in retirement as you might suppose. Better to come to that realization well *before* you retire, so you still have a chance to increase the size of your nest egg, not to mention the odds of it supporting you through retirement.

Can You Say "Longevity Risk"?

When we're accumulating money for retirement, most of us are aware that we're taking on investment risk, that is, exposing ourselves to the possibility that our stocks, stock funds, bonds, bond funds, and other investments might lose value rather than grow. During the late 1990s a lot of us began to overlook this risk as stock prices seemed to march inexorably upward. But the bear market that decimated stock prices in early 2000 reminded us that when it comes to investing, risk and reward are inseparable, and the higher the reward you shoot for, the more risk you've got to accept.

What many of us don't know, however, is that there's an additional dimension to risk when we enter the drawdown phase of retiremement planning: longevity risk. Basically, this is the all-too-real possibility that we'll outlive our money. In other words, after all our careful saving and investing, we may run through our retirement stash before we pass into the great beyond, leaving us to live out our golden years in a less than golden fashion. And even if we're aware enough to consider this risk, chances are we greatly underestimate it, much as we misjudged investing risk in the 1990s. Unfortunately, the consequences of overlooking or underestimating longevity risk can be as bad, if not worse, than the consequences many investors suffered from overlooking investing risk in the previous decade.

One of the reasons we either disregard or miscalculate the seriousness of longevity risk is that few of us have a real understanding of life expectancy statistics. So we tend to underestimate just how long our retirement portfolio is going to have to support us. And if your portfolio will be supporting you and another person—a spouse, a friend, a partner, whatever—then it's got to last even longer. One of the peculiarities about the actuarial calculations surrounding life expectancy calculations is that the odds of at least one member of a couple being alive at some point in the future are higher than the odds of either member of the couple alone. For example, while the odds of a sixty-five-year-old man living to age ninety are 30 percent and the odds of a sixty-five-year-old woman living to ninety are 41 percent, the odds that at least one member of a male-female couple both age sixty-five today will be around at age ninety are nearly 60 percent. All of which is to say that unless you know you've got a fatal condition or you're certain you're genetically programmed for a relatively short life, your assets have probably got to last you a good twenty-five to thirty-five years, possibly more, after you retire.

This has some profound implications on a practical level. At the very least, for example, it means that we've got to take care to factor inflation into our withdrawal strategy. Let's say, for example, you figure you'll need to withdraw $40,000 a year from your portfolio so that, combined with Social Security and any other pensions, you'll have enough money to meet your living expenses in retirement. But if you continue to withdraw just $40,000 year after year from your portfolio, you will eventually lose substantial purchasing power. Assuming economists don't find a way to do away with inflation, prices of goods and services will rise over time, so you won't be able to buy for $40,000 at age eighty-five what you were able to get at age sixty-five, and you won't be able to get at age ninety-five what you could get at age eighty-five. In other words, just to be able to buy the same level of goods and services, you will have to increase the amount you withdraw from your portfolio each year.

The amount of increase you need to stay even will depend, of course, on the rate of inflation. But even at modest levels of inflation, I think most people would be surprised at how much their withdrawals would have to increase. For example, if you begin withdrawing $40,000 a year from your portfolio at age sixty-five and inflation averaged just 2 percent a year—which is lower than the average of 3 percent or so we've experienced since the 1920s—then by age eighty-five your withdrawals would need to be just over $59,000 just for you to stay even. And by ninety-five, you would need to withdraw more than $72,000. If, on the other hand, inflation came in at its historical 3 percent average, then your annual withdrawal would have to total more than $72,000 at eighty-five and just over $97,000 by age ninety-five, or more than twice as much as your original forty grand. Clearly, increased longevity puts a strain on the assets in your portfolio.

Beware the Average Solution

Despite this harsh reality, many of us still seem to have this unrealistic notion that our retirement portfolio is a bottomless pot we can dip into for relatively large sums of money year after year for spans of thirty years or more. I suspect that one of the reasons for this is that the relatively high average returns we've had in financial assets over the past two decades give us an inflated notion of what kind of withdrawals our portfolio can sustain without running dry. But basing a withdrawal strategy on average returns can be dangerous.

To get an idea of just how dangerous, let's look at an example. Assume you've retired at age sixty-five with a $500,000 portfolio, 60 percent of which is invested in large-company stocks like those in the Standard & Poor's 500 index and 40 percent in intermediate-term government bonds. And let's further assume you want your retirement portfolio to support you at least thirty years, or until you're ninety-five. Considering that even after the bear market that began in early 2000 large-company stocks delivered an annualized return of more than 12 percent for the twenty years through 2002, that intermediate-term bonds returned roughly 9 percent, and that inflation averaged about 3 percent, you might assume that you could easily withdraw, say, 8 percent, or $40,000, from your portfolio and increase that amount for inflation each year without having to worry about running out of money.

But as the chart on page 250 shows, if you had embarked on exactly this strategy at the end of 1972, you would have run out of money in *less than ten years,* or before you hit age seventy-four. In fact, even if you lowered your withdrawal to what some people might consider a stingy rate of just 5 percent—an initial withdrawal of just $25,000—the money runs out in just under twenty-one years. In other words, your bank account will be empty just about the time when there's almost a 50 percent chance you'll still be alive and kicking for years to come.

How is it possible that an inflation-adjusted withdrawal rate even as small as 5 percent could fail so spectacularly? Well, the problem was a little thing known as the 1973–1974 bear market, which knocked the stock market for a 43 percent loss very early on in this example. That big loss in combination with the inflation-adjusted withdrawals put such a big dent in the portfolio that it wasn't able to recover in time to participate in the bull market that began in August 1982. The moral: Basing your withdrawals on average returns can be misleading. When you're

IT'S EASIER TO RUN OUT OF MONEY THAN YOU THINK

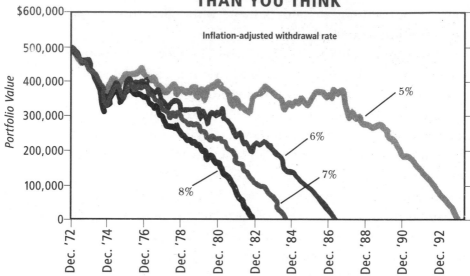

pulling money out of your portfolio, it's the combination of those withdrawals and the actual year-by-year returns, not the average return the portfolio earns over any period, that determines how long your portfolio will last. The big danger is that if you run into a period of lousy returns or an outright market downturn early in retirement, you could lose so much capital that your portfolio can be depleted much more quickly than you expect.

Keep It Real

So how do you set a withdrawal rate that can give you reasonable assurance that your money will last as long as you do? The single most effective thing you can do is to start out with a low withdrawal rate, probably something on the order of 4 percent. Now, that may seem awfully low, but let me be clear about what I mean. I'm talking about an initial draw of 4 percent of the value of your portfolio and then increasing that amount every year for a cost-of-living increase or inflation. So, for example, let's say you have $500,000 in retirement savings. If you set a

4 percent withdrawal rate, that would mean starting with a $20,000 withdrawal from your portfolio the first year. In subsequent years, you would increase this $20,000 to maintain your standard of living. You could do that by increasing the $20,000 by the previous year's rate of inflation, that is, the change in the consumer price index (CPI), which is widely reported in the consumer press or available at the Bureau of Labor Statistics website (www.bls.gov). Or you could set a reasonable inflation estimate, say, 3 percent, and increase your initial withdrawal amount by that percentage each year. If you find inflation is trending higher or lower than your estimate, you can make appropriate adjustments. Thus, if you started with a $20,000 withdrawal and increased that amount by 3 percent annually, your withdrawal would grow to $20,600 the second year, $21,218 the third, and so on, rising to just under $27,000 at the end of ten years.

Of course, an initial withdrawal rate of 4 percent might not give you as much income from your investments as you want or need. I'm sure most people would expect to be able to get more than $20,000 a year out of a $500,000 portfolio. (And I'm talking pretax dollars for the purposes of these examples. You would have to withdraw more than $20,000 to end up with $20,000 in spending money after taxes.) You've got to remember, though, that the higher you set your withdrawal rate, the greater the chances are that you will run out of money over the course of retirement. Tilting your portfolio mix toward stocks can somewhat lower the odds of running out of money because stocks have a good shot at raising your portfolio's return.

But as the chart on page 252 shows, increasing the percentage of stocks in your portfolio can do only so much. True, at higher withdrawal rates, the stock-heavy portfolios have lower odds of running dry within thirty years than bond-heavy portfolios. But even for an all-stock portfolio the odds are still what I think most people would consider unacceptably high—more than a 50 percent chance of running out of money. Look what happens, though, when you lower your withdrawal rate. All the portfolios do much better. Indeed, at a 4 percent withdrawal rate, portfolios with as little as 15 percent stocks have about the same odds of lasting thirty years as ones with 100 percent stocks. In short, by setting a low withdrawal rate, you can get decent odds of your money lasting through a long retirement without having to accept the huge ups and downs you would experience with an all-stock portfolio. Which is why I believe that the single best move you can make to increase the odds of your portfolio supporting you throughout retirement is to *set a low withdrawal rate.*

THE ODDS OF RUNNING OUT OF MONEY
DURING A THIRTY-YEAR RETIREMENT

WITH-DRAWAL RATE*	STOCKS-BONDS MIX					
	100% Stocks 0% Bonds	80% Stocks/ 20% Bonds	60% Stocks/ 40% Bonds	40% Stocks/ 60% Bonds	15% Stocks/ 85% Bonds	5% Stocks/ 95% Bonds
4%	13%	12%	10%	10%	13%	63%
5%	26%	25%	30%	40%	74%	100%
6%	43%	47%	57%	74%	99%	100%
7%	61%	68%	80%	94%	100%	100%

Source: T. Rowe Price
*Withdrawal rate is percentage of portfolio withdrawn the first year. That dollar amount is then increased 3 percent per year for cost-of-living adjustments. Probabilities are based on computerized simulations of historical performance of stocks and bonds over many decades.

Of course, if the financial markets deliver the generous returns we enjoyed during the 1980s and 1990s, a portfolio that's loaded with stocks not only might last the rest of your life but also could grow into a much, much larger sum. But there's no guarantee the future will deliver returns of the same magnitude we enjoyed during those boom decades. In fact, I think it would be foolish to count on it. And you've also got to remember that the higher the concentration of stocks or stock funds in a portfolio, the more its value will drop during market setbacks. Experiencing a huge setback during retirement can be especially frightening. Indeed, I'm sure many retirees who entered the bear market of 2000 with 80 percent or more of their portfolio in stocks probably wish they'd played it a bit more conservatively. All of which is to say that while an aggressive portfolio does better in computerized simulations, it's not necessarily the best way to go in real life. I would imagine that for most retirees, a stock position of 60 percent or so would probably be about as aggressive as they would want to go. Certainly anyone going beyond that percentage should do so only if he or she is aware of the risk and willing to accept some pretty steep downturns along the way.

Of course, there's no way to know in advance exactly what mix of stocks and bonds will make your portfolio last the longest or how you can set a withdrawal rate just high enough to give you the most income without your nest egg expiring before you do. In order to do that we would need to be able to predict the returns the financial markets will deliver year by year (or even month by month) over several decades, and we would need to know our precise life expectancy. We don't know either one of these things, let alone both.

But there are a few sophisticated tools on the Web that can help you set a withdrawal strategy that's at least realistic in terms of what we know about stock and bond returns based on the way they've behaved in the past. I'll mention one here that I've often used, and which is free: the Retirement Income Calculator in the Tools & Calculators section of the T. Rowe Price website (www.troweprice.com). You start by entering such information as your retirement age, how long you think you'll live after you retire, and the amount you would like to withdraw from your portfolio each month. You then select one of several model portfolios that range from as little as 5 percent to as much as 100 percent in stocks. Finally, you select a success rate—basically the odds that your portfolio will be able to deliver the income you want for as long as you would like. The success rate you pick can be as low as 50 percent (if you're a risk taker or have resources other than your portfolio to fall back on) or as high as 99 percent (if you really can't afford for your portfolio to run out). Hit the Calculate button, and bingo! The calculator runs computerized simulations that immediately tell you whether you're likely to achieve your goal. By tinkering with this calculator, you can see how dramatically the odds of your money lasting for, say, twenty-five or thirty years can change depending on the amount you withdraw and how you structure your portfolio. Or you can see how your odds of sustaining a specific withdrawal change depending on the mix of stocks and bonds in your portfolio. In short, you can get a pretty good idea of what combination of withdrawals and investment strategies makes the most sense for you considering how big or little a risk you're willing to take that your portfolio might expire before you do.

Annuities Can Help

There is a way to virtually ensure you'll always have money coming in no matter how long you live, and that's to buy an annuity. Yes, I know I was tough on annuities back in Chapter 4. But here I'm talking about using annuities for something different from accumulating a nest egg. I'm talking about using them for the purpose for which they were originally designed and have been used for thousands of years, namely, converting assets into income, in this case turning assets that you've accumulated for retirement into an income that can last the rest of your life. And when it comes to this purpose—converting assets into a steady income stream via a process called annuitizing or annuitization—I think annuities can actually play a valuable role, although you still have to be careful about which particular annuity you choose and what you pay in ongoing fees.

Annuities that provide a regular stream of income are known as payout or immediate annuities. And although annuities can get brain-numbingly complex in their little details and fine print, the basic premise of an annuity that makes regular payments is pretty simple. Basically, a payout annuity works like a life insurance policy in reverse. Instead of making regular premiums to an insurance company that pays a lump sum upon your death, you give the insurer a lump sum of cash in return for regular income payments you receive until you die or for a specific period. When it comes to payout annuities, you have two basic choices: a fixed payment that remains the same for life or a variable payment that fluctuates with the market but offers the possibility of a rising income over time. Each has its advantages and disadvantages, so it's important that you understand how both types work and what they can—and can't—do for you in terms of providing reliable retirement income.

Annuity Income Options

The size of the payments you receive from an annuity—and how long you get them—depends on which payout option you choose. The type of payout also determines whether your heirs receive money from the annuity after you die. Although most people opt for monthly payments, you can usually choose quarterly or even annual payments if you wish. Here's a rundown of the main choices as well as examples of how the payment changes depending on the option you chose.

TYPE OF PAYMENT	SIZE OF MONTHLY PAYMENT ASSUMING $100,000 INVESTMENT*
Lifetime income: You receive payments for the rest of your life. When you die, the payments stop and your heirs get nothing. This option usually provides the highest income because you assume the risk of being paid very little if you die well before the end of your life expectancy.	65-year-old man: $669 65-year-old woman: $630
Life with period certain: The annuity makes payments for the rest of your life or for a specified period, whichever is longer. So, for example, if you choose a lifetime income with a ten-year period certain and you die two years after buying the annuity, your beneficiary would receive the payments for eight more years (or, in	65-year-old man (10-year certain): $646 65-year-old woman (10-year certain): $616

many cases, have the option of taking the value in a lump sum). Your payment with this option is lower than with a straight lifetime income. Still, if you're in your sixties and choose a relatively short period—say, ten years—the difference in payments can be fairly small because your odds of dying within a few years are low. This option can be a relatively inexpensive way to ensure that your heirs would receive something were you to unexpectedly die soon after purchasing the annuity.

Joint survivor: The annuity makes payments as long as you or your designated survivor (typically a spouse, although it could be another relative or a friend) is alive. People typically choose this option to ensure that a surviving spouse will continue to receive income. Payments are lower than under a lifetime income option for one person. You can increase the size of the payment under this option, however, by stipulating that the survivor receive, say, only 50 percent of the original payment (50 percent option) rather than the full payment (100 percent survivor option).	65-year-old couple (100% survivor): $580 65-year-old couple (50% survivor) $666 while both are alive; $333 to survivor

Source: www.immediateannuities.com
*Payments are for fixed payout annuities as of October 2003. You may find higher or lower quotes depending on the current level of interest rates. Quotes can vary substantially from insurer to insurer.

The Pros and Cons of Fixed-Payout Annuities

A fixed-payout annuity is by far the simpler of the two types to understand. If you wanted to turn $100,000 into a guaranteed fixed income for life, for example, you would buy a fixed-payout or immediate annuity with your hundred grand, and the insurance company that issued the annuity would guarantee you a fixed payment as long as you live. (If you already had $100,000 in an annuity you had been using as a tax-deferred investment as described in Chapter 6, you would annuitize your balance, which is essentially the same thing as buying an immediate annuity.) The size of the payment would vary based on factors such as the insurer's estimate of your life expectancy and how much the insurer felt it could earn investing your money, typically in intermediate- to long-term bonds.

An annuity offers more than just a guaranteed lifetime income, however. It also allows you to draw a higher annual income from your assets than you could manage on your own earning the same rate of return as an insurer. How is it possible for annuities to pay a higher income than you can get on your own from the same assets earning the same rate of return? The answer is that while you must base your payments on a single life—your own—insurers can base annuity payments on a pool of many lives. Insurers sell their annuities to thousands, in some cases millions, of people. And they know that while some of these people will survive to their life expectancy and beyond, many others will die earlier. So insurers are able to boost their payments by, in effect, transferring the money of those who die early to the ones who die late. This amounts to an extra return for those people who are fortunate enough to live long lives. In fact, some people refer to this extra dimension of return that annuities offer as a mortality or longevity return.

In order to make that transfer from those who die early to those who die late, however, people who buy annuities must agree to give up access to their original investment. If you buy a life annuity for, say, $100,000, you no longer can get at that hundred grand, even if you need it for emergency expenses. You've turned it over to the insurer in return for the promise of a lifetime income. Similarly, if you die immediately after buying the annuity, your heirs would receive not a cent of your hundred grand. Any money you didn't collect from your annuity would constitute the mortality or longevity return that goes to the annuity owners who live beyond their life expectancy.

But even if you're willing to make the trade-off of access to your cash in return for a guaranteed fixed income, there's another factor you've got to consider. A fixed, guaranteed income may seem like the safest of all options, but even if prices were to rise at a relatively mild annual rate of 2 percent over the next twenty years, the purchasing power of your fixed annuity payment would decline by roughly a third.

A few insurers have tried to address this shortcoming by selling annuities with payments that increase annually with the rate of inflation or that rise at a predetermined rate, say, 2 or 3 percent a year. But to provide this buffer against inflation, these policies usually offer initial payments that are 20 to 25 percent below what you can get in a regular fixed-payout annuity. Because of their lower initial payments, these inflation-adjusted or cost-of-living-adjusted annuities haven't been particularly popular with retirees.

The Pros and Cons of Variable-Payout Annuities

There's a second type of annuity—a variable-payout annuity or immediate variable annuity—that doesn't offer the steady payments of a fixed annuity. Indeed, its payments fluctuate from month to month and can even go down under some circumstances. On the plus side, though, a variable-payout annuity has the potential of keeping the buying power of your lifetime payments ahead of inflation—and even offers the chance that your monthly payments could go up substantially over your lifetime, perhaps doubling or tripling.

The concept of an annuity whose payment can change over time isn't the easiest thing to get your mind around—hey, I warned you annuities can numb your brain—but here's a quick rundown on how variable-payout annuities work.

You start by choosing an assumed interest rate, or AIR, which is essentially a benchmark that, along with your life expectancy, determines the size of your initial payment. Some insurers allow you to pick your own AIR—typically within a range of 3 to 6 percent—while others assign a specific rate, often 3.5 or 4 percent. Next, you divide your investment among a number of subaccounts, which are essentially the same as mutual funds. Typically, you have anywhere from a half dozen to twenty or so choices, including growth, value, and large- and small-cap funds, as well as bond and international portfolios. If the subaccounts you've selected generate a higher return than the AIR, the payments from your variable annuity will increase.

If your subaccounts earn a lower rate of return than the AIR you chose, then your payments will decline.

The higher the AIR you choose, the higher the initial payment you receive. For example, a sixty-five-year-old man who invests $100,000 in a variable-payout annuity and chooses a 5 percent AIR might receive an initial payment of, say, $657 a month versus $566 with an AIR of 3.5 percent. So why not just go with the highest possible AIR? The reason is that the more your portfolio's return exceeds the AIR, the larger your future payments will be. So choosing a higher AIR will get you a higher initial payment, but it limits the potential for increases later on. Assuming your subaccounts earn 8 percent annually after expenses, for example, the $657 monthly payment with the 5 percent AIR would climb to just under $1,000 in fifteen years and a bit less than $1,200 in twenty years. That same 8 percent net return, on the other hand, would boost the initial $566-a-month payment under a 3.5 percent AIR to almost $1,100 a month in fifteen years and $1,325 a month in twenty years. So if you want more assurance that your income will keep pace with or exceed inflation, you're better off choosing a lower AIR.

Of course, this being annuities we're talking about, we've also got to take fees into account—and in the case of variable annuities, we're talking not one layer of fees but two. First, there are the annual portfolio fees for the subaccounts. The equivalent of mutual fund operating expenses, these charges typically run anywhere from 0.5 percent to nearly 2 percent in the case of some small-cap and international funds. Then come insurance charges, which usually run about 1.25 percent per year or more. Add the two types of fees together and total expenses can easily top 2 percent. Since it's the net return *after expenses* that determines your future payments, you'll likely see your payment grow more if you buy an annuity with low fees.

But even though variable annuities have a good chance of generating payments that will stay ahead of inflation, they also have some drawbacks you should be aware of. For one thing, payments go up and down each month depending on the performance of your subaccounts. That kind of uneven and un-predictable cash flow can make budgeting for living expenses tougher than if you're getting a steady income stream. What's more, payments can drop substantially over the short term if the markets go into a slump. For example, if you had been receiving monthly payments of $1,000 from a variable annuity invested in a mix of 70 percent stock funds and 30 percent bond funds at the end of 1999, you could easily have seen those payments slide 25 percent to $730 a month by the beginning of 2003 (although those payments would increase as the market recovered).

Insurers have been adding new features to variable-payout annuities to make them more attractive. Several insurers, for example, have designed annuities that give you access to at least some of your original investment even after you begin receiving lifetime income. Some annuities, for example, allow you to choose an access period of five to thirty years during which you can tap into the cash value of your annuity account should you incur unexpected expenses or simply want to indulge in a splurge. If you die during that access period, your heirs would be entitled to your account's remaining cash value. Others not only give you access to your cash but also guarantee that payments won't drop below a specified minimum—say, 80 percent or 85 percent of your initial payment—so your income won't be decimated by a prolonged market slump.

But while features such as a guaranteed floor on payments and access to the annuity's account value may make people feel more comfortable about buying an annuity, they also exact a cost. An access period option might add another 0.4 percent to the annual cost of the annuity, for example. And annuities that give you access to your money plus set a minimum on how low your payment can fall might add as much as an extra percentage point of costs. In short, you're adding yet another layer of expenses on top of the two layers of fees that are already built in. These higher expenses can significantly limit the amount your payments may rise when the market's cruising along to gains. Let's say, for example, you invest $100,000 in a variable annuity, choose a 4 percent AIR, and receive an initial payment of $628. If your subaccounts earn a steady 10 percent per year before expenses and your annuity deducts a total of 1 percent annually in fees, your payment would climb to $1,577 in twenty years. If you earned the same 10 percent return but your annuity deducted 2 percent a year in fees, your payment would climb to just $1,287, or *almost $300 a month less.* Thus, by opting for protection against occasional market setbacks, you could be relegating yourself to roughly 20 percent less income in fifteen years.

How Annuities Plus Other Investments Can Create a Retirement "Paycheck"

Fortunately, there is a simple way to take advantage of the one feature annuities have that no other investment does—the ability to provide an income you won't outlive, without giving up too much of that income to high fees and without giving up access to all your retirement assets; in other words, a solution that gives you the security of annuities and the flexibility and control of managing withdrawals from your portfolio on your own. Basically, that solution comes down to this: invest a portion of your retirement portfolio in one or more low-cost annuities that provide a lifetime income but none of the expensive options I mentioned above, and keep the rest of your money in a portfolio of mutual funds and/or stocks and bonds that you can draw from as needed to meet your living costs or to pay for unexpected expenses or the occasional splurge.

What's great about this solution is that it allows you to get more income from your assets than you could by simply managing your withdrawals on your own, plus it reduces the chances that you will outlive your money. And, just as important, it allows you to effectively create a retirement "paycheck" that consists of the income from your annuities plus withdrawals from your portfolio.

To get an idea of how this approach might actually work, consider the following hypothetical scenario I created with the help of the Chicago investment research firm Ibbotson Associates. Assume that a sixty-five-year-old man has savings of $500,000, from which he would like to withdraw 5 percent, or $25,000, in the first year of retirement and then increase that amount each year with inflation. And let's also assume this retiree has four different options for getting that $25,000 income adjusted for inflation each year. He can simply pull the required amount from his portfolio each year, a process known as systematic withdrawal (for simplicity's sake, let's assume that the portfolio is invested in mutual funds, 70 percent in large-company stock funds and 30 percent in intermediate-term bonds). Or he can get a portion of the $25,000 inflation-adjusted income by investing 25 percent of his assets in a fixed-payout annuity and the rest by taking systematic withdrawals from the remaining 75 percent of his assets that are invested in funds. Or he can get a portion of the $25,000 inflation-adjusted income by investing 25 percent of his assets in a variable-payout annuity and the rest from the 75 percent of his assets in funds. Or he can get a portion of the income from investing 50 percent of his assets in annuities (25 percent each in fixed and variable annuities) and the rest from the remaining 50 percent of his assets in funds.

Ibbotson ran computerized simulations using long-term historical results for stocks, bonds, and inflation to gauge our hypothetical retiree's chances of getting that inflation-adjusted income for the rest of his life under each of the four options above. The idea was to see which of the options had the lowest chance of falling below the target income level. The graph on page 263 summarizes the results.

Notice how the option of just pulling money out of the portfolio (line 1) works just fine for the first ten to fifteen years. Trouble is, when our fictional retiree gets beyond age eighty, the risk of his money running out rises rather steeply. If our retiree is lucky enough to have a very long life span, the chances that he'll run out of money can get pretty high. There's more than a 30 percent chance, for example, that his portfolio will run dry by age ninety-five and a higher than 40 percent chance it won't make it to his one hundredth birthday.

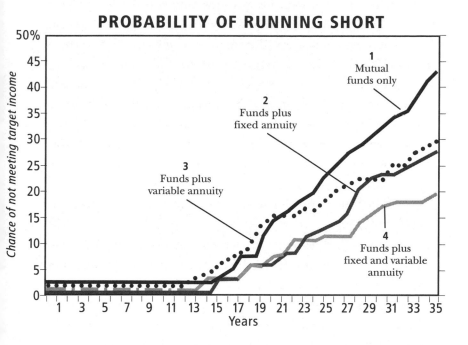

PROBABILITY OF RUNNING SHORT

But look at how the odds of falling below the target level of income drop when our retiree puts a portion of his assets into one or more annuities. For example, putting 25 percent of his assets in a fixed annuity (line 2) lowers the odds of running short by age ninety-five to less than 25 percent and by age one hundred to less than 30 percent. Similarly, investing 25 percent of his money in a variable annuity (line 3) also lowers the odds of falling below the target later in life. And the fourth option—investing in both fixed- and variable-payout annuities plus keeping assets in mutual funds (line 4)—does the best of all, reducing his odds of falling below the target level of income to just a bit over 15 percent by age ninety-five and less than 20 percent at one hundred—a big improvement from a straight systematic withdrawal strategy. In short, adding the annuities can substantially reduce the odds that you'll run short of money in retirement.

What's more, the hybrid approach I'm recommending has other advantages you can't see on the graph. If you rely solely on withdrawals from your portfolio and your portfolio runs dry, that's it. You're broke (although in reality you would probably begin taking smaller withdrawals before that happened). But when you own an annuity, the income never completely stops. You may fall short of your targeted withdrawals, but you will still get some income as long as you're alive. The graph also doesn't reflect the potential upside with a variable annuity. If the stock market delivers generous returns, it's possible the variable annuity payments alone could increase enough to provide your target income. Which means you could increase your target income and live a more lavish lifestyle—or you could let your regular portfolio's value rise and leave a nice legacy for your heirs.

Keep in mind, though, that these results are probabilities based on the types of returns the financial markets have generated in the past, not guarantees. If stocks and bonds deliver lower results in the future, the risk of running dry using my hybrid strategy will increase (although they'll likely increase even more if you rely solely on withdrawals from a conventional portfolio). This analysis also assumes you keep investment costs down by buying a low-cost annuity and that you invest in low-cost index funds in your regular portfolio. If you try this strategy with higher-cost annuities and higher-cost funds, your odds of falling below your target income will increase.

Remember, too, that this hybrid solution isn't all gain with no pain. In return for the security you get from investing a portion of your assets in an annuity, you give up control over some of your assets, which could restrict your financial maneuvering room in the future. And if you take the hybrid approach and you die before the end of your life expectancy, your heirs may end up with less than they would have gotten had you not allocated some of your money to an annuity.

How much money should you consider investing in one or more annuities to create a lifetime income? There are no handy rules of thumbs or guidelines that can lead you to a "correct" percentage. I can't imagine a scenario where it would make sense to annuitize all your assets, since that would be placing too large a bet on one investment. And since you would be giving up access to the assets you annuitized, you would be limiting your flexibility for dealing with life's unanticipated financial demands. Similarly, you may not need an annuity at all if you've accumulated so much wealth that your annual withdrawals would be so small relative to your portfolio's value that the chances are minuscule you would run out of money.

Beyond those extremes, however, deciding how much of your assets you might consider devoting to an annuity is largely a subjective affair. The percentage that's right for you depends on such factors as how much money you've saved, how much income you need, how long you think you're likely to live, how concerned you are about running short, and how much money you think you'll need on hand for unanticipated expenses and such. The greater you feel your chances are of living a long life and the more concerned you are that you might outlive your money, the more of your assets you would want to devote to annuities. Even then, however, you'll want to be sure to have enough money outside your annuities to meet unexpected expenses, to pay for the occasional vacation or other indulgence, or to leave a legacy to your heirs. One approach is to try to cover as much of your essential living expenses (the cost of food, clothing, housing, medical care, etc.) as possible with payments from regular sources of income such as Social Security, company pensions, and annuities, and then rely on withdrawals from the rest of your portfolio to fund discretionary spending and emergency expenses. All in all, however, I think it would be reasonable for most people who decide they need the stability of a reliable lifetime income to consider devoting somewhere in the neighborhood of 25 to 50 percent of their retirement assets to payout annuities.

Another major issue you must address if you think a payout annuity might be right for you is which assets to annuitize: the pretax money in accounts such as 401(k)s and IRA rollovers, or investments such as stocks and funds that you hold in taxable accounts. One argument for using taxable dollars to buy a payout annuity is that annuities offer a special tax benefit when they're funded with taxable dollars. A portion of each payment you receive is considered a return of your original investment rather than a gain on your capital, and thus it goes untaxed. This, in effect, increases the after-tax value of each payment. But annuities also have a tax disadvantage in that all gains are taxed as ordinary income, even long-term capital gains, which are normally taxed at lower long-term capital gains rates.

Because of this tax peculiarity, some financial advisers think you're better off using money in tax-deferred accounts like 401(k)s and IRAs to buy a payout annuity. They figure that the money you withdraw from such accounts will be taxed at ordinary income rates anyway, so why not use this money for the annuity and take advantage of the more favorable capital-gains treatment in your taxable accounts? Of course, when it comes time to retire, most of us will probably have the bulk of our retirement savings in tax-deferred accounts like 401(k)s and IRAs. So as a practical matter, these accounts will probably be the main source for any money we want to invest in an annuity. Still, if you have substantial assets in both taxable and tax-deferred accounts, you might consider having an adviser crunch the numbers both ways to see whether funding the annuity with taxable or tax-deferred assets, plus withdrawals from the remainder of your portfolio, works best in your situation.

Tips for Choosing an Annuity

The variety of payment options and different layers of fees can make it devilishly difficult to know whether you're getting a good deal on an annuity. You'll increase your odds of getting the best value for your money by following a few guidelines.

Get Quotes from Several Insurers

Since life expectancy estimates can and do vary among insurers, the payments you'll receive can also vary from insurer to insurer, often by 10 percent or more. Similarly, the initial payment you receive on a variable annuity can vary substantially. You can compare current quotes on fixed-payment annuities by going to the WebAnnuities.com site (www.immediateannuities. com). For a quote on the initial payment on variable annuities, you typically have to contact each insurer separately, although you can find quotes from a handful of insurers by going to the Product Center of the AnnuityNetAdvisor site (client.annuity netadvisor.com) and clicking on Annuity Payout Quotes.

Opt for Low Fees

With a fixed-payment annuity, you don't have to worry about annual fees. The payment already reflects the fees. With variable-payout annuities, however, you receive an initial payment that goes up or down depending on investment performance net of two sets of fees—insurance charges (often listed separately as mortality and expense charges and administrative fees) and portfolio expenses. By opting for an annuity with low expenses, you increase the chance your payments will rise in subsequent years. To find both insurance charges and portfolio expenses, check the fees section of the prospectus. One caveat: Some insurers keep expenses low by waiving a portion of their insurance charges and/or portfolio fees. But the insurer still has the right to boost these fees in the future. Since you're effectively locked into an annuity once you begin receiving payments, you should think hard before buying an annuity where the fees could jump substantially if the waiver is revoked.

Stick to High-Quality Companies—and Diversify

When you buy a payout annuity, you're counting on the insurer having the financial wherewithal to make those payments years and years into the future. (There are state guaranty funds to protect annuity holders, but their coverage is usually limited to $100,000 and can sometimes take a while to kick in.) So limit yourself to solid, reputable companies that get high financial strength ratings from firms such as A. M. Best (www.ambest. com), Standard & Poor's (www.standardandpoors.com), and Moody's Investors Service (www.moodys.com). For an extra bit of security, you should consider diversifying—that is, splitting your money among two or more annuities from high-quality companies. This way, should one insurer run into trouble, payments should continue without interruption from the others.

Don't Annuitize All Your Money at Once

To give yourself more financial maneuvering room in the event your needs change, consider annuitizing your money in two or three chunks over a few years rather than doing it all at once. Besides, the payment you get from a fixed-payout annuity depends largely on the current level of interest rates. If you put all your money into an annuity when rates happen to be very low, you've essentially relegated yourself to a lifetime of low payments. Annuitizing in stages makes it less likely you'll annuitize all your money at the worst possible time.

Develop a Tax-Smart Withdrawal Strategy

Ultimately, of course, your goal during retirement is to get as much income as possible out of the savings you've accumulated during your career—or, looked at another way, to make that money last as long as possible. One way you can squeeze the most out of your retirement portfolio is to draw on it as tax-efficiently as possible—that is, manage your withdrawals so that as little as possible gets siphoned off by the IRS and state tax authorities.

Again, there's no single strategy that guarantees you'll get the most income out of your portfolio or assures it will last the longest. But, generally, you have the best chance of minimizing the tax bite and leaving more money for you by following the following guidelines.

Start by Drawing from Your Taxable Accounts

If you hold investments such as mutual funds, stocks, bonds, and CDs in taxable accounts, it's likely they are regularly throwing off some sort of taxable gains in the form of dividends, interest payments, and, in the case of mutual funds, capital-gains distributions that you're being taxed on every year. In general, it pays to make these assets your first source of income. For one thing, you're already paying tax on the dividends, interest payments, and gains themselves, so you might as well spend them. And second, if you hold these assets, they'll continue to throw off gains that are often taxable at the highest income tax rates. Selling them for income, on the other hand, allows other assets that do a better job of sheltering their gains from taxes to grow, giving you access to a larger source of income after your taxable assets run out.

But not all your assets in taxable accounts are equally vulnerable to taxes. Municipal bonds, for example, generate interest that is free from federal taxes and in some cases state taxes as well. Individual stocks can also be tax efficient, in that you don't pay any gain on the increase in its share price until you actually sell—and if you hold the stock longer than a year, you pay tax at long-term capital-gains rates, which are lower than the rates on dividends, interest, and short-term gains. Even certain types of mutual funds—index funds and tax-managed funds, for example—allow you to effectively shelter much of their gains from taxes both by holding on to them for a long time and by paying tax on your eventual gain at the long-term capital-gains tax rate.

So when drawing from your taxable accounts, look first to the investments that tend to generate the biggest tax bills and then move on to more tax-efficient assets such as muni bonds, individual stocks in which you have built up large long-term capital gains, and index and tax-managed mutual funds.

Next, Move on to Tax-Deferred Retirement Accounts

After you've gotten as much as you can out of your taxable portfolio, you can then dip into tax-deferred accounts such as 401(k)s and IRAs. The reason it pays to avoid tapping tax-deferred accounts first if possible is that assets in tax-deferred accounts can grow more quickly than assets in taxable accounts because their gains aren't being eroded by taxes. Thus, the longer you leave your tax-deferred assets untouched, the more they can compound without the drag of taxes, and the larger a tax-deferred stash you'll have when you eventually begin drawing from it. Keep in mind, though, that at some point the government requires that you start pulling money from tax-deferred retirement accounts such as 401(k)s and IRAs (though not Roth IRAs). And if you don't withdraw the right amount, you can be hit with some staggering penalties. I'll deal with the required minimum distribution, or RMD, rules, on page 272.

Once you do begin taking money from these accounts, your withdrawals will be taxed at ordinary income tax rates. One exception: if you made nondeductible contributions to your IRA (or to a 401(k) that was then rolled into an IRA), then only the *gains* on those contributions are taxable. You've already paid tax on the nondeductible contributions themselves, so you aren't taxed again when that money is returned to you. Unfortunately, our tax laws don't allow you to withdraw all your nondeductible contributions first in order to create a tax-free income. If you have made nondeductible contributions, the IRS considers only a pro rata portion of each withdrawal a nontaxable return of your nondeductible contributions. After you've recouped all nondeductible contributions you made, the entire withdrawal is taxable.

Save Money in Any Roth IRA Accounts for Last

There are several reasons why you want to hold off as long as possible on tapping any assets you may have in Roth accounts. First, once you're over age fifty-nine and a half and the money has been in the account at least five years, all withdrawals from your Roth accounts are tax free. So not only are your investments in a Roth growing without the drag of taxes, neither those gains nor your original contributions will ever be taxed. Second, unlike a traditional IRA, which requires you to begin withdrawing money after age seventy and a half, Roths have no required withdrawals. So you can let the money rack up tax-free gains in the account as long as you want. Finally, Roth IRA assets can also be passed along to heirs free of income tax. Thus, the longer you let your money ride untouched in a Roth, the larger the tax-free stockpile of assets you will have in the future, either for your own retirement needs or to leave as a legacy to your heirs.

Of course, things don't always work out quite so neatly in real life. You may face circumstances that might lead you to draw down your assets in a different way than I suggest above. For example, if your retirement savings are so large (or your income need in relation to your assets so small) that it's unlikely you'll deplete your portfolio in your lifetime, then you might want to consider spending tax-deferred assets first. The reason is that assets in tax-deferred accounts are generally taxed more heavily than those in taxable accounts upon your death. If you plan on leaving assets to heirs, you're probably better off leaving them assets such as stocks or mutual funds held in taxable accounts since the cost basis of those assets steps up to market value when you die. That means your heirs pay tax only on gains earned after they inherit the stocks or funds, not on the unrealized gains that accumulated during your lifetime. There may be other reasons related to estate taxes that might lead you to draw from certain assets before others. Federal estate tax rules get complicated quickly, not to mention the fact that the revisions to estate taxes enacted during the summer of 2001 have a unique reversion provision that could be triggered in 2011 and put all the rules back to the way they were years before. (Of course, Congress could change that reversion provision in the meantime, so you'll have to keep tabs on what our esteemed legislators do between now and 2011.) If you expect to leave a sizable estate—certainly anything over $1 million—it's probably worthwhile to consult an estate tax attorney or financial planner who deals in such issues.

Similarly, there may be years in which you fall into a much higher income tax bracket than other years. In those years, you might want to sell stocks to produce gains that will be taxed at lower long-term capital-gains rates or, for that matter, take tax-free withdrawals from your Roth IRA to avoid paying additional tax at the high rate altogether.

There may also be opportunities for you to play the tax laws to your advantage by selling stocks or funds in your taxable accounts at a loss. You can then lower your tax bill by using that loss to offset other gains you may have taken; failing that, you may be able to apply as much as $3,000 of the loss each year against ordinary income. One warning, though: It's easy to get tripped up by the regulations covering securities losses and taxes. So before you begin selling securities for tax purposes, I suggest you take a look at the IRS publication that details all the government's nitpicking rules: Publication 550, "Investment Income and Expenses" (available at the IRS's website, www.irs.gov). It's not exactly a scintillating read, but it's better to know the ins and outs of this area beforehand rather than find you can't deduct a loss because you ran afoul of some arcane provision of the tax code.

Doing the Minimum

When you reach age seventy and a half, federal law requires that you begin pulling at least *some* money out of tax-deferred retirement accounts such as IRAs. (Roth IRAs are exempt from this requirement, and you can hold off taking distributions from your 401(k) as long as you're still working at the company.) This is *not* a matter of choice. You must withdraw at least the minimum stipulated by the IRS, or what is called your required minimum distribution (or RMD). If you fail to withdraw this amount, you can be hit with a big tax penalty—50 percent of the difference between what you should have withdrawn and what you actually withdrew.

It used to be that you practically had to be an actuary or a math whiz to figure out your RMD. But in a rare magnanimous gesture a couple of years ago, the IRS simplified the rules so that now even mere mortals can figure out how much they must withdraw each year. The new rules also require smaller distributions than in the past, which means that more of your assets can continue to grow free of taxes (assuming, of course, you can afford to withdraw only the minimum).

So, how do you determine your RMD? One way is to use the table on page 274. Let's say, for example, you reach age seventy and a half early in 2004 and will turn seventy-one that same year. By law, you must begin withdrawals from your 401(k) or IRA, although you can actually postpone making that first withdrawal until April 2005. To determine the size of your withdrawal, you take the balance of your IRA at the end of 2003 (the year before the required withdrawal) and divide that balance by the appropriate life expectancy figure in the table on the next page. In this case, the figure would be 26.5 years, since you turn seventy-one the year your required withdrawals begin. So if your IRA balance had been $100,000 at the end of 2003, you would divide $100,000 by 26.5 to come up with a required withdrawal of $3,774. As I said, you can wait until April 2005 to actually make that withdrawal. But if you do, you will still also have to make your withdrawal for 2005 by the end of 2005. In that case, you would take your IRA balance as of the end of 2004 and divide by 25.6, the life expectancy figure for age seventy-two.

There are a few other wrinkles you should know about. You use a different table to figure your minimum if the sole beneficiary of your IRA is a spouse who is more than ten years younger than you or if you are withdrawing money from an IRA that you've inherited. If you fall into either of those categories, you'll find the appropriate table in IRS Publication 590, "Individual Retirement Arrangements," which is available at the IRS's website (www.irs.gov). If you have more than one IRA, you figure your required withdrawal for each one, although you can total the separate minimums and take the combined amount from any one or more of your accounts.

Five Tips for Staying on the Yellow Brick Road of Retirement Security

Ultimately, your goal once you've finally retired is to do everything you can to ensure that the various resources you've accumulated during your career—your Social Security, your pensions, your investments—support you in retirement as well as they can for as long as they can. At the same time, of course, you don't want to spend every minute of retirement obsessing

CALCULATING YOUR MINIMUM DISTRIBUTION

YOUR AGE*	DIVIDE YOUR IRA BALANCE BY THIS FIGURE†	YOUR AGE	DIVIDE YOUR IRA BALANCE BY THIS FIGURE
70	27.4	93	9.6
71	26.5	94	9.1
72	25.6	95	8.6
73	24.7	96	8.1
74	23.8	97	7.6
75	22.9	98	7.1
76	22.0	99	6.7
77	21.2	100	6.3
78	20.3	101	5.9
79	19.5	102	5.5
80	18.7	103	5.2
81	17.9	104	4.9
82	17.1	105	4.5
83	16.3	106	4.2
84	15.5	107	3.9
85	14.8	108	3.7
86	14.1	109	3.4
87	13.4	110	3.1
88	12.7	111	2.9
89	12.0	112	2.6
90	11.4	113	2.4
91	10.8	114	2.1
92	10.2	115 or older	1.9

Source: IRS
*Age based on your birthday in the year you become seventy and a half.
†Life expectancy in years; IRA balance as of end of year prior to year of required withdrawal.

about your finances and agonizing over every investment move you make. After all, retirement is supposed to be a time when you enjoy life a bit, a chance for you to get to do some of the things you didn't have time to do during your working days.

But if you've set the stage for retirement in the ways I've described throughout this book, you should be able to achieve your goal of financial security throughout retirement while still leaving yourself plenty of time and opportunity to make your retirement years fulfilling. Toward that end, I'll leave you with five final recommendations that, along with a bit of thought and not too much effort on your part, can maintain your retirement plan for the rest of your life. Think of them as my five tips for staying on the yellow brick road of retirement security.

Set a Modest Initial Withdrawal Rate

You will vastly increase the chances of your retirement savings lasting for the rest of your life if you start with a conservative initial withdrawal rate—say, 3 to 5 percent of your portfolio. Granted, that may require you to live a bit less luxuriously than you might want to, especially if you've been looking forward to indulging yourself a bit after leaving the workaday world. But better to tighten your belt a little in the early stages of retirement than to find yourself with no retirement savings left at age ninety. Besides, if you're smart or lucky enough to earn good returns on your portfolio, so that its balance holds its own or even begins to swell, you always have the option of boosting the size of your withdrawals later on.

Take Taxes into Account

Your investing decisions during retirement shouldn't be solely driven by taxes, of course. But by managing your withdrawals to play the tax code to your advantage, you can increase the size of the after-tax withdrawals from your portfolio and/or substantially reduce the odds of your portfolio running out of money. So set aside a bit of time on several occassions during the year—and definitely a month or so before the end of the year, so that you still have time to make last-minute changes—to consider how your tax situation is shaping up for the current year and might look in the year ahead. Maybe the withdrawal strategy that was the pinnacle of tax efficiency a few years ago no longer makes sense for you because of changes in the tax code or changes in your investment holdings. Or perhaps a review of your stocks and funds will reveal holdings that you may want to unload for a loss that you can use to reduce the tax on other gains. The important thing to remember is that every dollar you can avoid paying in taxes is another dollar that can help pay your retirement living expenses or stay in your portfolio to extend its life.

Make Periodic Reality Checks

If there's one lesson we can all take from the experience of the last few years, it's that fast-changing conditions in the financial markets can have profound changes on one's retirement prospects. In the late 1990s, stocks were delivering such high returns and seemed so certain of continuing to do so that many retirees convinced themselves that they were sure to live out their golden years in luxury as long as they kept all or most of their money in stocks. That rosy outlook quickly turned much bleaker, however, when stock prices began their long slide in early 2000. But investment returns aren't the only variable that can change. Rising medical costs, a hike in property taxes, a spike in inflation, major house repairs—all these things and more can increase your living expenses and put unanticipated demands on your retirement savings. That's why it's crucial that you conduct periodic reality checks to see whether you're able to get by on the income you projected or whether your retirement income needs have increased. You'll also want to reevaluate the balance of your portfolio with an eye toward whether you can still manage the withdrawal rate you set originally. At the very least, you should go through the exercise I described earlier in the chapter of gauging the odds of your portfolio lasting the rest of your life given the amount of money you have remaining in your various investment accounts and how you have the assets in those accounts invested.

Make Adjustments Along the Way

A retirement income strategy isn't something you can create and then just leave alone—at least not if you expect it to remain effective throughout retirement. The fact is that no plan, no matter how well thought-out and sophisticated, can foresee all the possibilities you might have to deal with. So in order to keep your plan on track, you should expect to make some adjustments along the way. For example, if the conservative portfolio mix of 50 percent stocks and 50 percent bonds you set isn't generating high enough returns to sustain your withdrawals over your lifetime, perhaps you need to take a bit more investing risk and increase your stock exposure. On the other hand, you might consider looking for ways to pare back your withdrawals a bit. You could also could consider taking a part-time job so that you maintain the income you need but take some of the pressure off your portfolio. Or you might consider all three moves. What's most important, though, is that you address problems early on, when you have a better chance of solving them with small adjustments. The longer you wait, the greater the chance the problem will have grown so large that you may have to resort to drastic changes that could have a lower probability of success.

Have Fun

With all the emphasis on the financial aspects of retirement planning, it's easy to overlook the reason we go through the process at all: so that we can enjoy ourselves in retirement. So by all means, take the time to plan, monitor your progress, and make appropriate adjustments to your plan so you can attain a good measure of financial security in this stage of your life. But retirement planning is a means, not an end in itself. So don't let the planning get in the way of living a happy and fulfilled life. You get only one retirement. Enjoy it while you can.

INDEX

Index

ABOUT THE AUTHOR

Award-winning journalist Walter Updegrave is a senior editor at
Money magazine, where he writes the "Ask the Expert" column. He
also appears as "The Expert" on AOL Personal Finance and
CNNMONEY.com, where he answers personal finance questions
from online readers twice a week. Updegrave received an
economics degree from the University of Pennsylvania in 1974 but
has never let that prevent him from bringing humor and
commonsense analysis to personal finance. A Philadelphia native
and longtime "Iggles" fan, he now lives with his wife and son in
New Rochelle, New York, the hometown of Rob and Laura Petrie of
The Dick Van Dyke Show.